The
BEST
Women's Travel
Writing

2008

True Stories
From Around the World

T R A V E L E R S '   T A L E S

THE BEST WOMEN'S TRAVEL WRITING

2008

TRUE STORIES FROM AROUND THE WORLD

Edited by
LUCY McCAULEY

Travelers' Tales
an imprint of Solas House, Inc.
Palo Alto

Art Direction: Stefan Gutermuth
Interior design and page layout: Melanie Haage using the fonts
Nicolas Cochin, Ex Ponto, and Granjon
Author Photo: Gail E. Atwater

ISBN 1-932361-55-3
ISSN 1553-054X

First Edition
Printed in the United States
10 9 8 7 6 5 4 3 2 1

For Charles

Throw your dreams into space like a kite, and you do not know what it will bring back — a new life, a new friend, a new love, a new country.

— Anaïs Nin

Table of Contents

Editor's Preface

I've written before for Travelers' Tales about a long-held dream I finally realized a few years back: to hike the pilgrimage trail in northern Spain, the Camino de Santiago. What I didn't write about was the element of serendipity that accompanied the venture—the delightful phenomenon of happening upon something you don't expect. It's what travel often brings into play and what permeates many of the stories in this year's collection of *Best Women's Travel Writing*.

My pilgrimage included my daughter, Hannah, then eighteen months old. Because of her and the fact that I'd thrown out my back shortly before the trip, I decided to do only parts of the 500-mile pilgrimage, some of it by bus, rather than walking. I had planned everything carefully, set my itinerary, and packed a large bag with everything I imagined I could use on such a journey—probably more than I needed: a large supply of diapers; Cheerios and raisins for Hannah; bottles and a Ziplock bag of powdered milk; clothes and raingear for both of us; a travel guide and a selection of Hannah's books and toys.

The best part of the trip was when I left all of those things behind.

I hadn't planned it that way. It was the last leg of the pilgrimage, and I had decided on a daytrip with Hannah to Finisterre, what was once believed to be "the end of the earth." Lying on the northwestern-most point of Europe, Finisterre was the ancient finish-line of the pilgrimage trail, a few hours' bus-ride from the modern-day trail's end of Santiago de Compostela. At the time, I was struggling in my personal life, seeking some answers. The idea of traveling to the ends of the earth resonated with me somehow. I left my large bag at the hotel in Santiago and packed a small backpack containing only the barest essentials for the day, not even a toothbrush.

But in the space of a few minutes my plans changed when Hannah threw up on the bus, all over herself and partly on me, altering in that one uncontrollable act the rest of the journey. One minute she was happily singing "The Wheels on the Bus" and the next she was looking up at me pathetically, spewing great rivers of curdled milk and raisins all over the only clothes I'd brought for her.

A few minutes later we pulled into Finisterre, and on the dirt road outside the bus I stripped Hannah down and covered her in her little lavender windbreaker that I'd stuffed into my pack at the last minute. I wiped some errant splatterings from my shirt and looked at Hannah. She was still a bit green and looked so tiny and vulnerable in the jacket, her baby-bird's legs naked beneath.

I decided to find us a room. I wasn't sure how we'd manage without clothes and extra diapers, but I had plenty of powdered milk. I spotted a sign for a *pensión* just up the street, and that's when I felt it: the ripple of excitement. This little daytrip had suddenly turned into an adventure.

At the small, family-run *pensión*, the matron handed me a large bar of lye soap and pointed me to the backyard sink and clothesline. I scrubbed Hannah's shirt and pants while she played at my feet with the bucket of clothespins, wearing a shirt belonging to one of the matron's older grandchildren.

And we were fine. Without all of our stuff, we were better than fine. The local market of course had diapers for Hannah and a toothbrush for me. What else did we really need? A pilgrim I met along the trail, a young British woman, told me that she had begun the 500-mile journey carrying a pack full of clothes and books and hiking accoutrements. But as she walked she discarded things one by one, and then in great heaps and bundles, leaving them with locals she met in towns along the way. The more things she discarded, she said, the happier she felt—the simpler, and somehow more meaningful, the walk became for her, unburdened by the physical and psychological weight of all of those objects.

As I hung Hannah's clothes in the bright afternoon sun, I couldn't agree more. Trying to make do with what we had or could scavenge, I felt lighter, happier than I'd felt during the whole journey up to that point. And then there was that element of the unexpected. Travel sends us out of the familiar, hurtling us surely and certainly into utter *un*certainty, to a place where we can't help but yield to pure experience—to the new, the unexpected, to the change in itinerary or venue. To adventure.

Many of the selections in this year's *Best Women's Travel Writing* embody that phenomenon of serendipity. To name a few: Christine Sarkis finds her serendipitous moment at a fondue restaurant in France ("Dipping Fork, Flying Girl, Heart Attack"); Anne Lamott experiences it up-close-and-personal after a hard landing on a mountaintop ("Ski Patrol"); Mary Day Long encounters it on an overnight train from Turkey to Bulgaria ("Keep Breathing"); and in Mexico, Laura Resau learns of serendipity's transformative power when her date doesn't show up—again ("My *Ex-Novio's* Mother").

As for Hannah and me, in the end we stayed three days in Finisterre. Each morning we walked into the town's tiny *panadería* to buy fresh *bollos* of bread, which we ate with small packets of jam I found in my backpack, smuggled from the breakfast bar of our last hotel. In the afternoons Hannah toddled on the rocky beach, or next to the white walls that ran along the tourmaline bay. I'd hold onto her as she sat on the wall, the two of us looking out over the water. It was there that she said "ocean" for the first time, clearly entranced with it.

Each evening as we ate omelettes and *calamares* with spongy chunks of bread at a restaurant overlooking the water, I would decide to stay another day. Why not? I was happy to be away from the crowds in Santiago. Finisterre by contrast was so tranquil, with its views of ocean and mountains. The people were gentler there too, more open and friendly, compared to those in some towns along the pilgrim trail, the inhabitants jaded by the constant parade of foreigners. I felt utterly at peace there with my daughter, moving in and out of our days.

All too soon the pull of commitments back home and an unchangeable airline reservation forced us to board the bus back to Santiago. When I went to reclaim my things at the hotel there, I can't say I was happy to have them back again. Rather, I felt grateful for Hannah's indecorous moment on the bus. It had allowed us an oasis of time, there at "the end of the earth"—and it had transformed the journey.

—LUCY MCCAULEY

Introduction

LINDA ELLERBEE

The first time I traveled to a country not my own, the sixties were barely born. I was nineteen. I went to Bolivia as part of a student missionary program. The church said I was supposed to "bear witness." Which I did: In my letters home, I regularly wrote about the poverty of the Bolivian Indian population, the corruption that ran through every act and aspect of government I encountered, and the hypocrisy of most missionaries I met. My mother, certain they'd like to see what a good writer her daughter was, sent all my letters to the nice folks at the church's national mission headquarters. This was when I learned that what I called "bearing witness"—seeing what you see, hearing what you hear, and then telling others about it as truthfully as you can—will not make you popular. But it just might, one day, make you a journalist.

It did me. And it's been a great life.

Call it serendipity, at least according to my favorite definition of the word, which comes from crime writer Lawrence Block. *Serendipity*: Look for something, find something else, and realize that what you've found is more suited to your needs than what you thought you were looking for.

Take progress. Sometimes it's just one serendipity after another. For instance, Silly Putty, Teflon, Superglue, Cellophane, Rayon, Aspartame, Penicillin, laughing gas,

The Pill, x-rays, corn flakes, Wheaties, the microwave oven, Velcro, and Post-It notes have all played a role in my life, and in every case, their invention was due to you-know-what. The same is true of Viagra except for the part about it playing a role in my life. Except, possibly, indirectly.

Fine, but what, you ask, has serendipity got to do with the book in your hands?

Only everything.

Serendipity has been a singular part of the travel experience since God was a lassie, and yet it wasn't until 1754 that Horace Walpole gave us the word—in a letter to a friend—in which he explained where the idea for the word came from. "It was when I read a silly fairy tale, called *The Three Princes of Serendip*." (The ancient Persian name for Sri Lanka was Serendip.) "As their highnesses traveled they were always making discoveries, by accidents and sagacity, of things which they were not in quest of."

See, even the word had its beginnings in travel.

The concept, however, was by then already old.

It's hard to know if the sagacity mentioned above was involved in Leif Ericsson's case. But he *was* merely trying to escape a storm when, by accident, he became the first European to set foot on North America. And then Columbus "re-discovered" North America while searching for India. Nor should we forget Vincente Pinzon, who, while exploring the West Indies, stumbled upon Brazil. *Hello South America!* And then, of course, there was Albert Hofmann, the Swiss chemist who, when he accidentally ingested some Lysergic acid diethylamide, a drug he was studying, went on the world's first acid trip.

Nothing much has changed. There may be no more continents (or new psychedelic drugs) to "discover," but if you listen closely to the travel experiences of the women in this book, you will indeed hear the distant—and often not distant at all—melody of serendipity.

So how do you go about getting some serendipity in your travels?

In *The Last Voyage of Somebody the Sailor,* novelist John Barth wrote that "you don't reach Serendib (sic) by plotting a course for it. You have to set out in good faith for elsewhere and lose your bearings...serendipitously."

I disagree.

Once in a while it's why we go traveling in the first place (especially women, who so often seem to understand that the biggest part of being prepared is remembering to set a place at the table for the unexpected guest). Sometimes we go looking for one thing actually hoping that we might find another thing, even if we've no idea what that other thing might be.

We just know if it's serendipitous, it's good.

And if, on our journeys, we're ready for it, it's more likely to find us. But either way, journeys must be taken. As Block points out, you must be *looking for something* in order to find something else.

In celebration (or denial) of turning sixty, I loaded my backpack and flew to England, where I set out, alone and on foot, to follow the River Thames from its source in the Cotswolds to where it meets the sea some 200 miles down the path (and across the fields, past the villages, through London and most of English history). I meant to use the time to, as the Navajo say, "walk in beauty," to be conscious of the life around me, and my connection to it. Oh, hell, truth is, I was hoping to use this journey to make peace with turning sixty.

But I did not find what I was looking for, and what's more, in my rush to look for it, I finished what was meant to be a twenty-day walk in eighteen days, leaving me (two days before the big birthday) with no particular place to go.

Surprising even myself, I caught a plane to Italy, and on the dawn of the day that marked the beginning of my sixty-first year of life, found myself floating in the sea off the Amalfi Coast, where, over the space of an hour's floating, I finally and somewhat astoundingly made peace with my mother, who died in 1983.

Serendipità, as they say in Italy.

I have read that serendipity is said to be one of the ten hardest-to-translate English words. How encouraging, therefore, that today the word has been at least imported into so many other of this world's languages. In French, it's *sérendipicité.* In Spanish, *serendipia.* The Dutch call it *serendipiteit*; the Germans, *Serendipität.* And so it goes.

As, one hopes, do you.

Finally, is there an opposite of serendipity? Well, Scottish novelist William Boyd once made up the word *zemblanity,* which he described as "making unhappy, unlucky and expected discoveries occurring by design." To me, that would be just another word for "staying home."

I'm happy to say that while this book is filled with examples of serendipity, there is no zemblanity anywhere to be found.

Read on.

Happy surprises ahead.

Linda Ellerbee is an outspoken journalist, award-winning television producer, bestselling author, a breast cancer survivor, a mom, a grandmother, and one of the most sought-after speakers in America. With more than thirty years' experience as a network news correspondent, anchor, writer, and producer,

*Ellerbee has won several Emmy, Peabody, and Columbia duPont awards. She has written three bestsellers—*And So It Goes, *a rollicking account of her years in network television,* Move On, *a more intimate look at her life, and* Take Big Bites: Adventures Around the World and Across the Table, *a humorous account of her love of travel, talking to (and eating with) strangers. Today, Ellerbee heads her own television production company, Lucky Duck Productions, a supplier of prime time specials, documentaries, and limited-run series for television networks. Her news show for children,* Nick News, *airs on Nickelodeon, has won three Peabody Awards and five Emmys, and is the longest-running and most-watched children's news program ever.*

ॐ ॐ ॐ

La Zisa, La Cuba, and La Cubula

It started as a simple tour of Palermo.

"I'm taking you to visit La Zisa, La Cuba, and La Cubula," Maia, my elderly cousin informed me, folding her newspaper.

"Friends of yours?" I was teasing her; I'd seen them on my Palermo map. I'd had the great fortune of staying with her in her seventh floor apartment looking out on Monte Pellegrino for the last three weeks. She had escorted me to as many of her city's architectural pearls as we could pluck. She wanted to give me Sicily on a platter, wishing only that I would take it with me for a lifetime.

"You could say that. I haven't seen them myself for years. All three require a certain effort to locate, because they are hidden away. You will find them quite fascinating.

I have to say it again: I feel so young, rediscovering my own city with you here."

The section of town we drove through was bleak and modern. "Believe me, these buildings are worth the search. They are remnants of a tremendous twelfth-century pleasure park between Palermo and the golden shell of Conca d'Oro," Maia raised her voice, dodging traffic as if playing bumper cars. "These were the fantasy realms of the Arabo-Norman kings, where elaborate gardens and fountains, man-made lakes and pavilions covered the expanse, where exotic imported beasts roamed, where the royals luxuriated." We wound through harsh urban streets without a branch or blade of green anywhere. Maia turned into a sagging neighborhood of stone hovels and small vegetable plots guarded by a few retired dogs, roosters, and the top half of a crucified scarecrow.

"La Zisa. There," she yanked up the brake smartly and threw her door open, "as lovely as I remember it." The Moorish building rose lyrically from a palomino-colored field, its central arch soaring, its upper windows open to the morning air. Signs posted everywhere prohibited entrance.

"It's always in a state of restoration," Maia shrugged as we approached. "*Scusa*," she used her commanding-yet-polite-I-am-a-Palermo-senior-citizen tone in addressing a workman. "We'd like to look for five minutes, if you would be so kind."

"Sorry," he yelled back, "we're constructing a scaffold."

"Typical," Maia muttered to me. "We'll just stand inside for a minute, on the opposite end away from all the work," she called out. "All we want to do is see the light stream through the empty windows." To me she added, "The walls are said to have a beautiful apricot glow when the sun strikes them."

"Oooh, apricot," I gushed.

"Something could fall," he yelled.

"He's right about that. An empire for example." She proceeded gamely. "We have a visitor here from California. Surely you don't want to turn her away."

"Come back in ten years."

"This is not a laughing matter, my good man. You've been restoring and restoring. Why can't the public, who pays your wages, see the progress?"

He shrugged and walked away.

"Notice the line where the pond once was."

I slid my sunglasses down and squinted. "Maybe I see *something*. I'm not certain though."

"The entire park was once filled with coursing waters and reflecting pools. Eh, poets sang its praises," Maia half-closed her eyes at the faraway thought. "My husband and I used to picnic here, before we had our boys. Well, let's push ahead. We have the two other buildings to find, so that you can get an idea of the immensity of the park."

We drove through more gray slums stamped with impossibility. Everywhere, packs of young children mingled with older kids on the wasted streets.

"The poverty breaks my heart. Some who come here from the country regret the move, but then they cannot go back to a place they know full well is worse. What are we to do about our great problems, I ask you?"

I was seriously wishing I could formulate an answer when we merged into a thoroughfare cramped with vehicles. Maia circled to find parking in the chaos. She finally became so fed up—"Boh!"—that she pulled into a red zone. A bartender in the Caffè Nettuno leaned out his window.

"*Signora*, you might get towed," he warned.

Maia brushed aside the thought. "I don't think anything will happen. We'll only be here a few minutes."

We trudged up the crazy-cacaphonous boulevard to a military compound, Caserma Tukory, where we sought permission to see La Cuba. The guard, a rifle-carrying boy of twenty or so, scowled with an exaggerated authority that I wanted to laugh aloud at, especially since he had powdered sugar all over his lips. An incriminating partly-eaten brioche huddled on a plate in his office. He confiscated my passport and Maia's retirement card. Another grim soldier was summoned to lead us past barracks. He fixed his ramrod legs into the ground. "Here it is." Modest stonewalls faced us, and we faced them.

"This was the pleasure pavilion?"

Impatiently, the guard pushed a pebble around with his foot.

"We're standing in it. Notice what remains of the cube-shaped hall. Notice its similarity to La Zisa, although clearly much smaller. Can you imagine the sultans dallying with their consorts here in the shade, can you imagine zebras and peacocks roaming the grounds?"

"Yes, yes I can, because you paint a vivid picture." I couldn't really, but she had worked so very hard to get me here. The guard kept a suspicious eye trained on us and a suspicious ear tuned in.

"At ease, young man, we're leaving now. Onward to La Cubula." Maia wanted me to have nothing less than the full twelfth-century experience. We hit the street again. I struggled to keep up with her determined pace. Her walking shoes clicked briskly along the pavement.

The café proprietor ran towards us on bowed legs, waving his arms, leaning sideways at a dangerous angle. His eyes were frantic. "*Signora*, I warned you, I told you that this might happen," he moaned, "I told you so, but you wouldn't listen to me, and now this!"

My cousin, the color drained from her face, mutely stared at the empty red zone, but this man was undone. Customers in the bar poured out onto the sidewalk like an

opera chorus, crowding around to hear his riveting reen-
actment. He described the police pulling up with the tow
truck, the gruesome rattle of the chain, the hooks being
applied, the terrible scraping of the bumper along the
street, the sparks flying. He danced around the sidewalk
like a jerky Sicilian marionette, lunging, pacing, halting,
miming, weeping, arguing, not with Maia, but at the air. I
pinched my lips together hard and commanded myself, do
not laugh, I'm telling you. Someone handed him a handkerchief. He dried his face, then began again, holding his
head in his hands, wailing, "Oh me!"

"*Coraggio!*" (courage) shouted a bystander.

The café proprietor pointed to the space where the
car had been. The crowd wordlessly studied the void left
behind.

I wanted to say something helpful other than I'm sorry,
but I couldn't think of what it was. If it weren't for my
presence in Palermo my cousin wouldn't be chaperoning
me all over the city to show me this disintegrating ruin and
that obscure sight. She wouldn't be parking in forbidden
zones. The fault rested with me. Mea maxissima culpa.

The man was still at it. This would never happen back
home. Americans don't run out of cafés to witness the
aftermath of a towing. My eyes stayed fixed on the red
paint. How the poor man must have carried on during the
actual confiscation. Now he sat on the curb, fanning himself while the murmuring crowd slowly dispersed.

I tagged after Maia into the café. "Let's go get your car
wherever they've taken it."

She waved away that idea with her hand, disappearing
into a wooden phone booth. I paced up and down the length
of the counter past gleaming brass fixtures, past rows of
gelati in their trays—*cocco, caramella, zabaglione, pistacchio,
kiwi, cassata*—past pastries fashioned into pianos, drums,

violins and harps, treble clefs and sixteenth notes. I was a distracting and expensive influence on my aged cousin, who was wearing herself out watching over me. Her taut voice threaded from the booth. She emerged insisting that we take a cab home.

"What a pity that you cannot now see La Cubula. It is truly lovely. To pick up the car, we must first go to a magistrate, pay the fine, and procure permission to retrieve the vehicle from a separate office before they issue us the right papers to present at the car-storage facility. Too close to lunchtime now. All the offices will close for three hours. At any rate, there's nothing to do but go home. Three different places all over the city I have to go." She held up three fingers. "It would take all day."

"Aye-yi-yi," I slapped my forehead, "what bureaucracy. It could unravel a person."

"It does, all the time. My son will handle this," she stated firmly. "Sons are good at this kind of thing. Would you like an espresso and maybe one of these biscotti?"

That was it. I was weighing on her, even though she had daily insisted I could stay with her as long as I wanted. I had to leave. The taxi pulled up. I looked back one last time at Mr. Caffè Thespian, crumpled on a tall stool, a cigarette dangling lifelessly between his lips, a vacant gaze on his face. He felt so much. So much!

Our cab did its best to advance in the midday jam. I glanced at Maia, who stared out the window, her mind clearly on the recent loss. Our driver decided to maneuver crosswise over to the first intersection, and we were treated to yells, honks, and gestures I had not yet seen around town. He sang throughout, cheerful as a cherub, eyeing me in the rear-view. I eyed him back.

"There's my car," Maia shrieked. Ahead by half a block the nose of her white Fiat bobbed in the metal sea.

"*Permesso, Signora,* I shall chase it down for you," the cab driver announced and up on the sidewalk we went. He caught sight of me in his mirror and winked.

After much deft maneuvering, we actually came abreast of the tow truck.

"*Permesso.* I will ask him to give you your car. For a small fee."

I gaped at Maia, astounded. Go ahead, she gestured, if you can. But he couldn't. The towman was devoted to the rules of the city. No bribes today. Maia sighed, and away we were driven to her apartment building. She and I fought over who would pay. I won.

As she headed towards the lobby our driver said, "*Signorina,* it has been an incomparable pleasure transporting cargo such as yourself." He kissed my hand and took off.

෴ ෴ ෴

Natalie Galli's articles have appeared in the San Francisco Chronicle *and* The Berkeley Monthly. *Her work of creative non-fiction,* Three-Cornered Island, *details her search for Franca Viola, the first woman in Sicilian history to publicly refuse the tradition of coercive marriage.* Ciao Meow, *her children's book about a freewheeling cat, boasts illustrations by her sister. Look for her contributions in* Travelers' Tales Italy *and* Italy: a Love Story. *She lives in San Rafael, California.*

❧ ❧ ❧

Dipping Fork, Flying Girl, Heart Attack

There's more than one way to get up from the table.

I can't eat fondue all the time, but there's just nothing like the occasional pot of molten cheese to stir the senses and soften the belly. On a recommendation, my sister Kathryn and I ventured out with two friends one cold November evening to a small restaurant at the edge of Montmartre known for its inexpensive *prix fixe* menu and generous glasses of wine.

The narrow room was lined by two long rows of small tables packed so tightly together that their edges touched. When we arrived many of the tables were already filled; groups clustered around heavy pots and vied for dipping rights across from couples clinking glasses. The whole room was warm from the heat of the kitchen and the air was rich with the dense aroma of melted cheese and cherry brandy.

The waiter showed us to our table. With effort, he wedged it out from between its neighbors so that Kathryn and I could slip through to the bench seats against the wall. After tucking us in, he brought large glasses of wine and a tiny bowl of olives that we savored as more people poured through the door and squeezed into the remaining few seats. By the time the fondue came—a substantial pot balanced atop a small flame and flanked by squares of bread—the dining room was packed and people stood waiting outside. Those of us already inside were trapped in our seats by the piles of food, the people sitting shoulder to shoulder, and the aisle so narrow that the waiters had to navigate it sideways. But we didn't care. We were eating fondue and drinking wine, we were laughing and telling stories: the one about trying to ask for a quart of milk but through an error in pronunciation ending up with a torso-sized wheel of cheese; the sighting of the fat parakeet among the pigeons at the Jardin de Tuileries; and the cautionary tale about why it's a terrible idea to eat chocolate cookies next to a heater while wearing wool pants.

The fondue was dangerously good. I ate with an abandon I was sure I'd regret within the hour, dunking each piece of bread completely and not bothering to let the excess cheese drip back into the pot before popping it in my mouth. I drank only wine with my meal because I'd once heard that drinking water while eating fondue causes the cheese to cool and form a giant rubbery ball in the stomach. Kathryn hypothesized that carbonation would prevent rubber ball formation, so she felt safe ordering and drinking a large bottle of sparkling water.

Though Kathryn and I had both worked diligently during our Paris sojourn to blend in with the culture—to walk for miles in high heels, wear scarves well, give the *pouf* of non-committal thought, and buy our produce at open-air

markets—we never did master the French art of drinking without peeing. It was a remarkable skill exhibited by
French women, and one that I'd seen again and again at
dinner parties, bars, and clubs; where after long hours of
revelry I would be unable to stand the pressure any longer
and would sneak off to the bathroom in shame while these
women with bladders of steel continued sipping and nib-
bling, comfortably ignoring the very foundation of human
digestion, at least until a more convenient hour.

We'd given up on the fondue and finished a second bottle
of wine by the time Kathryn's cultural physiology caught
up with her. "I'm so sorry," she said. "Really sorry. But I've
got to pee. I'm going to need to get out." She squirmed and
grimaced to illustrate the gravity of the situation.

We considered the options. Our table was still piled
too high with pots, utensils, wine, and glasses to consider
moving it safely. The two Frenchmen at the next table
overheard the conversation and suggested that Kathryn
crawl under the table, but after scrunching down to test the
plausibility of the maneuver, she realized that she was too
tall to slide beneath it. Someone waved our waiter over. He
crossed his arms and smiled confidently; he had obviously
been in this position before and knew exactly what to do.
He told her to stand up on her seat and jump across. The
men at the table next to us nodded approvingly.

"I will catch you, you see?" He held his arms out, rolled
up his sleeves, and flexed. He did have excellent muscle tone.
Kathryn looked at all of us. Taken with the idea that soon,
with the blessing of the management, she might sail high
above the table, I grinned and said, "He will catch you, you
see?" She bit her lip and looked at each of us again to make
sure we weren't kidding. Then, on wobbly heels, she climbed
up on the bench seat, steadying herself on my shoulder, shaking her head at the thought of what she was about to do.

For a minute, Kathryn just stood there. We waited, giddy and breathless, watching her debate between stepping on the table and leaping over it. In every way, the latter was the best option. We had been taught very specific things about table manners growing up: no feet anywhere near the table, use a napkin not the tablecloth, and don't ever discuss rats. Remembering the no-feet rule, I could see she was having a very hard time envisioning her slightly muddy high heel on the white tablecloth. And, while stepping on a table felt like a true transgression, jumping over it somehow didn't seem quite as wrong.

From our lower elevation, we could see that the fondue pot was perched precariously on its little burner, and that a jolt could send both Sterno and cheese liquid into one of our laps. And I suspected that fondue, if mixed with flammables, would be dangerous for the same reason that it's not a good idea to wear polyester close to a campfire. With one hand, I smoothed my napkin all the way across my lap, just in case.

She took a long, slow breath. The man sitting at the next table cheered her on with a hearty "Courage, mademoiselle, courage." The waiter bent his knees and signaled for her to jump. Kathryn nodded, braced herself against the wall, and then flung all of her five feet nine inches over the table. She jumped with extended legs and eyes wide with terror, her foot missing the cauldron of cheese by an easy six inches. The waiter caught her in his arms and lowered her safely back to the ground. We clapped, the waiter bowed, Kathryn blushed, thanked him, and hurried off to the bathroom.

The waiters of Paris square off each year in a uniformed, tray-carrying race through the center of the city. I feel sure that someday, when the race inspires an entire Waiter Olympics, patron catching will be event number two.

When Kathryn returned, the two men next to us got up and moved their table out so that she could slide back in. Through the cheese and wine haze I briefly wondered why we hadn't done that initially.

As they moved the table back into place, the shorter of the two asked us if we'd enjoyed the fondue. He touched the edge of his now-empty pot as he asked. We all agreed that it had been great. He then asked, with feigned surprise, if we were finished already. Our pot still sat half full on the table, but I couldn't imagine eating any more cheese without blacking out. Kathryn indicated that we'd finished, and that's when he asked if he and his friend could eat the rest.

It was a surprising request. Here were two middle-aged, reasonably fit, well-dressed Parisians asking us for the leftover two pounds of our fondue. I shrugged a *"oui"* and we passed it over. They thanked us and promptly polished off the rest of the pot, summoning the waiter to replenish their supply of bread halfway through. After they finished, the man next to me leaned over, smiling and kneading his chest with his fist. And in a voice mixed with the bliss of satiation and casual fatalism, he said, "Tonight, I might die."

Christine Sarkis is an associate editor at SmarterTravel.com. Her work has also appeared on USAToday.com, and in Spain from a Backpack. *Her sister Kathryn has not jumped over any more tables since the fondue incident, and has no plans to reinvent herself as a dining-room Evel Knievel.*

❧ ❧ ❧

My Ex-Novio's Mother

Maybe she was better off without the boyfriend.

One sunny afternoon, in the flowered courtyard of my apartment in small-town Oaxaca, I was washing clothes when my elderly landlady emerged from the banana leaves, and out of the blue, exclaimed, "Laurita, did you know that some people in this world don't believe in the mother of Jesus?!"

"I've heard that," I conceded, squeezing out soap suds and wondering what had prompted her inquiry—possibly a recent Jehovah's Witness visit despite the *This home is Catholic* sticker vehemently plastered on her door.

She shook her head, bewildered. "But Laurita, we must believe in the Virgin. You know why?"

"Why?"

She wagged her finger at me—a squat, apron-bedecked sage. "Because we pray to Her. And then She tells Her Son what to do. And He does it. That's how it all works."

She scrunched up her face and burst into nasal laughter. "Mothers have the real power. Remember that!"

Four years later, I'm sitting on a narrow bed in a raw cement room on the outskirts of the same small town in Oaxaca. After living in the U.S. for two years, I'm now renting out this tiny room as a base for my anthropological fieldwork. Apart from the bed, the room is nearly bare except for an unstained wooden desk and chair that I bought literally off the back of a carpenter.

The lack of seating is the excuse for my ex-sort-of-boyfriend, Baruc, to sit next to me on the flowered sheets. He's careful not to wrinkle the button-down shirt and khaki pants that fit him like a model's. I gaze at his dimpled half-smile and remember all over again how his manicured hands used to make my skin tingle.

He's helping me form questions for my Master's thesis interviews with Mixtec women, and over the past two hours, the space between us has grown smaller and warmer. Baruc was my first friend in Oaxaca, the one who taught me Spanish and Mixteco, the first to invite me to an indigenous festival and feed me goat in *mole* sauce. The fruity smell of his shampoo brings back the magical feeling of exploring a new land. Once we finish drafting the interview, I resist the urge to sink into him, and instead ask the question that could send him running from the room. "So, four years ago…why didn't you let us get closer?"

He stares at the ceiling, uncomfortable. "I figured you'd be leaving. All the English teachers come for a year or two, then they leave for good."

"But I might have stayed. Look at me. I can't stay away."

He sighs. "Now I know that. But I didn't before. And my mother…" Another sigh.

Aha. His mother.

Back when we were sort-of boyfriend and girlfriend, he never spent the night at my place, always returning to his parents' house by 11 p.m.—even though he was twenty-six. I'd assumed the motive was noble: to protect my already dubious reputation as a twenty-three-year-old woman living alone in small-town Mexico. The culturally appropriate place for unmarried sex was a dark alley, involving a skirt furtively pushed up, no mention of condoms, and often, a belly mysteriously swelling a few months later. But two adults spending all night in a real bed, using birth control, maybe even showering together and lounging around naked—well, that was just morally depraved.

After a long pause, he continues. "My mother was worried you'd take me to your country, and then all her sons would be there."

His three brothers have been working as undocumented immigrants in Chicago since they were teenagers, risking desert crossings every few years to come back for visits. There seems to be an agreement that Baruc would be the one to stay. After all, he has a college degree, accounting job, and even his own car. In rural Oaxaca, grown sons traditionally live on their parents' property with their wives and children. The exodus of young people to Mexico City and the U.S. has thrown a wrench in the custom, yet Baruc's parents have evidently held onto these hopes for him.

"My mother says she couldn't bear it if I left, too."

His mother always treated me with polite reserve, never affectionately calling me Laurita, as my other local friends did. She didn't even call me Laura. I remained a generic *güera*—white girl—to her. I'd chalked it up to her personality, but maybe she simply saw me as a heartless foreign creature with pale skin that might snatch her son.

After a while, I touch Baruc's stiff sleeve, probably ironed that morning by his mother. "Seriously. I might have stayed with you."

He strokes my arm with his perfect fingers, and then, just when I'm starting to melt, he pulls away. "Laurita, I have to go. I have to run some errands for my mother."

I'm starting to kick myself when he says, "Let's go out tonight. I'll pick you up around six."

"Really? You promise?"

"Of course."

In the past, the pattern was familiar: he'd ask me to go out, tell me what time he'd pick me up, and then he wouldn't show. Usually, at the university the next day, I'd stop by the accounting office and ask him what happened in a voice designed to sound as unhurt as possible. "Oh, right," he'd say breezily. "I had to help my mother with something." I assumed he was lying, and I tried not to care too much. I imagined his obstacle to commitment was another woman in a dark alley—but I never suspected his mother.

This time is different. I'm four years older and wiser now, and I've run out of patience. He will have to play by my rules. "You really, truly promise you'll come?"

"Yes, Laurita. I promise."

At six I'm all dressed up, watching the occasional burro pass by on the dirt road. In the yard, chickens peck at corn as the landlady's teenage granddaughter gyrates to the song blaring from her boom box: *"...un movimiento sexy, sexy, sexy..."*

By seven o'clock, my stomach is rumbling and I'm cursing my gullibility.

At eight, it starts raining. I need to get food, which means finding a taxi to take me to town. I run down the dark, muddy street in the rain, soaked and pathetic. Once I plop inside the taxi, I decide that this time *will* be different. Indignant, I shake the water from my hair, and give the driver directions to Baruc's parents' house.

Fifteen minutes later, he drops me off at the roadside by their house. I stomp through mud puddles to the locked metal gate, and I ring the buzzer and pound on the metal gate, clanking the chain like a lunatic. His mother, Doña Esperanza, pokes her head out the door and squints at me through the dark rain. A shawl draped over her head, she comes outside, her wide body lumbering down the steps.

"*Güera*," she says, fumbling with the keys. "White girl, what are you doing here?"

She still doesn't know my name? No way am I pretending to be nice to this woman anymore.

I am not the type that yells. Especially not at other people's mothers. But the words spout up like boiling lava. "WHERE IS YOUR SON?!"

What I really want to shout is *WHERE IS YOUR* PINCHE *SON?* Or better yet, *WHERE IS YOUR* PENDEJO *OF A SON?!* but I manage to hang onto a few threads of self-control.

She looks at me, stunned, and slowly opens the gate.

"WHERE IS HE?!" I screech.

"He's running some errands."

"Well, that—" I swallow the words *hijo de puta*. "Well that son of yours was supposed to pick me up at six. I've been waiting for TWO AND A HALF HOURS!"

She blinks, shocked. I'd never been anything but polite and gracious to her. She'd probably thought of us *güeras* as soulless Barbies—skinny, plastic, smiling dolls, incapable of red-hot fury.

"Come in, *güera*." She ushers me into the tiny, gray cement kitchen that smells of dried chile, and sits me down at the table where her mother is seated.

Doña Elisa watches us curiously with cataract-muted eyes. A polyester skirt-suit peeks out from under a checked apron, and a ribboned white braid snakes down her back. "What's happening?" she asks.

I'm afraid I'll yell at this old lady, so I keep my mouth glued shut and let her daughter answer. "Baruc said he'd pick up the *güera* and he didn't." She bites her lip and the corners of her mouth turn up, suppressing laughter.

I glare. "I AM *HASTA LA MADRE* WITH YOUR SON!" Essentially, *I've f-ing had it with your son.*

They stare at each other for a split second, then double over, clutching their large bellies, shaking with laughter.

"Ay, *güera!*" the grandmother says. "You need some *agua de espanto.*" Fright water. "That will cure you."

"But I don't have fright, I have ANGER! AT YOUR GRAND-SON!" *And at your evil daughter,* I add silently.

More laughter. "The *agua de espanto* works for *coraje*, too," Doña Elisa assures me. "Don't worry, *güera.*"

Many Mixtec people in rural Oaxaca feel that anger and fright cause illness, that these emotion-energies can harm your body or lead to your spirit being stolen. So now the important thing is to cure my anger before it causes real damage. From the top shelf, Doña Esperanza grabs an old Coke bottle, filled with clear liquid. She pours me a small glass and sets it on the flowered vinyl tablecloth.

I sniff. It's a hard alcohol—probably *mezcal* locally made from fermented agave nectar and steeped with herbs and spices—strong, tingling ones like cloves and anise.

"Drink," Doña Elisa says, smiling, wiping tears from her face.

I gulp it. For a moment, it burns, then flows through my empty stomach and seeps quickly into my bloodstream. Little by little, the *coraje* floats out and dissipates.

"Have another, *güera,*" Doña Esperanza says.

I down a second glass.

By the third, every last trace of rage has gone. Now we're cracking jokes and telling stories. Over and over, Doña Esperanza imitates me in the rain at the gate. Screwing up her face, she fake-yells, *where is your son?!* And this sends Doña Elisa and me into cascades of belly-shaking giggles.

On the fourth glass, a truck pulls up and headlights flash across the wall. Quickly, I try to compose myself and smooth my rain-frizzy hair. A minute later, Baruc strides in, looking as handsome as ever, especially model-like with rain dripping from his sculpted face and his mouth parted in surprise. "Laura! What are you doing here?"

His mother and grandmother launch into the story, offering bits and pieces between giggles, and collapsing in hysterical laughter on the *where is your son?!* part.

Baruc stares at me, then the bottle of *agua de espanto*, and then back at me. "Are you drunk, Laura?"

I grin. "It's medicine. To get rid of my *coraje*. To avoid killing you." *And your mother,* I recall, glancing at her fondly.

He looks at us like we're crazy. "I'm hungry, *Mamá*."

She hops up and plucks some tortillas from a basket. Yes, it's quite an arrangement they have—he follows her orders in his romantic relationships; she follows his orders in domestic tasks. A fair bargain.

One day in my apartment, years ago, Baruc told me to get him a glass of water. It had sounded like a command, so I promptly replied, "Get it yourself." He laughed, but an uncomfortable feeling hovered in the room.

I gaze at his mother now, suddenly grateful, wondering if she ended up saving me from a life of waiting hand and foot on her son.

"I'm going to change clothes," Baruc tells us, annoyed, and disappears to his room.

We women snicker. For a tiny moment, I imagine life with these ladies as my in-laws. It would be entertaining— but only with enough *agua de espanto* to keep the *coraje* at bay.

We chat as Doña Esperanza heats up beans and *mole* and chamomile tea. She sets them in front of me with a basket of steaming tortillas. "Eat," she says warmly, with a genuine smile. "Eat."

As I chew, she takes my hand in her pudgy one. "Oh, Laurita," she says. "Why don't you stay? Why don't you stay and marry my son, Laurita?"

And just like that, something shifts. In her eyes, my anger has melted away the pale, plastic, Barbie-doll skin of a nameless *güera*. For the first time, she sees me, really sees me...just a little too late.

Colorado-based Laura Resau is an award-winning author of two young adult novels set in rural Oaxaca: What the Moon Saw *and* Red Glass. *Her travel writing has appeared in anthologies by Travelers' Tales and Lonely Planet, as well as numerous journals and magazines. Visit her web site at www.lauraresau.com.*

❧ ❧ ❧

Cave with a View

In the Himalayas, a traveler looks for solitude and finds companionship, yearns for hardship and finds comfort.

I sit in a pink plastic lawn chair in front of my borrowed meditation cave. The afternoon is perfect, a warm cedar-scented breeze sighing through the branches of the deodars on the hill. Tiny birds chirp in the underbrush. My rosary drops onto my lap, my mantra recitation slurs to a halt.

Past my bare toes is a gulf of bluish, haze-softened air. Far below, the sacred lake glints like dull-green jade. The high Himalayas are visible today, low and pale across the horizon.

I've wanted to meditate in a cave ever since reading those first hyperbolic yoga books as a teenager. But I thought I'd be eating weeds, fighting off leopards and even a demon or two. Privation and loneliness would be the whole enlightening deal. I'd end up luminous and scrawny, wearing nothing but a diaper.

Reality, here, is quite the opposite. I'm getting fatter by the day. By the time I go home, after a month, I will have gained eight pounds. My cave has electricity and linoleum on the floor, keeping dust at bay. It's not exactly a cave, but an overhang under a cliff, beefed up with a front wall, door, and curtains on the windows. The effect is reminiscent of a rustic stone house you might see in the Alps, but with bigger spiders.

Yes, I'm surrounded by mini-beings: spiders, centipedes, flies, mosquitoes, beetles, silverfish, moths, and cockroaches. Through the pitch-black night I hear them crunching in each other's jaws, plus the scuffling of rats, mongooses, feral cats, and snakes, fighting and mating in the roof. Not to mention the living presence of the mountain, dropping the occasional clod onto my bed as she takes another baby step toward the sea.

These things all provide occasion for forbearance, and a tale of hardship I can tell the folks back home. But vermin and the danger of collapse aren't the main duress of being here. It is accepting the extraordinary love I'm being given.

One night I dream of my mother, alive. She died in 1983 but I know what the dream means. I haven't been cared for like this since I was an infant.

Three weeks ago, armed with introductions and a few small gifts, I arrived in Rewalsar, as the Indians call the lake and town a thousand meters below this cave (for Tibetans, it's Tso Pema, Lotus Lake). Ani Choe Lhamo was the first person I contacted. She is a nun, about forty years of age, and speaks a little English. We hung out. "You and me, same!" she said, laughing, the day she learned we shared a root guru, the late Nyoshul Khen Rinpoche. A few days later she offered me her cave. I'd mentioned envying her but honestly, I didn't mean it as a hint.

"If you or I meditate in my cave, what difference?" Then she laughed maniacally again.

But I'm cautiously in agreement that we may have been sisters in some forgotten past life. It's a feeling. Laughing together, lying side by side on a bed, eating mango sprinkled with Chunky Chat spice powder, I felt inexplicably close. Rationally, I tell myself this is simply what it feels like to hang out with someone who practices being unselfish, compassionate, and wise every day for years. Still, being here feels like stumbling into the bosom of a long-lost, alternate family. Or maybe I don't even have to call it alternate. It's real. Resonances deep as blood.

"I will miss you," she said, and walked off around the shoulder of the hill.

So my cave is full of her absence, an austere, demanding gift in its own way. I'm sleeping in her bed, sitting in her pink lawn chair gazing out at this view—while she shares a room with her eighty-year-old great-uncle at a monastery down the hill.

And this is only half the story. For the cave is a duplex, and another nun lives in the other half: rotund, gossipy Ani Choenyi, sixty-one.

"My" side of the cave is slightly bigger than hers. Still, from the bed, where I usually meditate, I can reach everything without uncrossing my legs. Book, teacup, incense, light switch. It is delightful to be snuggled into the mountain's dark stone belly, upheld by the sturdy rhythms of Ani Choenyi's practice.

I love listening to her drum and bell, the strange wail of her thighbone trumpet that wriggles through the air as soon as darkness swallows the mountain. She is practicing Chöd, offering her body to demons, hungry ghosts, and presumably the human being next door. I

know she thinks I'm hungry, given the way she feeds
me during the day.

I've been fantasizing a lot about my life unrolling forward from here, especially when it rains and the outer
world literally vanishes behind low, rolling clouds the
color of dirty rags. Or when morning light comes in
the window. And even when dozens of spiders spiral
around the walls. Of course I know this is like a dream.
I won't be here long—very soon, my karmic debt to
this community would go from overwhelming to dis-
graceful. Like the *New Yorker* cartoon of a wife coming
to retrieve her husband from a similar mountaintop.
"Sheldon!"

For now, it's obvious that love is the practice I am
meant to be doing here. Especially since this lake is
where Guru Rinpoche, aka Padmasambhava, the yogi
who converted Tibet to Buddhism, fell in love twelve
hundred years back.

A few hundred yards from where I sit, he and
Princess Mandarava disappeared into the stony bowels
of this mountain. Though her mind was freed by their
tantric practice, it's hardly surprising that her father, the
king, got upset. There are still some pretty wild ascetics
wandering around India. Just a week ago, down by the
lake, I got creeped out by the coals at the bottom of a pair
of eyes I'd made the mistake of looking into. I wouldn't
want my daughter running off with him!

The king tried to burn Guru Rinpoche alive but the
saintly magician turned the pyre into a pond; and, as in
all such stories, the king bowed down as a disciple.

The actual lake is kind of small; but around here,
the mythical proportions of things are more important.
There is an island said to migrate around the lake; I

finally figured out it was a tiny mat of reeds, decked with old white offering scarves.

Tso Pema is in the Mandi district of Himachal Pradesh, a region known for prosperity. Indeed the foothills seem less deforested than elsewhere and the villages better off: ample stone houses with slate roofs, a few satellite dishes. Each hamlet is rich in invisible wealth too. Veritable armies of yogis have reached enlightenment in the cave-riddled forests—some famous, like the siddhas Naropa and Tilopa, but many more are anonymous practitioners in a luminous tradition that continues to the present day. When I arrived with my list of folks to contact, several were unavailable, in *tsam*, sealed retreat. Old folks meet daily to pray; and in the monastery dorm, many rooms have curtains drawn across the doors, indicating the tenant is in retreat.

You can't miss it. Everybody feels it. A sweet energy dances in the air. How to absorb it? Do you just sit there? It's fun, but weirdly difficult. Love, surrender, and interconnection are surely part of it; but I keep bumping up against neurotic guilt and self-doubt.

Another dream: I'm in a Hindi spy movie, full of paranoid intrigue, but wake up just as I'm finding out everything's actually O.K.

Luckily I have two career cave yoginis, showing me how it's done. I can see they are not living in any outward paradise. Both of them have medical issues and rely on sponsors in far-off countries to send them the $40 a month they need to live on. Ani Choe Lhamo has stuck a Buddha image in the biggest ceiling crack, presumably to ward off a collapse of the entire cliff above.

What I notice is that they don't let their minds get the better of them. Ani Choenyi hates the bugs in her cave, but she'd never kill them. "What? And ruin the blessings?"

The longer I am here, the more people I hear the two of them are helping with their monthly $40.

One day Ani Choe Lhamo shows up to check on me, but I think she wants her cave back and offer to move out. She scowls good-humoredly—I'm being tiresome. The next time she comes, I can't resist offering again. The truth is, I can't imagine moving out of my house in Boston for her.

That was the night I had my Hindi spy dream.

As for Ani Choenyi, she's been waiting on me hand and foot. Buttered chapatis at breakfast, stir-fried vegetables at lunch, piping-hot corn porridge at dinner. "Eat, eat," she cries, ladling a third helping onto my plate. Tea—I must be swilling forty cups a day. Sweet milky Indian tea, Tibetan butter tea, plain black tea (*suja, pocha, ngakja* in Tibetan). Every afternoon she comes, with a cup of *suja* and a cookie, in case I'm hungry and tired from all my practice.

I have to receive this love. What else am I going to do, go home early and pay a penalty to the airlines?

Ani Choenyi is a Chaucerian character, stout and honest, with a face as rough as the earthen walls. We spend mealtimes laughing, having elaborate conversations in a blend of pantomime and baby-talk Tibetan. She's taught me many of the things a mother would teach her child. The names and uses of my fingers, for example. First finger: Eating Finger. Middle finger: Ring Finger. Third finger: Secret Finger. Fourth finger: Little Finger. Sticking her two Secret Fingers into her nostrils, she tells me this is a foolproof method of easing childbirth. The baby will pop right out, she assures me, nodding vehemently with her fingers still stuck in.

And, as it often used to happen in those romantic old spiritual books, she's teaching me things I could learn in no other way, the rhythms of a practitioner who's in it for the long haul: wake up between 3 and 4 A.M. and practice until 8 A.M.; take the rat you trapped last night and release it far away (the supply of rats is endless); enjoy a leisurely breakfast, then meditate until lunchtime; post-lunch you nap, do chores, or perhaps receive a visitor; then, what? more meditation; dinner is small; then practice until late: 10 P.M.

Ani Choenyi saw her mother and sister killed by the Chinese. "I went to my teacher, Golok Ani, and I said, 'Let's go.'" Golok Ani, the Ani from Golok, was her teacher for thirty years, but Ani Choenyi never learned her personal name. The two of them took trains and walked to India. They stopped in Sikkim to see Dudjom Rinpoche, then in Bodh Gaya, arriving here in 1962.

Back in the old days, the hill was "empty," natural. Villagers said the deep narrow cave at the top of the mountain was where Guru Rinpoche and Mandarava practiced. She and Golok Ani joined the great meditator, Wangdor Rinpoche, living in small caves, *phuk-pa chum-chum,* amongst the piled rocks. Snow would blow in. Golok Ani died, sitting up in meditation; then Ani Choe Lhamo came along, a new cave-mate.

After Wangdor Rinpoche emerged from his practice, temples were built around him. More refugee practitioners keep arriving. Now there are fifty people at least up here. Most are young nuns from Derge, his region of Tibet. Lama Wangdor Rinpoche supports the community as best he can, bringing money back from teaching tours to the U.S. and Europe. He installed electricity and water pipes and donated furry blankets to everyone. But now he's seventy-two and finds it more difficult to travel. Some of the foreign sponsors got tired of sending money to people they've never seen. And now that caves are chockablock, the local villagers are reportedly resisting new arrivals.

Back in the old days, Ani Choenyi tells me, it was better. Not so crowded. But certainly less convenient. They lugged water from a spring an hour's walk downhill and begged for food in the villages.

It makes me cry when she talks about how the Indian people helped Tibetans. In the early days, a locket bearing the Dalai Lama's image was a train ticket, meal ticket, and room for the night. "We owe them everything," she says simply. Soon I learn from a teashop owner that Ani Choenyi put him through school and is now paying for his children's education. Then there's Malka, the sad homeless widow who roams the hillsides, kicked out by her family. She keeps a change of clothes in Ani Choenyi's woodshed. When the milk-seller's husband gets drunk and beats her, she too pours out her heart to Ani Choenyi.

But Ani Choenyi is no fool; she has what in the West we call "good boundaries." Time to meditate? She kicks out her friends and locks the gate. One day the teashop owner invites her to the christening of a new baby, and Ani Choenyi comes toddling home from the party after half an hour. They were drinking alcohol, she grouses. A nun has no business lingering at that sort of party.

She's confided in me her opinion of Westerners. The ones she's met are a little cuckoo. Emotional. "Should I do this practice, or that practice?" she mimicked, guffawing; I winced with recognition.

Today the only reason I'm alone, out on this veranda, is because she's chanting in a ceremony downtown—a feast offering for an unsuccessful itinerant clothing vendor. Afterward she'll go to the market and buy food for the two of us.

It's actually funny—I was secretly relieved she'd be away so I could finally skip a meal and eat the chocolate Luna Bar I'd been saving. I told her not to arrange a lunch and she slyly pretended to agree. As soon as I'd gobbled the Luna Bar there came a shy knock at the blue metal gate. I unbolted it and sure enough, there stood Ani Ngejung from two caves down, holding an enamel plate piled high with rice and eggplant curry. She sat and watched me eat, then silently took the plate away.

After she left, I tried to meditate indoors. But it's mid-July, hot season in India. Stuffed and drowsy, I came out where it's cooler.

A flock of tiny birds dips in and out of the bushes. Soon the mongoose slinks out from behind the water tank, liquid and silent as the snakes it feeds on. Seeing me, it slinks back.

Alas, if I am to embody a Tantric deity, it will be a distracted one.

Downhill a house is being built. Stonemasons' hammers clink, each blow clear but tiny. Fainter still is the tumult of the pilgrim town. Bus motors grinding, dogs yapping, laughter, shouts, an occasional temple bell. The thousand-meter drop provides a contemplative distance my unruly mind cannot. The worried world looks doll-house-sized. Leaning forward I can see the town rimming a button-sized lake. Tibetan *gompas* with yellow corrugated roofs; the Sikh *gurdwara*'s powder-blue dorm, the fat white spire of the Hindu *mandir*.

The mayor, who also runs the dry-cleaning shop, tells me that fully half of the local population consists of pilgrims, a stable flux of six thousand. This supports local farmers and shopkeepers. July is the high season, plains dwellers heading for the hills, bringing their children before school has started. All the passes down from Ladakh are open, too. Huge Sikh families are continually disgorged from SUVs, cameras ready to point and shoot at any Westerner. Busloads of Ladakhis—indescribably dirty and devout—come to prostrate in all the *gompas*. Not to mention the trickle of new Tibetan refugees arriving day by day. And the odd foreigner, like me.

Who *must* force herself to go back to visualizing her wrathful deity.

He's squashing me under his big toe. "*Rulu, Rulu!*" he roars, then disappears into space again, leaving me to my fatuous thoughts.

"Why do people practice in caves?" I ask Tenzin Wangyal Rinpoche, the Bön Buddhist lama, a month after I return to the United States.

He laughs and says that back in Tibet, if you didn't want to be a nomad or a town dweller any more, the caves were right there. Free housing.

I press him. "Is there an energy in the earth?"

Yes, he said, making a circular gesture in front of his belly. But hardly anybody knows how to work with it. Sacred energy is easier—the energy from previous meditators. Your efforts enter a kind of multiplying circuit, enhanced and eased by those who came before you.

It sure feels that way.

The deodars sough quietly in the gentle breeze. Hundreds of colorful prayer flags flutter like laundry of the gods. Their shadows dart jerkily, unpredictably in the thin, dried-up thorn branches that edge the nuns' terrace. This homemade security fence has seemed threatening and unaesthetic up to now, with its inch-long thorns poking through damp grubby laundry, trapping food crumbs from the dishwater Ani Choenyi tosses down the nearly vertical hillside. Suddenly the fence reminds me of a sculpture I saw once in a gallery: a room-sized, impossibly fragile construction made of toothpicks by a Polish artist. Hers lacked the element of movement, this mesmerizing flitting from depth to surface, point to point. I fantasize shipping the whole caboodle to New York, then lapse into a purer contemplation of the ephemeral movements of light. Is anything actually moving? Does the light inherently exist? Is it different from the shadow that follows it so closely?

Finally I hear a rattling at the blue gate. Ani Choenyi coming home. I straighten my back, begin to move the *mala* through my fingers. I've missed her; I wouldn't want her to think I'm slacking off.

In a few days I will leave this sacred place and time. Ani Ngejung will insist on carrying my suitcase on her head all the way to the bus stop. Ani Choenyi will accompany me down, to a restaurant where I'll treat her and Choe Lhamo to meat *momos*.

"Come back in two years!" they'll say. "We'll set you up in a sealed retreat. Now that we know you, we can really help you!"

Kate Wheeler is an award-winning fiction writer and journalist. Once upon a time she was a Buddhist nun, but is now married and lives in Somerville, Massachusetts. She teaches and practices meditation, and travels as much as she can. She's now at work on her second novel.

❧ ❧ ❧

Eros in Venice

There's more than one way to capture romance in the capital of love.

Don't go to Venice alone. I should have known that before I got there, but didn't. Of all the places in the world to visit without a lover, here was the city of Don Juan, of masked balls at Carnivale, of ducal intrigue behind the luminous pink stone of the Doge's palace. Honeymooners throw open broad shutters to views of the Grand Canal before falling, breathless, back into bed. Gondolas ply past endlessly with couples curled into each other in the fading light. I suddenly wanted to warn single women everywhere—to post it in bathroom stalls and on message boards—*Don't go to Venice alone, or live to regret it.*

From the first, Venice shimmers and dazzles. I had arrived on the train from Romeo and Juliette's Verona, and nearly fallen, head over heels, into the jade green waters of the Grand Canal. I wandered around that first day guppy-mouthed, doubtful of the city's very reality. Around every corner I half expected to find pulleys and Hollywood prop-men holding up the whole façade—and lovers, more and more lovers, hidden away with their private affairs on back sets.

Instead I found the palatial beauty of Campo San Marco choked with the tourist hordes of summer, chattering like monkeys in a cacophony of languages and posing with over-stuffed pigeons atop their heads and outstretched arms. Even then there was something romantic and grand that belied the chaos. Bathed in the light of the Adriatic, the golden mosaics of the onion-domed Basilica gleam. The bell tower, the *Campanile*, reaches high from the low horizon of the sinking city inspiringly. The porticoed buildings of the Procuratie, where the highest ranking officials of the Venetian state held their offices, are graying but noble; and the two tall columns that flank the square, crowned with the lion and the saint, stare out to the lagoon like wistful lovers themselves waiting for ships to return.

At night the pigeons disappear—completely. They roost somewhere silent and unseen, replaced by an unworldly calm. Lights flicker on under the arcades of the Procuratie, and white-tuxedoed orchestras take up their instruments under the velvetine sky. And in the grand ballroom of St. Mark's Square, the bevy of tourists become balletic couples, wheeling and waltzing under the stars.

Cradling my knees to my chest I perched on a pigeon-stained step, watching. They danced mostly to schmaltzy American showtunes, I told myself contemptuously, and overpaid for thorny roses hocked by chip-toothed gypsies. But in truth, I envied them. I thought of cheering myself with a Bellini cocktail, invented at nearby Harry's Bar, but somehow I couldn't bring myself to claim a seat at the linen-covered tables. I told myself the rent for one of those café spots was too steep, but who was I kidding: despite so many travels alone, here I felt like an outcast, unworthy of a place—love's reject in a city where eros, musky and mysterious, wafts through the very air.

That night I boarded the *vaporetto*, Venice's slow-chugging waterbus. Leaning over the railing, I saw heat lightning crackling overhead. At the steps of an ancient palazzo, enormous stone bowls brimming with flame beckoned to guests arriving in sleek boats two by two, to an elite, clandestine world, where silhouettes passed like wraiths under chandeliers of jewel-toned Murano glass.

The gloved attendants of the vaporetto threw thick coils of rope around a piling and pulled the boat to my stop at Ca D'Oro...*Palace of gold*. I repeated the name to myself, rolling the "r" of D'oro sumptuously. Yet my room near the palace was a single windowless cell (the rooms I had seen on their web site, with quaint views of hidden canals, were reserved for couples, I learned at check-in). As I stepped off the dock I looked over my shoulder at the shadowy guests. I wanted only to be one of them; to be welcomed in through one of those clandestine back canals; to take a warm hand and be led; to hear, from some half-darkened room, a soft voice call my name.

Venice doesn't boast the sorts of major tourist sights of Paris or Rome or London. There are quiet art galleries to be visited, graceful canal-side *palazzi* with rooms filled with fleshy Tiepolos and spacious Canalettis and countless views of the Grand Canal out of Arabic windows. There is the dark, domed Basilica, with its Byzantine secrets. And there are the artisanal jewelry shops that line the arced stone back of the Rialto Bridge. But days in Venice are long and slow moving, inviting a visitor simply to wander, compelling one in its labyrinthian innards to be lost and found and lost again.

Beyond San Marco, Venice's narrow alleys, scrawled with unexpected and abundant graffiti, give way to *camp-ielli*—postcard-size squares with dripping wells and stone churches, from whose dark interiors come plaintive strains of Baroque concertos. Dark bars called *bacari* offer dozens of *cicheti*: small glistening plates of polenta and squid and mushrooms, paired with pale glasses of the local Veneto wine.

I discovered *frittare*, fried bread drizzled in balsamic vinegar and fresh fragrant basil, ate it *al fresco*, and learned the pride of finding my way back through the baffling maze for another serving the next day. And in Dorsodoro I found my own café, under a cerulean blue umbrella, sipping the best-priced tea in the city near the creaking wood of the Accademia bridge. There I spent my afternoons, unhurried, soaking in a view free from billboards and Home Depots, and rich in warm-toned stone: sienna and salmon, mustard and pumpkin. Time acquired a texture we don't appreciate in all our usual busy-ness; hours felt thick and viscous. And I became attuned to stillness and silence, to this cityscape without Vespas, buses, and backfires.

Slowly, imperceptibly, Venezia was casting its spell. The city of hot-blooded romance is also *La Serenissima*, "the most serene," languishing in the long summer days like a well-sunned cat. It's a city where locals meet late in the afternoon at the sweet shops for a festive, fizzy *spritz*—wine and seltzer and a shot of kool-aid bright Campari. It's a city where one of the most astounding things to do is to board the #1 water bus, claim a lone seat at the prow, and ply the Grand Canal's full serpentine length at sunset, when the water becomes an Impressionistic canvas; or to sit at night drinking wine from a paper cup at the foot of the Rialto Bridge where, if you look very closely, tiny crabs turn over in the water in slow, undulating waltzes of their own.

But the gondolas continued to wound me. Moored at the docks or gliding past with their glistening bows, the *ferro* that crowns the metal prow shot through me every time I glanced their way. Those sleek and gleaming glammed-up canoes became not only a symbol of Venice, but a painful reminder of my lonely experience there. They were not meant for a single person; the prohibitive expense of an hour's ride and their sneering, heart-shaped double seats made that fact abundantly clear. But to visit Venice without riding in a gondola seemed as awful as being in Venice without a lover. It rang of deprivation.

I felt the snub every time I passed a *stazio*, where brawny gondolieri charmed the tourists into their boats. They were gregarious, flirtatious, and sometimes gallant as I passed, tipping their ribboned straw hats and posing, with flexed muscles, for my snapshots. But they only rarely tried their sales pitch on me. As frustrating as it was to have to turn them down when they tried to hock a ride I couldn't afford on my own, it was even worse when, seeing that I was alone in the throngs, they didn't even try.

On my last day in Venice I was moving through the alleyways, lost yet again but serendipitously stumbling into hidden squares, where buildings dilapidated gracefully in pastel, fresco-like tones. Over one of the hundreds of tiny bridges, another gondolier called to me.

"Can't afford it," I turned to reply over my shoulder.

"But I give you good price," he replied.

This bartering business was really breaking my heart. "I'm on my own—I can't afford it."

"On your own?" he paused. "By yourself?"

He had to rub it in. "Yes," I said, pausing for a moment. "Sorry."

"But I give you good price," he repeated.

I sighed. "How much?"

No answer, just a smirk.

"*Quanto costa?*" I repeated.

"How much you got?"

"Not much. It's my last day. I'm just about out of money."

He paused, looked around with his hands on his hips. "Then I give you ride for what you got."

What was it he said? I asked myself as I tore through the square to the nearest ATM to coax a few more euro from the machine. Had he offered, had he *promised*, a one-person rate for a one-person ride—just for me? I was afraid it might be a trick or a joke, but when I arrived back at the stazio a few minutes later my gondolier hadn't disappeared, but was rubbing a cloth over his boat like a teenager with a back-alley hot-rod.

He was one of those fair Venetians, with curling, golden hair and pastel blue eyes, young and almost impossibly beautiful. His skin was deeply tanned from countless hours in the sun. Leaving his hat on the pier, he donned slick black shades and helped me into the boat. His bicep flexed conspicuously under his black-and-white striped shirt as he rotated the oar in a full-body circle to navigate us out of our narrow canal.

It was supposed to be a cab-ride in reverse, with the driver behind me. But I found myself wanting to look over my shoulder so often that I swung around on the seat to face him.

"What's your name?" I asked.

"Eros," he responded, without a whiff of irony.

I looked up to see him, blond and burnished, haloed in the Adriatic sunlight.

"*Eros?!*" I repeated. And his smile gleamed.

I can't remember all the questions I sent his way in those

giddy first few minutes of my gondola ride—about what it was like and how it was done and where we would go. But before I knew what was happening he was beckoning me.

"Come," he said, "You try."

He approached, sure-footed on the rocking boat, and took my hand. I followed as best I could, stepping across the benches to the stern. He stood close behind me; wrapped his arms around me; placed his golden head over my shoulder. He took my hands and positioned them on the huge wooden oar. I felt its weight, his breath, as he began to guide me through the steering motion.

Now I was a bit breathless myself. Somehow I found myself with a gigantic gondola oar in my own hands and a god-like gondolier standing close behind me. Within a minute of being left to bear the oar's weight on my own, I dropped it, losing it forever, I immediately feared, into the murk of the canal. But Eros caught it and rutted it deep into the water, one-handed, bending his knees with gymnastic agility, and bringing it back to my nervous hands.

He used his feet, too, like a Chinese acrobat, to push off the exteriors of canal-side *palazzi* when I steered us into walls. And he chatted and flirted, inviting me to go "a-sweeming" off his motorboat in the Lido before I left town.

Strangely, I felt myself more interested in asking him questions about the city, about the history of gondolier families, who have passed down the trade from fathers to sons for hundreds of years; about the meaning of the striped poles and striped shirts, which differentiated those families like medieval crests; about the real Don Juan who famously escaped from the prison in the Ducal palace but not so famously hid in an uninspired stone building he showed me. There is nothing a gondolier doesn't know about his city and nothing he does not love. Listening to Eros, I was becoming the initiate I dreamed of being, gliding through those narrow canals one can only see in a gondola, where laundered unmentionables drip dry and low music issues from half-opened shutters in the late afternoon.

How many thousands of travelers ride shoulder to shoulder in Venetian gondolas, low in the city's endlessly changing waters? And how many are offered this opportunity of learning to steer their own? I knew that none of those cuddly couples had done so, and I doubted if many had experienced the city the way I was experiencing it, standing on the stern of a gondola, alone with my own guide whispering intimately into my ear.

I had come to Venice alone and found myself, literally, in Eros's boat. But in the end I didn't take the man up on his offer to ride with him on his motorboat and go "swimming." I didn't need to. Maybe what I had wanted all along wasn't a lover but a love affair—that feeling of dizzy rapture; that experience of being lit from within; that deep abiding sense of belonging. Steering my own way through hidden canals, I realized it had happened already. As I stopped and listened to the lapping water, I could almost hear the city whispering my name.

Jennifer Carol Cook received her Ph.D. from Brandeis University. She currently teaches writing and American literature at Bentley College and is the author of Machine and Metaphor: The Ethics of Language in American Realism. *She continues to write both fiction and creative nonfiction, and her next major project is a book focusing on the painter Johannes Vermeer.*

❦ ❦ ❦

On the Dark Side

Two kayakers test their moxie on a windswept
adventure in Patagonia.

On a pebbly beach in a small village in southern Chile,
my friend Katie turned to me and said, "You know
you've misdressed when the guys around you are wearing
rubber pants."

Katie had on yoga-like stretch pants in a cotton-polyes-
ter blend. I wore a pair of waterproof pants that flared at
the ankles to accommodate hiking or ski boots. Both were
ideal clothing options for something other than a wilder-
ness kayaking adventure down Patagonia's glacial-fed Río
Serrano. Luckily, our guides came prepared. Not with the
latest women-specific latex trousers—that would be too
good to be true—but with Gore-Tex paddling jackets, dry
bags, and all the kayaking equipment we would need.

Katie and I wanted to explore what one of our guides
called the "dark side of the park," an area of Patagonia's

famous Torres del Paine National Park that could be reached only by boat. Our plan was to paddle fifteen miles down the Río Serrano, past glaciers, through avalanche zones, and by craggy granite mountains to a fjord where the river meets the ocean. It was a two-day trip that we hoped to do in one day. Or, rather, in one afternoon: It was 2:30 p.m. by the time we finally slipped away from shore.

We launched our kayaks from a clearing on a road with no name, near the village of Pueblito Serrano. The narrow river snaked through a landscape where beech trees and slabs of grass dangled from eroded embankments, grasping to hold on in the high winds and swift currents. A condor hovered overhead, looking like a prehistoric vulture on the prowl. And just beyond a sandbar at the edge of the woods, three wild horses stood perfectly still and watched us paddle by.

The Río Grey soon emerged on our right, bringing with it milky-gray water that had traveled down from a glacier several miles away. It was one of dozens of rivers and streams that dumped near-freezing glacial water into the Serrano, which then whisked it out to the Pacific Ocean. After our guides, Miky ("Micky") and a Turkish ex-pat named Cem ("Jam"), carried our boats around a waterfall, the landscape opened up, revealing mountains with razor-sharp rock towers and serrated peaks, and glaciers hanging in their valleys. Cem stopped paddling to tell us there were two areas we needed to cross and then we would be fine.

"They can be windy because they're so wide," he said.

The wind had been a constant adversary in all of our Patagonian adventures. We had seen it sweep grown men off their feet and nearly topple our horses as we rode along a cliff-top with a precipitous 3,000-foot drop. Gusty winds had also turned a three-hour hike into a five-hour journey.

"Just keep paddling and get across as quickly as you can," Cem said, as we approached an area where the river was hundreds of feet wide.

We made sure water bottles, spare paddles, and dry bags with cameras were tightly lashed onto our boats and then began paddling. At first, there was hardly a breeze, giving us a good chance to focus on Monte Donoso looming above us. Then, within a paddle stroke, a strong, unforgiving wind started blowing, steadily increasing and kicking up waves until the river looked like a trail of speed bumps.

I get nervous on the water, especially when there are strong currents or big waves: I once nearly drowned in the ocean and, another time, got caught in a flash flood in the middle of a jungle. As the wind gusted up to fifty miles per hour and the waves swelled, I put my head down and paddled as hard as I could. I glanced over several times to make sure Cem was still near me and then behind me to make sure Miky and Katie were O.K. The third time I looked back, I stopped paddling. Something didn't look right. I squinted to focus and realized Katie's kayak rudder was sticking straight up in the air.

"Cem, Katie's gone over!" I yelled.

"Stay here," Cem said, as he spun his kayak around and took off to help rescue her.

Miky floated next to Katie's upturned boat. I couldn't see Katie anywhere, just her kayak bobbing in the waves. I wanted to go help, but knew Miky and Cem could save her better than I could. Miky had grown up hiking and paddling in southern Chile and considered Patagonia his backyard, and Cem was Turkey's first whitewater kayaking champion and had competed internationally for a spot on the Olympic team. I was just a recreational kayaker whose sense of adventure often exceeded my skill.

I kept watching until I finally saw Katie's head pop up out of the water. Then I headed straight for shore. If I flipped, there was no one nearby to rescue me.

Cem and Miky helped Katie crawl back into her boat and then they paddled to the beach where I stood shaking from adrenaline.

"Are you O.K.?" I asked Katie. "You must be *freezing*."

"What a crazy thing that was!" Katie said, as she climbed out of her boat. "The waves kept getting bigger and bigger and then one just tossed me."

"Well, this is Patagonia," said Miky, as if it were really no surprise. "I saw you with a happy face and then thwap," he said, flipping his hand over. "It was *loco*—crazy!"

"I had a total Zen moment while I was upside down," Katie said, still breathless from the icy water. "I just sat there and chilled out, and then I yanked myself out of the boat."

"Next time, rubber pants," I said, looking at Katie's soggy, drooping pants and handing her a pair of thermals.

Katie quickly changed and ran up and down the beach to warm up, while Cem made tea and Miky prepared ham and cheese sandwiches with a chili-cream cheese spread. We sat under a giant, old beech tree eating sandwiches and sipping black tea while a wild horse grazed nearby.

Once Katie warmed up, we set off again, paddling across the second dicey area without any trouble. Eventually, we arrived at a big beach where Cem and Miky typically camp on their two-day trips. It overlooked the majestic Tyndall Glacier, a major arm of the enormous Southern Patagonian Ice Field. If we stopped there, we would have plenty of time to pitch our tents and make dinner while it was still light. But Miky had tempted us. The second campsite was on a fjord at the end of the river, just fifty yards from a lagoon that was full of icebergs and overshadowed by a steep, cascading glacier. It had mountain views, real bathrooms, and a friendly ranger named Pancho who would let us hang out in his warm hut.

My heart was set on the second campsite, but I hadn't been the one who had gone swimming in a glacial river that day. We still had five or six miles to go and it was about two hours before sunset.

"Maybe paddling will keep Katie warm," I thought, while I listened to our options. "Or maybe she'll hate me by the end of this trip."

"I vote to keep going," I said, even though we'd be cutting it close time-wise, "but I'll do whatever you all decide."

Katie thought about it and said, "I can keep going, but I probably won't be able to go any faster."

"All right, let's go!" said Cem.

What Katie and I didn't hear, after we had decided to continue, was a conversation between Miky and Cem that went something like this:

Miky: "Hey, did you bring a headlight?"

Cem: "Yeah, did you?"

Miky: "Yeah."

Cem: "Good." Long pause.

Miky: "I've never done this trip in one day."

Cem: "Me neither!" Laughter. "Let's see how far we get. We should make it."

Cem kept a close eye on us as we paddled. I was a little nervous, but I trusted our guides. We paddled through the Golden Hour, when the drooping sun doused the landscape in fiery yellow light and lit up a flock of white geese as they flew toward the Tyndall Glacier. Since passing the spot where the Río Tyndall emptied into the Serrano, the speed of the current had definitely increased. Trees and branches choked the river in many places, creating eddies and sections of whitewater that we carefully avoided. Gray clouds began to appear and the wind started kicking up again. My watch, which had a barometer, predicted rain.

"A farmer lives here," said Miky, pointing to our right, though we couldn't see any buildings or other signs of life. "And there's a hermit who lives a little farther down. They're brothers and they don't talk to each other anymore. The story is they both fell in love with the same woman and the farmer won her heart."

Luckily, the farmer still talked to the outside world. It turned out he had spotted us as we paddled by and radioed ahead to several people in Seno Ultima Esperanza, or Last Hope Sound: Pancho, the park ranger, and the owners of a nearby lodge. The farmer knew it was late for four kayakers to be paddling downriver and told everyone to watch for us.

Meanwhile, we continued paddling and drifting and floating and paddling. As it grew darker, the landscape began to appear more ominous. Even the sound of water rushing over downed logs seemed amplified and more unnerving.

"Don't go too close to the left," warned Cem, as we approached a mountain that was dripping vegetation. "There are landslides."

I stayed in the middle of the river and watched for falling rocks, logs poking above the surface and eddies. I followed Cem, like a duckling, whenever we came upon a tricky area. As we approached a sharp bend in the river, where a sheer cliff rose up in front of us, I could feel the river twisting and pulling in awkward directions. My kayak fishtailed and I paddled frantically to bring the stern back around, still trying to keep in line with Cem. Then the current pushed me sideways toward the cliff. My heart was pounding, but I paddled hard and focused on the back of Cem's boat and the flat water ahead of us.

Eventually, we all made it through the area without capsizing and then Cem said, "This is where the kayak broke." As it turned out, this was one of the most treacherous sections of the river. The previous year, a couple in a tandem kayak had capsized here, as they paddled through the funky currents. They were rescued, but their boat got stuck between a V-shaped, downed tree and broke in half. It would take a lot of force to make a rigid, plastic boat break, so I was glad to hear that story after we had safely made it through.

We still had a good forty-five minutes to go and light was quickly disappearing. The details of the landscape had also faded away: We could see the outline of the fjord's steep walls, but not the texture of the trees or rocks along the shore. In many ways, it felt like "the dark side" of the park. Not only were we losing light, but if something were to happen to us here, it would be a long time before we were rescued. We had only seen two people in six hours, heading upriver in a motorboat. Suddenly, on 7,000-foot Monte Balmaceda off to our right, a slab of snow let loose and rumbled down the side of the mountain.

"Avalanche!" I yelled, pointing.

The thunderous sound echoed off the mountains around us, but we were well out of harm's way.

"You'll hear those all night long," said Cem.

"But there's no danger, right?" I asked.

"Not at all," he promised.

We rounded another bend and the river began to open up. Ahead, we could see a thin line of trees and a large body of water.

"This is where the river joins the ocean," said Cem. "We may have waves here," he added, and sure enough, small swells started rolling toward us. We kept paddling as darkness fell—so dark, at this point, that we'd lost sight of Katie and Miky behind us.

Around that time, Katie later recalled, "Miky says to me, 'Are you O.K.?' and I'm thinking, 'What choice do I have? I have to be O.K. We're in Patagonia, it's getting dark, no one knows we're here, the wind's coming in, the waves are getting bigger and my arms are going to fall off!'"

Then, in front of us, like a beacon, we could see Pancho's flashing light guiding us in and showing us where to land. It was 9:30 P.M., about half an hour after sunset and ten minutes before total darkness. It wasn't until we were about thirty feet from shore that I could see Pancho's figure. Cem and I landed in a muddy clearing that had hoof prints from wild cows.

"*Hola, amigo,*" Cem said to Pancho, a good friend of his, and the two embraced and slapped each other's backs. "*¡Muchas gracias!*"

Pancho had apparently been standing on the beach flashing a light for over an hour. He lit a big bonfire, so we could warm up while we pitched our tents, and Katie and Miky pulled up about ten minutes later.

As we were sitting around Pancho's roasting-hot kitchen, watching Cem and Miky make a wonderful pasta dish with fresh veggies and cream sauce, Katie raised her glass of mango sour and said, "I'd like to make a toast to survival!"

"And to heroes," said Cem, motioning to Pancho.

"Heroes!" cried Katie, saluting Pancho, Miky, and Cem.

"And rubber pants," I added.

ॐ ॐ ॐ

Kari Bodnarchuk is an adventure-travel writer who has talked many friends into going on crazy journeys, although never the same friend twice. She has written books on Rwanda and Kurdistan and earned awards for her writing and photography, including two Lowell Thomas Travel Journalism awards for stories on Rwanda and recreational tree climbing. She writes for publications like Outside, Backpacker, The Miami Herald, *and* The Boston Globe, *and has contributed to numerous travel anthologies, including* The Best Women's Travel Writing 2005, 2006, *and* 2007. *She lives in Bellingham, Washington, with her husband and cat, and a fancy new pair of rubber pants.*

᠍ ᠍ ᠍

Ski Patrol

On a mountaintop, she proved the theory
of gravity, "once and for all."

ot too long ago, I was skiing in the mountains
where my son, Sam, and I spend a weekend most
winters. Nowadays, he instantly disappears with the hordes
of snowboarders. I believe he is somewhat embarrassed to be
seen with me: once, standing next to him and his friend at
the bottom of a hill, I fell over for no reason. And in fact, the
very first time we went skiing together, I skied in a strangely
slow, inexorable path for a hundred feet or so, straight into
a huge net at the bottom of the slopes, erected to protect the
small Ski Bear children from being crushed. Then I got
tangled up in it, like a fish.

After Sam disappears, I usually take the chairlift to
the top of the pony slope for a couple of runs, which
anyone can manage. And I triumph. I roar down the

slight incline, pretending to be an Olympic skier. Filled with confidence, I try the easiest intermediate slope, where I mostly fall or slide down on my butt for the first run, and then have a few extended runs of four or five minutes where I am actually skiing. By my second run down an intermediate slope, I am on my feet almost the whole time, skiing triumphantly for America.

But this time, as the chairlift carried me to the top of the intermediate slope, which I had just skied down, I experienced a moment's confusion, born of hormones, high altitude, and a light snow falling. I suddenly could not remember whether the stop we were approaching was the same one I had just skied down from. The chair slowed and lowered for us to disembark, and my seat-mate got off and zipped away like a swallow, while I sat there torn between wanting to get off and thinking that mine was the next stop.

The chair jerked forward and resumed its ascent. I looked around for landmarks but saw only brightly col-ored skiers in clusters, and I was pretty sure that this was not the right stop...until a second later, when I realized I was mistaken—it *was* the right stop. By then the chair was four or five feet off the ground and rising. But I did not let this stop me. I took a long, deep breath, wriggled to the edge of the chair, and flung myself off into the snow—flung myself, the way stuntmen fling themselves onto the backs of speeding trains, or a clown flings him-self from a bucking bronco, mugging bug-eyed for the crowd.

I estimate that I was five or six feet off the ground for the timeless instant of eternity before I crashed down into the snow. I landed hard, proving the theory of grav-ity once and for all. I was somehow still on my skis, for a moment, until I fell over.

I do not imagine anyone had seen anything like this before, someone hurtling into outer space with such force, from such a low starting point. I felt like Icarus, near death in the snow, with melting skis instead of wings.

I was immediately aware of two things: that I was not badly hurt, and that most people were pretending not to have noticed, out of kindness, or horror, or mortification. I am ever my mother's daughter, and so my first impulse was to smile with confidence to a few who were watching, wave like a politician campaigning from a rarely used horizontal position.

"I'm O.K.," I said to two pretty women who came over and offered to pull me up. I continued to wave nonchalantly, as if this sort of silly thing happened to me all the time. I told them that I just needed to catch my breath. They made sympathetic cooing sounds, and skied away. I sat up and leaned back on my hands in the snow.

By the time I finally stood up, my hands were frozen. I was winded, ashamed, confused, bruised—grateful only that Sam hadn't seen me. He'd have died. He would have stabbed himself repeatedly in the head with his ski pole.

Just when I thought things couldn't get much worse, nausea struck, wave after wave, like morning sickness, and I thought, I'm going to throw up in the snow! Ladies and gentlemen, now for my next trick...I pretended to pinch my nostrils against the cold, but was actually pressing my hand to my mouth to hold back the tide. My head spun, and I prayed, Help me, Jesus, help me, the way a very old woman at my church named Mary used to pray at her most afraid and delirious, right in the middle of anything—sermons, songs: "I know my change is gonna come, but touch me *now*, Lord."

I don't know how long I stood there with my hand clamped to my mouth, only my poles and a frayed, consignment-store faith to support me. All I knew was that help is always on the way, a hundred percent of the time. Rumi said, "Someone fills the cup in front of us." I know that when I call out, God will be near, and hear, and help eventually. Of course, it is the "eventually" that throws one into despair. For instance, even now, I know America will be restored again, eventually, although it is hard to envision this at the moment, and it could take a century or more for the nation and the world to recover from the George W. Bush years. But they will. God always hears our cries, and helps, and it's always a surprise to see what form God will take on earth: in the old joke, a man whose plane crashed in the tundra bitterly tells a bartender that God forsook him—that he waited in vain for divine intervention, and would have died in the snow...if it hadn't been for some fucking *Eskimos* who came by. So maybe a tall, strong man with a medical toboggan would be by soon, or the two pretty women, or Jesus in earmuffs.

Instead, a short, plump woman pulled up on skis a few minutes later. She was wearing an orange cap and an official jacket from the ski resort.

"I think I'm going to throw up," I said, so she wouldn't get too close.

"Well, then, let's just stand here a moment," she said. She had acne and chapped cheeks, and small brown eyes.

"I think I might need help," I said, which is something I force myself to say every few years.

"You landed *so* hard. I saw you from up above."

I shook my head, bewildered, on the verge of tears. "Are you on the ski patrol?" I asked.

"Sort of. I'm here to help in non-emergency situations like this. Why don't you come with me." She stepped out of her skis and stood on my bindings so that I could step out of mine. We picked up our skis and I trudged after her through the snow.

We walked to a wooden ten-by-ten shack away from the lift and went inside. It held two long benches, a folding chair, and shelves laden with first-aid equipment, bottles of water, used coffee cups, a walkie-talkie; and it was warm from a kerosene heater. There were two shabby windows, through which you could see snowy pine trees outside. The woman poured me a miniature Dixie cup of water, but my face was so cold that I couldn't get my lips to work, and I dribbled water down my front like an aged, numbed-up woman at the dentist's.

She took the cup away from me, "Let's take off your gloves first," she said, and pulled them off, as gently as if they were mittens connected inside my jacket sleeves with a string.

She laid my gloves on the chair near the heater and pulled off her own. "Mine are nice and toasty," she said. "You can wear them for a while, until yours warm up. I'll be back soon—there are only a couple of us working this spot today." She went outside.

After a while, I stretched out on one of the benches and closed my eyes. The kerosene smelled like lacquer, and I kept feeling waves of nausea. My bones were cold. I could isolate the icy scent of pine trees that sneaked through the walls. Sometimes grace is a ribbon of mountain air that gets in through the cracks.

I practiced concentrating between each wave of nausea, the way I did when I was in labor, savoring ice chips and apple juice between contractions. Miles from home, holed up deeply alone in a smelly hut, I had the old, familiar feelings of separation: from myself, from God, and from the happy, pretty people outside.

I thought of the woman from the ski patrol, with her small brown eyes. She looked like the monk seals that swim ashore in Hawaii to rest on the sand. The adult seals are six and seven feet long, and they all look like Charles Laughton. The newest tourists on the beach think they are dying and need to be rescued, but anyone who has been there even a day knows that they come onshore to rest. Pool workers from the beachside resorts always arrive, with yellow safety tape and traffic cones, to rope off a space for the seals to rest in. The first time I came upon one in the sand, I thought it was trying to make eye contact with me—I was its last, best hope of being saved. It had sand around its eyes and lots of shark scars. My guy Rory, who surfs in Hawaii every year, laughed and explained that the seals are perfectly fine, and when they are rested, they waddle back to the ocean.

This is how I feel about the world much of the time, when I am not feeling too far gone. Things are how they are supposed to be, all evidence to the contrary. Life swims, lumbers across the sand, rests; lumbers, swims, rests.

I lay there on the bench immobilized. If I were a monk seal, I could have waddled up into a sitting position, slid off the bench, and pulled myself by my flippers back into the ocean. Rory once saw a mother monk seal teaching her pup how to rest by swimming up onto the sand for a while before slipping back into the waves. The two of them practiced over and over, then disappeared into the water. Remembering this made me miss Sam terribly. I felt discarded, and I needed for time to pass more quickly. I would be fine with life's contractions if they would simply pass when I am ready for them to, so I can be O.K. again and remember what, after all, I'm doing in labor. Being human can be so dispiriting. It is a real stretch for me a lot of the time.

I put my nose to a crack in the wall so I could smell the pine.

I couldn't wait any longer for the ski patrol woman to come back. Where was she? She'd *said*. She was my only real friend, and I was such a mess. Her voice was gentle and kind—"O that today you would hearken to His voice," the psalmist wrote, and "harden not your hearts." O.K., *fine*, I said to God, and then noticed that I was much less of a frozen mess than I'd been earlier. This was a lot. I could have sat up, but I wanted the ski patrol person to see the full extent of my suffering—if she ever in fact returned.

I thought of the people I know from church and political circles who are doing a kind of psychic ski patrol in the world, noticing when people are in trouble, refusing to look away, offering an ear and their own warm gloves to wear.

Twenty minutes later, my ski patrol woman did come back, rubbing her bare hands together. "How you doing?" she asked. At first the enthusiasm in her voice worried me, because she sounded as if we might now move on to calisthenics. Then I could tell that she knew I was fine, better, rested. I was peaceful: she was my own private pool-worker, my own mother seal. I sat up and breathed in the fresh air from the open door.

She gave me another Dixie cup of water, and I hoisted it Germanically.

She walked over to the heater and checked my gloves. "They're all ready to wear again if you'll give me mine back."

I stood up. I felt like my old self, which is to say creaky but O.K.

"I'd take the chair down," she said. "Unless you really want to ski."

I really wanted to ski. I'd already had one great run down this slope.

She made a huge fuss over me when I left, as if I'd been in an avalanche. I pulled on my gloves and headed out onto the huge white ocean of ice. I glided and fell and got back up and skied little by little, the very best I could, all the way down the mountain.

Anne Lamott is the author of six novels and four bestselling nonfiction books including: Operating Instructions, Bird by Bird, Traveling Mercies, Plan B, *and* Grace (Eventually), *from which this essay was excerpted. She has been a book reviewer for* Mademoiselle, *a restaurant critic for* California *magazine, and a columnist for the* San Francisco Chronicle *and* Salon.com. *She lives near San Francisco.*

ℬ ℬ ℬ

The Basket

She came face to face with one of life's mysteries: the
random nature of privilege.

*I*t was my mump that taught me the most about Nepal.
Or rather, my mump and the woman in the basket.
This wasn't what I expected, since I went to Nepal to find
exotic customs and cultural difference. I wanted to know
about brightly colored gods, sacred cows, Tibetan Buddhist
Om-chanters. And I did find these there, but in the end I
found that the most profound difference between my life
and that of the Nepali people was a chasm deeper than all
the sacred temple pools and holy rivers put together, and
existed in the space between my mump and her basket.

A few days before a trek into the Himalayan foothills,
where I first saw the woman in the basket, I had awoken in
a blockish hotel in the tourist town of Pokhara with a golf
ball-sized lump in my neck. It bulged painfully just below

my right earlobe, behind the jawbone. I got out my emergency medical guide and matched myself to a drawing of
a man with a hampsterish, swollen face. Mumps. Infected
saliva glands. But the guy in the picture had lumps on both
sides, not just on one. So, I had a mump.

Clenched with anxiety (could a mump be deadly?),
I careened in a taxi to the dusty, fly-speckled Pokhara
Hospital emergency room. The mump jounced painfully
as we hurtled through ruts like dry creek beds, swerving
wildly to avoid immovable cows and frantic bicyclists. In
the sultry air of the hospital, I sat in a dingy, linoleum-tiled
examination room where fat flies buzzed loudly, spiraling
drunkenly around my head. A message scrawled in English
on a marker board read: "Help prevent the spread of AIDS
and Hepatitis: don't leave used needles lying around." It
dawned on me that this was a far different Nepal than the
one I had come looking for.

Although reassured by the lack of dirty syringes on
the floor, I balked when the doctor picked a glass thermometer out of a drawer and wiped it on the sleeve of his
white coat. My mind groped desperately with my limited
Nepali, trying to conjure the phrase "I refuse to put that
in my mouth." Smiling at my alarm, he indicated to my
relief that I should use my armpit. After the brief examination, which included reading the thermometer (normal)
and prodding the mump (still swollen), he informed me
in blessedly perfect English that I would swell up and
resemble a puffer fish for a full week. I would have pain
and maybe fever. Then it would just go away.

The next day, I strode purposefully up the hiking
trail on the way to the Sherpa town of Simigaau in the
Himalayan foothills, my head wrapped in a handkerchief
like a cartoon character to ease the painful jarring of my
swollen face. The trail, the same that eventually heads

toward Khumbu and the Everest base camp, was a glorious, meandering climb through terraced hillsides and
wooded valleys chaperoned by vast, white-fanged peaks
angled into clouds.

It was hard not to admire the scenery, but I was distracted as locals and fellow trekkers openly gawked at
me. I could see in their eyes that I looked like a freak. At
the height of the swelling, I peered into the mirror to find
that I appeared to be a 400-pound woman who could only
afford liposuction for one side of her body. Covering up the
left side of the mirror, I looked like me in thirty years after
a steady diet of Cheetos and Macadamia nuts. Covering up
the right side, I looked like my normal-sized self.

I plodded along, wallowing in self-pity, cursing the
injustice of becoming such a monstrosity, and that's when I
saw the woman in the basket. In Nepal people carry things
in large, conical baskets that rest on their backs, supported
by a strap lashed across the forehead. Sherpas carry these
up mountains in flip-flops, loaded down with everything
from trekkers' backpacks to glass bottles of Coca-Cola.
The basket in front of me on the third day of the trek, on
the back of a small, sturdy man who served as one of our
group's cooks, was designed with an open space at its back,
a window from which the woman watched me. Her dark
eyes were big and sad above the blue surgical mask strung
across her emaciated cheeks to check the spread of her
tuberculosis. She was young and frail, wrapped in a blanket, her skeletal fingers pinching its edge to her pointed
chin. Her stick-like legs folded like a collection of kindling
underneath her.

I looked at her, wondering if her tuberculosis could
spread despite the face covering. Should I fall back and
walk somewhere else? Did having mumps make me more
vulnerable to other diseases? The slender trail forced me

into a tight single file behind her, so I trudged on face to face with her, contemplating the terrible thinness of her body, the imperceptible rise and fall of the mask as her weak breath pressed it to her mouth.

"They've tried every drug available in the country," a friend whispered, coming up next to me as the trail broadened. She looked at the woman in the basket, frowning slightly. "If she was in Boston, no problem, she'd be cured. But here, I guess she just dies." The basket-woman, my friend had discovered, was the sister of the man who carried her, and had visited Kathmandu three times for treatments that never worked. She was returning from another failed round of drugs, headed home to her village to wait for the inevitable.

I walked on behind the basket, my fear of her germs overtaken by the sudden and stunning understanding of the vast gulf that separated the two of us, despite our faces hovering only yards apart. There I was, like her a young woman on a trail in the middle of Nepal, also ill with an infectious disease, also in pain as we lurched down the rocky trail together. But at the same time I was miles away from the reality of her hopelessness. No matter how deep into the third-world countryside we traveled, I remained tied by an invisible but unbreakable thread to the promise of first-world safety.

If the doctor at the hospital a few days before had told me I had tuberculosis instead of mumps, I would have been immediately on my way to world-class care by doctors better educated than any the woman in the basket had ever laid eyes on. Possible obstacles to my care simply did not exist in this country. At the hospital, for example, I didn't think twice about paying the ten-rupee fee, which amounted to pocket change for me but was a damaging amount for many of the patients. Without question, I could get the best medical care Nepal had to offer, and if things got bad a helicopter would come and take me somewhere better. Without question, this woman would die before she was even twenty because the drugs she needed were elsewhere.

When we arrived in Simigaau, a village stair-stepping up a terraced mountainside, green with fields of rice and millet, I was confronted by some of the cultural difference I had come to Nepal to find. I attended a Sherpa Buddhist service that was as much liquor-swilling, circle-dancing party as it was solemn, gong-banging, monk-chanting ceremony. When I told the children in faltering Nepali that I came from America, they asked if that was farther away than Kathmandu. But despite these newfound fascinations, I couldn't stop thinking about the woman in the basket. While I took language classes on the sun-drenched patios of mud-brick farmhouses, my mump slowly but definitely diminishing, she sat somewhere in some dim room, heaving her last shallow breaths of life.

The most profound difference I found in Nepal, despite witnessing throngs of women in red saris dancing in temples on holidays, bodies burning on riverside cremation pyres, and ascetic Hindu holy men with hair as long and matted as the crusted ropes of ships, was the difference of possibility. Walking along that hiking trail, the woman in the basket watched me with vacant eyes as the possibility of her life slipped away. What I saw as I looked at her was the finality of hopelessness. What she saw as she looked at me was a person with a temporarily disfigured face who knew that all of her trouble would, as the doctor had said, just go away.

❧ ❧ ❧

Katherine Gustafson's personal essays regularly appear in publications such as The Christian Science Monitor *and* Transitions Abroad, *and her fiction was recently named a runner up for the* Iowa Review Award *for Fiction. She works as a nonprofit development writer in Washington, D.C., and has recently returned from Asia with a lifetime supply of green tea, an inability to properly pronounce a single Chinese word, and a burgeoning love of Japanese gardens.*

KRISTIN BARENDSEN

~ ~ ~

Why Tuk-Tuks Make the Big Bucks

A *farang* tries to tame the wildest creature
of Thailand's urban jungle.

*I*t looks easy, like driving a car, except that the gas is
a flick of the wrist. But when I take a deep breath
and turn the key, I understand why *tuk-tuks* make the big
bucks.

"Right hand, fuel!" Pon shouts from the back seat.
The engine sputters and roars to life. "Left foot, clutch,
let go!"

"I'm not in gear!"

"Gear number one!"

I move my right hand from the throttle to the gear
stick between my knees. The engine dies instantly.
Sweat and sunscreen drip into my eyes.

"Shift with left hand, not right hand," Pon insists.

"I can't shift with left hand," I protest. "I'm a *farang*!"

We're in a sprawling, deserted parking lot on the outskirts of Chiang Mai, Thailand's northern metropolis. I've accepted the outrageous offer of Pon, one of the country's few women *tuk-tuk* drivers, to teach me, a *farang* (gringo), how to drive a three-wheeled auto rickshaw. But so far I am failing this most unusual Driver's Ed lesson.

The wildest creatures of the Thai urban jungle, *tuk-tuks* can weave through gridlocked traffic and pull a U-turn within one lane with room to spare. They're a cross between a tricycle and a torpedo, with toy-sized wheels, open sides, a convertible canvas roof, and space enough to cram three tourists (or eight Thais) in back. The term "*tuk-tuk*" echoes the sound of the two-stroke engine that provides a rhythmic backdrop, even a pulse, to every Thai city. Attempts to ban further manufacture of this top noise and air polluter have fizzled in the face of high tourist demand and the popular opinion that the *tuk-tuk* is quintessentially Thai, a symbol of nationalistic pride.

Like every expat in Chiang Mai, I had spent many an evening shoehorned into the back of a *tuk-tuk* with other passengers, careening through intersections at Hail-Mary speed. But never had I seen a fellow *farang* behind the wheel; Thais have the driving market cornered. When Pon had proposed to alter this balance of power even for an afternoon, the significance had not been lost on me. How many *farangs* ever have this opportunity, and how many would dare seize it? How would people react to the sight of me, female and blonde, driving down the road in this contraption?

I try to restart the engine, but nothing happens. "Close the key," Pon says. "If you forget to close key, big fire!" I watch in the rearview mirror as she illustrates her point with waving hands and explosive sound effects. "Not after one minute, but after ten. Because if not close key, gas stay on."

I close the key, then open it and rev the engine. The *tuk-tuk* heaves forward, a rough beast slouching towards Bethlehem.

"Don't forget brake, right foot!" Pon warns me that her former student had forgotten the brake and "almost make big accident."

I hit a speed bump dead on, sending Pon airborne and then back to the plastic bench with an audible *thud*. "Hey, brake, I say!" she complains, rubbing her backside. "Sorry, girlfriend," I offer, but I can't help laughing. Karmically I've just repaid all the *tuk-tuk* drivers who have sprained my coccyx on the unforgiving seat.

I try to shift into second but grind the gears and stall. If you neglect the gas even momentarily, the engine dies into deafening silence. This is why, in Chiang Mai, there's never a still moment absent the slicing rev of the two-stroke engine.

"Shift with left hand, not right! I tell you already."

Eventually I can navigate the vehicle, which Pon has named "Betsy," with relative ease, making ever-tightening circles. Pon relaxes a little, reclining with her feet up on the side rail and peeling mandarin oranges. While giving reverse gear a try, I tilt my head back and accept an orange slice into my mouth. The fruit is a burst of cool on a blazing hot day. I realize my back and legs are soaked in sweat.

"Should I take her into town?" I ask, but the question is rhetorical, as I've already decided I'm too chicken.

"Oh, *mai pen rai,*" Pon replies, invoking the Thai national motto, "never mind." It's a philosophy that can be considered extreme denial of—or extreme adaptation to—life's difficulties. It's perhaps best epitomized in the way Thais drive any vehicle: turning onto busy streets without noting the status of oncoming traffic, weaving recklessly with ultimate trust in reincarnation.

I'm not sure if Pon means "never mind the possibility of death, let's take her into town," or "never mind that stupid idea, let's leave it for the day." *Mai pen rai,* I agree to leave it, and give her back the reins.

I first met Pon while navigating my bicycle slowly through a late-night traffic jam along Chiang Mai's "moat road," a multi-lane myriad of one-ways and U-turns that follows the moat around the old city. I heard insistent honking and turned to see a *tuk-tuk* commandeered by a stocky woman wearing flannel, a bandanna tied like a sweatband around her boyish haircut. Flashing a crooked-toothed smile, she reached a hand toward me with her business card. Though a motorbike was trying to cut between us, I extended my arm and grabbed the card. "Pon's *Tuk-Tuk* Service," it read. She winked.

It was an unusual way to flirt, but anything goes in Thailand.

One rainy evening a few weeks later, I was walking past the Night Bazaar, the city's outdoor gift market, where throngs of *tuk-tuks* lay in wait for the tourists swarming past. "Hey, beautiful!" a voice called. It was Pon, grinning and offering a bag of mandarin oranges. I climbed in her vehicle—not to flirt back, as she was too butch for me, but because I could tell already she was one of "my people," and a fascinating woman.

I remarked to Pon that I rarely saw women *tuk-tuk* drivers. Pon confirmed that out of over 600 drivers in

Chiang Mai, there were only "fifteen women maxi-mum." We set off to find one of her female colleagues, but on the way the rain became a monsoon deluge that stranded us under the awning of a Shell station for an hour and a half.

When the storm let up Pon treated me to dinner at her favorite restaurant, a florescent-lit noodle shop, where she barked orders at the wait staff until our meals arrived. My bowl featured broth with noodles, pickled eggs, and a gray-purple block of cow's blood. *Another only-in-Thailand moment,* I thought as Pon gave me a pointed stare. "On the bicycle you look so beautiful and young," she said. "Now you look old and tired. Why?"

I told her that in my country, such a statement would be considered rude. When she repeated her observation even more emphatically, I replied, "You're not looking so good yourself, sistah." She laughed, but I could tell she hadn't caught the meaning.

"You want to drive a *tuk-tuk*? I teach you." It was my turn to laugh, but the seed was planted.

Since that evening I had run into Pon several more times. She kept me updated on her love life and its impressive cast of female and male characters who would exit stage right and re-enter on cue. I complained about my oppo-site, and ironic, problem—my house-arrest celibacy as a white woman in Asia, even as one who, like Pon, prefers both genders. While I told Pon the details of my failed dates, I was careful not to invite her to break my streak of purity.

Pon confided in me about former girlfriends, usually other drivers, who had abused her considerable generos-ity. "I want to help her, you know. I give her 4000 baht, then 2000 baht. She not pay me back. I think her good, her no good." She said that altogether she had lent 50,000 baht (about $1588 US) that she'd never seen again.

Pon, forty-six, was born in Bangkok and has lived in Chiang Mai for fifteen years. She learned how to drive "a bicycle age six, motorbike age nine, car age thirteen." She had survived near-fatal accidents while piloting a motorbike and car, but *mai pen rai,* she got back on the diesel horse and started driving professionally two years before. She claimed to have mastered the art of *tuk-tukking* in just ten minutes. "Why you don't believe me?" she asked.

Pon rents "Betsy" from a *tuk-tuk* dealer for 180 baht per day. Named after Pon's first crush "on American girl like you," Betsy is standard-issue black with yellow trim and plates, stickers advertising tourist attractions, and a masculine love-life talisman hanging from the rearview mirror. The gear-stick handle is a pool ball, green number 6. Pon also owns a new SUV that she uses to drive customers to farther-flung destinations like the mountains. She has six mobile phones, "because one might be out of order." Somehow she manages to run a side business renting motorbikes and bicycles. "You must be the wealthiest *tuk-tuk* driver in Chiang Mai," I observed. She laughed, but neither confirmed nor denied.

Granted, Pon works hard for her money. She sleeps a maximum of six hours per night, and she plies the tourist-thick streets between Tha Pae Gate and the Night Bazaar for fourteen to eighteen hours a day. This staggering figure does, however, include frequent breaks to hang out with customers and colleagues. "I like foreigner," she waxed with a wistful smile. "Because they have more money. And my heart same-same American people."

"Same-same, but different," I qualified.

Whenever I saw Pon on the street, she would offer feed-back on my appearance. "Why you gain weight?"

"Because I visited my family in the States, and I ate a lot of bread and cheese."

"Why you do that?"

This was why I kept procrastinating my driving lesson—it wasn't every day that I wanted to be called *uan,* fat.

Finally I resolved to make the date. I called Pon sev-eral times over the course of a week. "I have customer now. I call you later," she said each time.

Then one morning she showed up unannounced at my guesthouse, ready to teach. As we took off in a cloud of blue smoke toward the parking lot that would serve as my train-ing grounds, she turned to face me. "Kristin, you skinny now. Why you lose weight? You look better before."

After our lesson we drive away from the lot, Pon once again in the pilot's seat. I refuse her offers to take me to the umbrella factory, the bungee jump, and her cousin's marble shop, venues that will pay her a commission for my white-skinned output of cash. I want to treat her to Japanese food, which she has never tried. While we wait for our combination platters, I complain about the absence of a lesbian bar in Chiang Mai. Pon narrows her eyes, asking me why I would want such a thing. I explain, "I'm from San Francisco, where there are lots of places—bars, cafés, bookstores—to meet people like us, make friends. Wouldn't you want that here?"

"My whole life is like a lesbian bar," she replies. "Why would I want to pay for whiskey?"

"A lesbian bar on three wheels," I add. "Touché."

To illustrate her point, Pon takes four wrapped tooth-picks from the dispenser on our table. She places one toothpick in opposition to the other three, which, lined up side by side, represent her current lovers—French woman, Thai woman, Canadian man. None live in Chiang Mai, none know about each other, and all are planning to visit during the same two-week span. I express my admiration of the seductive prowess that got her into this mess.

"Big problem, Kristin. What should I do?"

"You should say, 'I have customer now. I call you later.'"

She mimes the single toothpick running away from all the others. I mime them chasing her, yelling, "taxi, taxi!"

When we part for the day, I give her an American hug and 200 baht (US $5.50) for her expertise. But something feels incomplete: I haven't really done it. I still long to take the *tuk-tuk* on the road—the real Thai road in all its raw insanity. I long to make an unforgettable spectacle of myself.

The next morning, I see Pon parked outside Tha Pae Gate, the ruins of an ancient city wall that borders the moat. She waves an orange at me. "I want to do it," I beg. "Let me drive just down Loi Kroh."

"You sure?"

"Yes, sure."

"You sure?"

I turn the key. And with the honking red-truck taxis and silver SUVs bearing down on me, I understand how much Buddhist equanimity is required in this job. "*Mai pen rai*," I whisper to myself, drawing in a long breath and trying to slow my heart, which revs like a two-stroke engine. As Pon in the back seat waves traffic around us, I give Betsy the gas and we take off down the moat road. Never mind that I am driving down the left side of the street—this I am used to by now.

I turn onto Loi Kroh, a street lined with girlie bars and swarming with tourists. I spot an elderly *farang* gentleman and his twentysomething Thai companion, and I slow to attract them. "Hallo Sah!" I call in my best Thai accent. "Sah! *Tuk-tuk*?"

I expect this couple, and indeed everyone on the street, to drop their jaws and stare. *I* would have stared. But they don't even glance in my direction, just give me exasperated waves of the hand.

I realize they are jaded by touts and I am doing the accent too well. "Speak American!" Pon urges. I try a Texas drawl. "Howdy, y'all, taxi!" The man looks at me, but his face registers blankness—what he sees does not compute.

I stop at the Night Bazaar, where Pon explains our antics to her smiling colleagues and competitors parked there. When I see two women walking with heads lolling under the weight of their mammoth backpacks, I call out, "Taxi, Madame!" and honk enthusiastically. They politely decline with an English-accented, "Thanks, we're just walking to our hotel." They don't seem the least bit fazed. Maybe they are fresh off the plane and can't appreciate the import of what they are seeing. Or maybe they're already living by *mai pen rai*—here translated as, "Yeah? So what."

I want to be noticed; it's one of the reasons I live abroad, to have an unusual life. Normally just riding my bicycle I turn heads, inspire cries of "Hallo *farang*!" from children playing on the sidewalks. So why, I wonder, am I now being treated as just another of the city's 600 *tuk-tuk* drivers?

I continue down the busy Night Bazaar road, choking on fumes and watching my mirrors, which show red-truck taxis weaving desperately to pass me as my engine screams in second gear. A few street vendors smile, and one gives me a thumbs-up. Still, not the reception I had expected.

The next foreigner I see looks like he's been on a bender for days. "*Tuk-tuk!*" I cry and pursue him onto a side street, stopping in front of him so that Betsy blocks his path. He gives me an addled glance and starts to walk around us. "Ride to your hotel, forty baht!" I offer.

"Twenty baht," he counters.

"Thirty." He climbs in back with Pon.

"Where to?" I ask. Lucky for all of us, his guesthouse is only a few blocks away. He reeks of cheap whiskey and the formaldehyde that is said to be a key ingredient in Thai beer. Gavin, from Sydney, says he came to Chiang Mai on holiday a month ago and deliberately missed his flight back. "It's the girls," he candidly slurs. "They're not like the sheilas back home." Pon murmurs encouragement; I choose not to touch that one.

I approach a busy, signal-less intersection where a smirking policeman stops traffic in all directions to wave me through.

"By the way, this isn't exactly legal, is it?" Gavin asks. We laugh.

"No way!" Pon replies. "You need license." She says *farangs* can take the licensing exam if they can read and write Thai.

"I heard you can just pay more and not take the test," Gavin says. "I mean, for any driving license."

"Oh sure, just pay more."

A few blocks down, three Thai teenagers on a motorcycle slow to let me lurch past as I struggle to shift into third. "*Farang khap tuk-tuk!*" one exclaims, and they all giggle. This is more like it.

I stop at Gavin's guesthouse, "John's Place," at $2.50 per day among the cheapest digs in the city.

"Okay, Gavin, what do you think about me, a white woman, driving this *tuk-tuk*?" I ask.

"Well you know, it's kind of unusual I suppose, but this is Thailand. I saw things last night that would shock you to high heaven. This is just, well, a bit of a laugh." He weaves up the sidewalk to John's.

He's right. Only-in-Thailand meets *mai pen rai*. I'm just an expat driving a *tuk-tuk*, and Pon is just my butch mentor. In a country where the extraordinary is ordinary, this is only another moment of another day. But with that realization I feel a giddy surge of love for this bizarre, marvelous, polluted place I am calling home.

When we return to Tha Pae Gate, I park on the shoulder and let Pon take over. We slap hands in a victorious high-five. Pon appreciates my triumph, even if no one else does.

"Were you afraid?" she asks me.

"A little. Were you?"

"A lot!" She laughs so hard and long that I see she must have been terrified. I give her a kiss on both cheeks as reassurance, apology, and thanks. "But you drive great," she says. "*Farang khap tuk-tuk.*" She takes a deep breath and holds out a slice. "Orange?" she offers. I open my mouth wide.

Kristin Barendsen writes about travel, yoga, and the arts from her home in Santa Fe. She is author of the forthcoming book Photography and New Mexico.

ಱ ಱ ಱ

Roof Dogs

In Mexico, the top isn't necessarily the best place to be.

Javier is speaking to me in Spanish and I nod, hoping to imply a comprehension that completely eludes me. I'm having my morning coffee on the lovely terrace of his guesthouse, from which the crazy quilt of colors and shapes that is Guanajuato spreads out gloriously in all directions. I'm not yet fully awake, and the urban roosters and dogs are competing with Javier for my attention, but I'm listening very carefully, trying hard to understand. Some words I recognize: *bello, soleado, bueno, caliente*, but I'm having difficulty combining them into coherent thoughts. It would have been better to come clean, at the outset, to a working ignorance of Spanish, but here I am, alone in Mexico, and some misguided wariness of exploitation inhibits this disclosure. As proprietor of the guesthouse, something will pull him away any minute now, and I think I can sustain the ruse.

"*Perro de techo*," he says, pointing to his neighbor's beautiful deep blue house. The steep hills surrounding the guesthouse are covered with multi-hued homes and churches built in the seventeenth and eighteenth centuries during Guanajuato's prosperous heyday as a silver capital. The one next door is particularly elegant.

I nod, smiling "*¡Si, muy bonita!*" I try not to inflict my so-called Spanish on innocent natives, but I do know how to say "beautiful." (Later I will learn that I have committed yet another blunder, as it appears Javier was complaining about the barking of the dog on the roof next door.)

As soon as Javier leaves, I finish my coffee and climb down four flights of stairs to the kitchen for a refill. I pass a small crowd of laughing, jostling American adolescents on the stairwell and realize that I'm staying in a glorified hostel, which suits me just fine.

When I return to the terrace, the adolescents are seated around the only table, sharing an assortment of large pastries and beverages. They invite me to join them, but I crave solitude right now, and I politely decline, preferring to stand at the other end of the terrace (I see they've appropriated all of the chairs) and watch the rising sun wash over the hills.

Mexico is notorious for attracting all sorts of people, some respectable, on the right side of the law, and some decidedly not. I haven't committed any crime, but I feel that I've somehow strayed to the wrong side of my destiny. And, while not exactly a desperado, I'm on the run—not from the authorities, but from a job I can't bear to keep and am equally afraid to lose.

I have a wonderful life in Cambridge—this I know. My home is in a charming neighborhood walking distance from my spacious art studio, Harvard Square, a prismatic network of friends, family, and lovers, and just about everything else that nourishes a rich, multifaceted life. But in Boston I sit miserably at the helm of a research center created to solve problems that matter deeply to me, while the center expends its energy on everything *but* the population of children that it was designed to serve. I can't reconcile deserting the children to whom we have pledged so much and, to date, have offered so little and thus, I haven't had the heart, or, quite frankly, the guts, to form a Plan B.

During my first visit two years ago, Guanajuato burrowed deep under my skin. Maybe your aesthetic has to gravitate toward joy and whimsy, toward more rather than less, to truly appreciate the grandeur of Guanajuato. Even on bad days, the city exudes a certain élan, reminding me of the gleeful lady I saw once, in the bathroom below Penn Station, coloring her white hair with Crayolas. No two buildings are painted the same color, apparently, by mandate of the local government—or so I *think* I was told by a cab driver whose English was scarcely better than my Spanish. This is a city of such visual exuberance that it stands out in a country that expresses itself in uninhibited saturated colors, whose trees boast blue flowers. And to my painter's eye and desperado soul, it's the perfect environment in which to flounder around a bit until a better idea takes hold. There's no injunction to do, say, or perform anything in particular, which works well for me, and for the others who have fled to this country to live purely as our hopes and dreams dictate, if only for a sliver of time.

My thinking has been shaken loose. Maybe too loose. As I stroll past the stately university, I find myself thinking, *Hey, maybe I could teach there!* I decide to visit Diego Rivera's brilliant scarlet childhood house cum museum and think, *Hey, I could paint here!* Even, as I enjoy a superb chicken mole for lunch at Truco 7, my favorite cheap haunt in Guanajuato, and notice that the wait staff is overextended, I think, *Hmmmm…waiting tables…I've never done that before but, hey, I could do that!* My brand-new caffeine induced optimism is responding exuberantly to the stimuli around me, completely undeterred by the sobering Laws of Reality. (Law #1—you can't live in Mexico and Cambridge simultaneously without a generous benefactor underwriting the lifestyle.) But such are the beginnings of life renovation. Gather competing plans, assess which one offers the best balance of form and function, and then choose the one you really want regardless.

The next morning, I'm invited to a sumptuous breakfast in the home of Bill, a retired American newspaper editor from South Carolina, and his wife, Charlotte, whom I met casually during my previous visit to Guanajuato. They live in a stately crimson mansion that came cheap and fully furnished with stunning antique Mexican furniture. The graceful Spanish architecture and complex tile work typical of old colonial buildings are striking, but the clincher, accessible by a rickety ladder, is the rooftop, which provides 360 degrees of steep hills covered with multi-hued homes.

Bill fills my plate with a large serving of *chilaquiles*, a traditional breakfast dish of shredded tortilla, onion, and cheese, in a spicy tomato sauce. Additionally, there's a delicious Mexican omelet, and a platter of succulent tropical fruits. The plan is to spend the day with Bill in Santa Rosa, a tiny town that he and Charlotte love, high in the mountains just outside of Guanajuato and, I'm guessing, it's safer to fill up now rather than partake of the hygienically suspect offerings of Santa Rosa.

I remember to ask Bill a nagging question from the day before. "So, what exactly is *perro de techo?*"

"*Perro de techo* is roof dog, a dog that lives on the roof of the house. People here keep them for protection. That barking that you hear all the time, that's the roof dogs."

I contemplate this over my second helping of *chilaquiles*, which tastes better with each bite. It's Mexican comfort food.

"You mean they *never* come down?" I'm appalled, and also surprised. I've seen dogs aplenty walking the streets of Guanajuato, with owners immoderate in their displays of affection.

"Nope, they spend their whole lives on the roof."

This strikes me as unbearably sad. As a fugitive from misery, my emotions are still raw, and I identify with the dogs, sequestered as I am at the top of my profession with no obvious way down. What would happen, I wonder, if I snuck out under cover of night and freed them, house by house? What would happen if I freed myself? We'd probably all end up together on the street, foraging food from trash bins and kind strangers.

I ask Bill to pass the *chilaquiles*.

The road to Santa Rosa winds through the hills surrounding Guanajuato, an ascending spiral with hairpin turns and breathtaking vistas. Barren hills yield to surprisingly verdant mountains, and civilization recedes into little specks dotting the scenery far below. Everything I thought I knew about central Mexican climate and terrain is challenged by the increasingly lush, forested landscape. We are in the middle of nowhere, climbing and weaving through undomesticated mountains. If I ever had any trust issues about the man I hardly know at the wheel, this would be the logical moment to panic. I choose instead to be dazzled by the panoramas around each bend and feel grateful to the semi-stranger steering me through all this, come what may.

When we arrive in Santa Rosa, the first thing I notice is the crisp clean air. Let it be noted, for the record, that my passion for colonial Mexico would be tempered by its environmental shortcomings if I were a strictly rational person. Suffice it to say, cleanliness, be it water or air, is not the magnet that draws one to this country.

But Santa Rosa is another world altogether. No filter exists between the land and a pristine indigo sky, nothing to mute the cheerfully painted assemblage of dilapidated buildings. Whereas Guanajuato is a masterpiece of vertical panache, Santa Rosa, at the zenith of a mountain, flaunts her charms horizontally. The old cobbled road suggests a heyday long past, as though this sleepy town of colorful low-slung buildings once thrummed with purpose and vitality and has now retired for a century or two of rest. The cool air is invigorating and as we walk down the street, roasted corn wafts from an open door. People smile warmly. I am in love.

Bill explains that Santa Rosa is known for its fauna-and-flora decorated pottery, which, it appears, has been its key to survival. The state of Guanajuato (in which the city by the same name resides) is studded with ghost towns that once staffed the now obsolete silver mines, but this town still has a pulse, however languid.

It's actually more like two little pueblos, one above the other. We begin in upper Santa Rosa because it has a little café in which to relax and refresh. They know Bill here, as I'm pretty sure they know all of their patrons, past and present, given the nature of middle-of-nowhere business. No sooner have we seated ourselves, than a handsome walnut-skinned man with a long ponytail comes up to greet Bill. Bill introduces me to Carlos, a local artist, who apologizes that he can't sit with us because work is being done on one of his studios.

"Studios?" I inquire. My ears are perked—if I had a tail, it would be wagging.

"Yes, I have four." His black eyes are shining and I wonder if he's playing me or just under the influence of something or other. Or both.

Just as I begin thinking *Hey, I can make art here...* my reverie is interrupted by Bill, who tells Carlos that I'm a painter. Carlos smiles alluringly and says, point blank, that he has an extra studio (*more like three*, intones the running narrative in my head) if I would like to move here. His eyes, the proverbial windows to the soul, seem to have the shades drawn, but I think it's a genuine offer. Of course, I know that there's no way I'd indulge this fantasy. Still, this is great material to animate my imagined alter-life.

Bill, who has professed a superficial knowledge of Spanish, orders our coffee and chats with the waitress in brisk, cadenced Spanish. I begin to wonder who this man really is, and indeed, I'm about to learn.

"I'm writing a book," he says.

"Really?" All I know about Bill is that after leaving his newspaper career and moving here, he has taken up painting as a new hobby and has demonstrated some genuine talent.

"I thought you were intent on becoming the next great Mexican artist?"

"No," he drawls, "I'm a recovering alcoholic, and I'm writing about a stint in a crooked Mexican rehab. I went in and, long after I was thoroughly sober, those bastards wouldn't let me out."

I'm looking at Bill more intently, trying to revise several of my assumptions about him. To begin with, he's clearly not the uncomplicated, fixed-income retiree I imagined. He seems happy enough now, but it occurs to me that maybe he was once a roof dog, too.

"We should've done our homework first," he continues, "but I was in bad shape. Didn't really think much about why the place was surrounded by high walls. High walls with glass shards on top—that's usually a bad sign. But otherwise it looked respectable enough." Bill's face flushes, and I can see the residue of the trauma overtake his usual joviality.

"Every month they got a fat check from my family, and as soon as they saw I was a cash cow gringo, they had no intention of letting me go. There were others like me, but they were old, no fight left in them. We were all cut off from our families, from everything."

He goes on to tell me how he tried and failed on several occasions to escape, how his wife was told that his sobriety was in jeopardy and that she too was conned, at least for a while, into passive acceptance. This is the dark side of the lawlessness that, in theory at least, also makes Mexico so intriguing to me. The climax of the story, the harrowing escape, is amazing, and I'm convinced that Bill is writing a *New York Times* bestseller. He knows it's a great story, but I can tell that he's driven by an imperative to save others from the same fate. Someone else will have to be Mexico's next great artist. *Hey, I can do that!* chimes the little voice in my head that responds well to caffeine but heeds no logic, no responsibility, and no allegiance whatsoever to reality.

Our next stop is lower Santa Rosa, which includes a once grand crumbling church with a modest shady plaza, and a quintessential dusty road, replete with free-range donkeys, free-range dogs, free-range chickens, and free-range children chasing each other and an assortment of the free-range creatures around. I think I even spot a wandering black bull farther on down. There's a clearly upstairs/downstairs aspect to Santa Rosa, and we have arrived at the bargain basement. The area is littered with discarded old cars and their respective parts, and the occasional abodes are a shade too derelict to earn the moniker of house. Some show signs of life—one painted bright orange and cobalt blue has a goat tied to its fence, but others look abandoned.

Here I can't help but notice the beggars, most of whom are traditionally-dressed native women with young children, for whom "possibility" is stunted to the most basic of needs, daily sustenance. I share what I can, which won't make the slightest ripple in this vast sea of need. My inner-city children have it hard, but this is a whole new level of deprivation, however quaint it may look at first blush. Like the problems at my research center, there's no way I can fix this. But hopeless as it feels, is it better to stop trying? This, I think, is the central issue I need to resolve before I go back. And it's a doozey.

Before my companion can stop me I walk up to the old, forlorn billy goat, scratch his head, and murmur a friendly salutation, from one mammal to another. In a genuinely touching moment, figuratively and literally, he gently nudges his head against my ribs.

"See," I say to Bill, who is shaking his head, "He's just a big puppy dog, as sweet as can be."

"That's not the issue, my dear." Almost instantly, I catch his drift. For the next several hours, I will reek of eau d' billy goat. To this day, I have yet to encounter an odor as tenacious, as soap-and-waterproof, as Mexican billy goat.

We go to sit in the shade of the plaza and imagine the former glory of the church. Two scruffy young boys come to join us. No words are exchanged, it seems they're just there to keep us company. I decide they must be brothers, as they're wearing identical blue shirts. Bill buys them

drinks and they reply in unison "*¡Gracias, señor!*" I offer a
few pesos and off they go to chase more dogs.

Just then, the roving bull sashays past us and walks into
the church with doors left open to welcome all in need. Bill
shoots me a welcome-to-Mexico look. This should be interesting, I think. Moments later, he is loping out with shrieking, flailing priests and villagers at his heels. Back outside,
the bull is encircled by a group of rangy barking dogs. He
tries running away, but the dogs are faster and spoiling for
a fight, so instead he lurches at them. The dogs immediately scatter, knowing the balance of power has shifted, and
the bull saunters back down the road in peace. This little
vignette seems a fitting representation of life up here: take
it easy and if that doesn't work, crank things up a notch.
But conserve as much energy as possible. I'm pretty sure
we could profit from this kind of approach back home.

"You know, Bill," I say. "Until this pious bull incident, I
haven't witnessed any tension up here."

"Right you are," says Bill. "This is life in the slower than
slow lane."

"It's a shame I'm such an urban creature," I admit.
"Otherwise I might take Carlos up on his offer."

"Well, sure. Carlos could use another wife. I think he
only has two or three right now."

For no apparent reason, this makes me incredibly happy.
I suppose it's knowing that there are still places where people can live like this, even though I know it's not in cards
for me. I've already begun engineering the elusive Plan B,
and it will be launched in Massachusetts, sans views, sans
bulls, sans Carlos. Its contours are just coming into focus,
but the core, where the children reside, is crystal clear.

We sip our bottled drinks and listen to the oak leaves
rustling overhead. The breeze is playing with my long

hair, re-styling it in collaboration with the local jet stream. I push it off my face and the breeze blows is right back. I'm about to go back to the car for a rubber band, but Bill indicates that it's time for us to head back to Guanajuato anyway, so we both take a good look around and then go.

As we snake our way back into the city, everything seems welcoming and familiar, as though I've broken through the membrane separating the tourists from the converts. The streets and sidewalks are awash with brightly attired children. For some reason, I never noticed how many children roam through this city. Then I notice that they're dressed up, and I ask Bill if perhaps today is one of Mexico's many holidays. Bill brightens, "Oh hell, yes, it's Day of the Children. I completely forgot." Day of the children, I smile, could the universe be any less subtle?

I know that it's not merely serendipitous that I landed in a country defined by contradictions: beauty, brutality, joy, poverty, and laws seemingly written to be broken. Bring an open mind, comfort with ambiguity, and a measure of recklessness, the siren breathes in your ear, and each day will be exhilarating. Still, when I hear the barking, there's no way to avoid the melancholy it arouses. I know my limits, know that there will never be a way for me to reconcile the way this country loves and torments its dogs, that Santa Rosa and Guanajuato will live on as a dream, and that my love for Mexico, her colors and spirit, will always be intense and imperfect.

Back at our plaza, El Día de los Niños is in full swing and the entire area has been transformed into a noisy dance arena. Children, released for a day from the confinement of school and the burden of homework, are doing a line dance to "Achy Breaky Heart," a frothy once-popular American country song blaring from a boombox.

The sea of kids slides to the left and twirls around en masse. They move back, step to the right, pause, and swivel their hips. This undulating sea of color and movement presents an arresting image, a unified energy field moving as one. Like most of my young constituents back home, many of these children probably live hand to mouth. They live without electronic toys, new clothes, or health insurance, but as I watch them turn and shimmy, I wonder if we really do have it better in the U.S. Evidence to the contrary is mounting, or, more specifically, dancing with abandon.

Surreal is a word that I try to avoid when depicting Mexico, as it's easy to overuse, but there's no other way to describe this moment. There's no escaping the giddiness, and I find myself moving in rhythm to the song, as carefree as the swirling and dipping children. I try not to think about going home, but when I do, I think my nine days away have lent some valuable perspective which, I realize, is the most I could have expected. In particular, I have come to realize that some problems simply can't be fixed, that the only sane response sometimes is to cut losses and move on. It's the center that I'm going to abandon, I have decided, but not the cause. Where and how I do this is still a bit up in the air, and I'm vaguely concerned that this may be a facile south-of-the-border resolution, but if it is, I implore Mexico and the world beyond, please feel no obligation to inform my achy breaky heart.

The song ends, and the children break formation, only to reassemble as pairs for the next song, sung in a rhythmic Spanish. The roof dogs are surprisingly quiet right now; perhaps they too are mesmerized by this spectacle. I wish they had better lives, but there's not much I can do for them. It occurs to me that perhaps they are loved by their owners, and, maybe, I hope, some family members play with them on the roof, lavish them with affection, offer treats. As for me, I'm no longer feeling quite so trapped, so there's really nothing left to do but join the children and dance.

Andrea Oseas is currently living the life of a painter and sometimes writer in Cambridge, while being subsidized by consulting for a business school in Boston. She is still intent on making the world a better place for children, and if you want to hire her for that purpose, or to offer her free plane, train, or boat tickets to virtually any destination, please Google her email address ASAP.

ℬ ℬ ℬ

Lavaland

A family vacation becomes a seminar on fire fountains,
cinder cones, and rift zones when the author invites along
her father, eminent writer John McPhee.

*H*aleakala, House of the Sun, is so named because
the demigod Maui once stood upon the summit
and caught the sun in a net to slow its march across the sky,
making the day last longer—Hawaiian time. Thirty-three
miles long, twenty-six miles wide, rising 10,025 feet above
sea level and sinking another 36,000 feet into the ocean
floor, so heavy it depresses the ocean floor by a good 16,000
feet (like a bowling ball pressing into a mattress), Haleakala
is considered by some geologists to be, from base to summit,
the biggest mountain in the world. A perfect shield volcano,
it dominates the landscape of Maui. Indeed, it *is* Maui. Its
slopes crash into the sea, cows graze its arid plains, sugarcane fields and jungles thick with banana and passion-fruit
trees cover lava flows that started rising above the surface

of the Pacific 1.1 million years ago, when Maui, second-youngest island in the Hawaiian chain, sat directly over the geophysical hot spot that created it.

Also on the back of Haleakala, of course, are the hundreds of thousands of tourists who visit each year, ascending by the busload to watch the sunrise, coasting on bikes in orange-helmeted packs down its north flank at dawn, hiking and riding on horseback into its caldera, golfing, hang gliding, parasailing, windsurfing, surfing its fringe of giant waves, lying lazily along its shores sipping mai tais, and sporting leis beside the serpentine pools of resorts dripping with bougainvillea. "Designer tropics," my father muttered, after a look at those hotels. We'd come to Hawaii for a vacation on the volcanoes, a lesson of sorts in geology. Geology is one of his subjects. Over a span of twenty years, from my teens to my early thirties, he wrote books on geology that were ultimately collected in the large tome *Annals of the Former World*. It did not take much to persuade him. "When do we leave?" he asked.

At first, I'd had the idea that I would take this trip alone with him, leaving my husband and children at home. My father had taken me to Hawaii when I was twenty-one years old, to accompany him for a piece he was writing on Iceland about attempts that had been made there to control a flow of lava and save a town and its harbor from destruction. He had wanted to deepen his understanding of volcanoes and to see firsthand the molten outpourings of the Big Island's Kilauea, one of the most active volcanoes in the world. I was not even faintly interested in his agenda, so he parked me in a hotel with a pool, and I passed my days reclining on a chaise, slathered in lotion, working on my senior thesis, and missing my Italian boyfriend 10,000 miles away.

Now, twenty years later, I was interested in that geologic history. It was my turn to take him.

Mark, my husband, naturally felt when I mentioned Hawaii that he and the children would like to be there, too. I told my sister Jenny of this predicament and she dealt with it by inviting herself, her husband, and her two boys. Before long, another sister, Laura, a photographer, offered to bring her daughter and to take the pictures. All together we numbered eleven and had thirty pieces of luggage. As we got ready to leave, a friend of Dad's referred to us as "the Joads."

And then we were there, the eleven of us, on top of Haleakala, just after dawn. In the surrounding distance, we saw volcanoes everywhere: the Big Island's Mauna Loa and Mauna Kea looming above the clouds across a stretch of water to the south: to the north, Molokai, Lanai, and West Maui (attached to the rest of Maui by an isthmus). Hawaii is a collection of volcanoes that form in clusters above the hot spot that creates them, and this fact is made spectacularly visual here. Molokai and Lanai and Maui are all parts of one cluster. Erosion and rising water levels after the melting of the last Ice Age have given them the illusion of being separate.

As our guide, my father had come prepared. He'd spoken with geophysicists, geochemists, and volcanologists. He'd studied maps. He'd brought the most recent edition of the book *Roadside Geology of Hawaii*, by Richard Hazlett and Donald Hyndman. He had typed a list of highlights, stops, and excursions, interspersed with advance directives for his grandchildren ("Tommaso, put that iPod away. Go out and collect xenoliths!"). In six single-spaced pages bound in folders, he informed us about tholeiite basalt and alkalic basalts and where to

find lava bombs, lava trees, lava tubes, xenoliths (bits of
the earth's mantle carried upward unmelted and intact,
and other bits of crystallized magma), and the *ahinahina*,
a fabulous Dr. Seuss-like plant that grows on the summit
of Haleakala and nowhere else on earth. He had notes
for each island we planned to visit—Maui, Kauai, and
Hawaii—outlining what we should do and see. But the
real lessons simply came from listening to him as he rode
in the front seat, as he walked by my side, as he sat at all
the various picnics and dinners, making comments about
what exactly it was we were looking at. He was reading
the land as if it were a book. I love this about my father. At
any given place he has always tried to suggest to me what
sort of world we are in and what and how it was made.
Mountains rise and fall, oceans disappear within a matter
of sentences.

Looking fifteen miles down Haleakala's southwest
rift zone, you see Kahoolawe and Molokini. The latter rises from a submarine continuation of Haleakala's
southwestern flank. Seeing it gives a sense of just how
big Haleakala is, just how far its slopes descend beneath
the water's surface.

The east rift zone, on the island's other side, is 100
miles long from summit to base in the Hawaiian deeps,
and 90 miles of it are below sea level. Typically a shield
volcano has three rift zones radiating spokelike from
its summit crater. A rift zone is created when molten
magma inside the volcano rises to a weak area and opens
up a very long fissure, like a scratch with blood in it.
Cinder cones develop around vents along the rift, sending up fire fountains almost in single file, as if they were
marching down the slope of the volcano.

The most recent lava flow on Maui occurred in the
southwest rift zone some time between 1490 and 1600,

near La Pérouse Bay. After exploring this area, standing at sea level we looked up toward Haleakala's summit across gorgeous swaths of color in fields bisected by a black river of frozen lava of both kinds: the jagged aa (rough lava) and the swirling pahoehoe (smooth lava). Before we could stop them, the five children were on it. My nephew Leandro (age five) thought the aa would be soft, like crumpled dirt, because it gives that illusion. Then he fell and cut his knee. "Page 1, line 1," my father said cryptically, and went into a peroration about shield volcanoes and rift zones.

When people think of volcanoes, they usually picture stratovolcanoes—Fujiyama, Mount St. Helen's, Mount Vesuvius—which may blow in violent, destructive bursts, burying towns and killing great numbers of people. Generally a stratovolcano starts in a subduction zone (where one tectonic plate dives beneath another). Shield volcanoes, dangerous enough, are subtler and gentler in shape. Looking at Haleakala, you might think you could walk up there easily, but just try it. The mountain is beyond human reference; it tests one's ability to imagine its scale. The violence associated with a hot spot is often most extensive at the start, when a plume of heat and hard rock comes up through the mantle and penetrates the earth's crust, pushing out huge volumes of now melted rock known as flood basalts. Late-stage eruptions—which occur when a volcano, as a passenger on a tectonic plate, is moving away from its source of heat—can also be quite violent. Over the hundreds of thousands of years in between, the lava oozes out. One flow on top of another, spilling from the center down the sides—growing, as my father said, "like wax from a candle dripping down the sides of a bottle." He paused, letting this image sink in, then looked at me and said,

"That'll be a hundred bucks." My father is used to being paid by the word, but—forget it—not by me. A consummate Scot, with the word *phee* in his very name, he presents his bill of sale. When he turns a phrase I might want, I'll try a preemptive strike, and say, "That's mine." When a turn of phrase is flat-out bad, I tell him, "You can keep that one."

He pointed to a line of hills, some bare and black, others covered in a fine layer of grass, signs of their relative age. "Each bump is a cinder cone that once shot fire fountains as high as 1,900 feet into the air." I stood at his side, obediently taking notes. Laura set up her camera and took pictures. Mark, Jenny, and Luca, her husband, asked questions. The kids played hide-and-seek in the lava. I looked toward the ocean, then to the bumps descending from the summit and the black-lava rivers cutting through arid terrain on the island's dry side. I could almost see those bumps come to life, shooting their fountains of liquid rock. "It's not hot," declared Livia, my five-year-old daughter, touching the pahoehoe. "I thought lava would be hot."

"Kula volcanics," my father said, looking up from *Roadside Geology* to identify the rock spills we were passing through as we began a day's journey completely around Haleakala—perhaps one of the most spectacular drives on earth. The road cuts through tropical forests with waterfalls, thick ferns, and the brilliant red flash of the flame tree. My father mumbled Conrad: "...the earliest beginnings of the world, when vegetation rioted on the earth and the big trees were kings." Then, on the northern stretch of the park's ring road, pouring down the slopes of Haleakala to the Keanae Valley, came a vast black stripe of lava running into the surf, which had cut it into spires and spikes. In the terminology of Hawaiian geologists, the Hana volcanics had covered the Kula volcanics, and then both had gone under the Honomanu volcanics. We all loved these names. And, looking up the slopes of the mountain, we could see what they referred to, as we had seen from above—the successive lava flows layering each other as they dramatically cascaded over cliffs. Ten thousand years old, some of the Kula flows were essentially without vegetation, black as ever, as if they had happened yesterday.

We drove south along the coast on the Hana Highway, through the sleepy town of Hana and across the east rift zone. You could see it descending from the summit like a spine, cutting through town and continuing right out to sea. In Hana, we hiked a narrow trail beside steep drops and came to a red-sand beach, where we swam inside a cinder cone called Kauiki Head—as it happens, near a nude beach, something that the children, not to mention the oldest member of our group, found infinitely fascinating. We stopped again to walk beside the pools of Oheo—twenty-two of them—which carve their way down Haleakala's southern slope to the ocean, one pouring into the next, each one in a different lava flow. We continued on under the desolate south side of the volcano on a stretch of road that guidebooks warn you against but is not that rough and should be ventured. Charles Lindbergh is buried in this remote region, near Kaupo Valley, which was blue and serenely beautiful in the afternoon light as we looked up into it to the rim of the summit crater.

My mind went back to all of us on the summit, hiking into its crater—a moonscape of sorts (used to train NASA astronauts for that very reason), with cinder cones and lava bombs scattered all about and a penetrating silence that allows you to feel entirely alone, even if you are not. We hiked separately, raising little puffs of lava dust with each step; the air was so clear—diamond-sharp. If you apply a little imagination to a landscape like this, it can turn molten again and thus, indeed, the word *frozen* seems to be the most accurate—as if all the action had stopped suddenly. It was windy and cold as we hiked out, my large and intrepid family, all the little kids here and there, decorating this surreal terrain.

Descending in our caravan of two big cars—as we passed through a eucalyptus grove that flooded the air with its fabulous scent—my father said, "It feels like we're halfway into next week, but it's only 11:15 in the morning. It's a dubious honor to be part of a family to whom sleep means nothing." Looking back at Haleakala from a field of sugarcane, he said he deeply regretted that the mountain—and all the rest of the fiftieth state—could not be towed around Cape Horn and north to replace Florida.

To understand the geology of Hawaii you must have some knowledge of a geophysical hot spot beyond its definition as a fixed locus of thermal energy originating deep down near the earth's core and rising in a plume of heat intense enough to break through the plate lying over it. After a hot spot's first, often violent eruption, which inundates a vast area with molten rock, activity settles down into a consistent rhythm of eruption and accumulation. Typically a hot spot lasts about 100 million years—not much of the total history of the earth. "About one forty-sixth, if anybody cares," Dad said. Hot spots don't move. The plates above them move, carrying away the volcanoes the hot spot has produced. Imagine a sewing-machine needle punching holes in fabric. The moving fabric is the plate, the holes the volcanoes, the needle the hot-spot plume. (Don't even ask how much that image cost.)

Worldwide, there are about forty to fifty active hot spots, among them Yellowstone and Iceland. Of them all, Hawaii is the easiest to see, because there are no continental landmasses or other competing geologic features. The chain of volcanic mountains that includes Hawaii is about eighty million years old and 5,000 miles long, starting just south of the Big Island and reaching all the way to Alaska. After Hawaii, the submarine remnants of an island can be found on average, every forty miles along that 5,000-mile line. And, as if on a conveyor belt, they are all being carried north to the Aleutian Trench, into which they will ultimately descend and be consumed as the Pacific Plate dives beneath the North American Plate. From Kauai northwestward, the chain includes some 1,500 miles of subaerial atolls, but mainly the former islands are seamounts, or submarine mountains. Halfway to Alaska the chain bends and turns north, marking a shift in the motion of the Pacific Plate that occurred forty-three million years ago. At the bend, the former islands become the Emperor Seamounts, so called by the Japanese oceanographers who discovered them in the 1930s and named them for specific emperors of Japan, in chronological order—the oldest emperor being on the precipice of destruction at the Aleutian Trench.

From Maui we flew to Kauai, the oldest island in the state of Hawaii. Beautiful Kauai, the garden isle, includes one of the wettest spots on earth, where nearly 500 inches of rain falls annually. (New York gets 47, Seattle 37, London 23.6.) This very wet spot is an area near the top of Mount Waialeale, a shield volcano whose spires and craggy peaks are covered in a green so rich it seems gemlike. Kauai's incomparable landscape has been used as the setting for movies—*South Pacific*, *Raiders of the Lost Ark*, and *Jurassic Park* among them. It was good to have seen Maui first. Haleakala offers the eye a splayed Euclidean angle, massive and obtuse. Kauai is a lesson in erosion: only the imagination, connecting the ribbed and sculpted palis (steep slopes), could reveal the shield volcano as it was a few million years ago.

We spent the afternoon visiting Lumahai Beach, a perfect, palm-fringed crescent near Hanalei, strolling the shore, watching the winter waves roll in thunderously, with nothing but ocean between us and Alaska. We looked for xenoliths and swam in a small pool protected by a tall barrier of lava, against which those waves crashed, causing white cascades to flow among us. Lumahai Beach—known locally as Luma-die because of a ferocious undertow that has carried swimmers to their deaths—was the setting for the hair-washing scene in *South Pacific*. All of us, my father included, agreed that we'd give up our careers if we could become film-location scouts.

At the crack of dawn, with our thirty pieces of luggage—my son Jasper ricocheting here and there, a pinball of testosterone, and my father suggesting that he be put in a kennel—we boarded a plane for the Big Island, and to put Hawaiian geology into general perspective, these are some things to consider: Kauai, at five million years, is the same age as the formation of the Red Sea and the separation of Baja California from the Mexican mainland. The Big Island of Hawaii, a cluster of five volcanoes, is only about 750,000 years old. And, of course, the fresh flows of Kilauea have an initial age of zero.

On the Big Island, you do not need imagination to see the volcanoes and the way in which they all fit together above the hot spot. Simply drive north from Waimea toward Hawi on the Kohala Mountain Road. Look around. You'll see Kohala, Hualalai, Mauna Kea, and Mauna Loa, their vast shields convex and climactic. Like biscuits in a tin, these massive, gentle mountains fit snugly, pushing up against one another. On the slopes of Kohala there are cattle farms as large and lush as some in Virginia.

You can drive to the top of Mauna Kea, the White Mountain, gradually rising above the cloud line and ending at the summit, one of the world's most spectacular cul-de-sacs, nearly 14,000 feet above sea level. From its base on the ocean floor to the place where you stand, this mountain is 25 percent higher than Everest. Craters and cinder cones pock the landscape. You look on a level line across twenty-seven aerial miles to the summit of Mauna Loa, the Long Mountain, the largest active volcano in the world, which, volcanologists report, is swelling, preparing to erupt once again.

The following day, we set out for Hawaii Volcanoes National Park. At the summit crater of Kilauea—a third as high as Mauna Loa and nestled into its evening shadow—offerings to the goddess Pele appear on the rim: flowers, incense, Ritz crackers, pineapples, bottles of gin and vodka. When Mark Twain looked into the crater in June 1866, he found the scent of the sulfurous vapors "not unpleasant to a sinner." Kilauea was in eruption for the entire nineteenth century. A renewed eruption began in 1983 and hasn't stopped. The action is not in the summit crater but down in the eastern rift zone; a whole fishing village was obliterated in 1990, buried thirty feet deep.

As we descended Kilauea on Chain of Craters Road, ropy pahoehoe was all around us, and the children described it using bathroom humor. But soon we all looked up, and the children's language went up some distance, too. "Awesome!" "Incredible!" "Wow!" "Beauteous!" Several miles away across the lavascape was a high-rising plume of steam created by new lava pouring into the ocean.

The road turned toward it, paralleling the coast. We drove as far as cars are permitted to go and then got out and walked on until the road disappeared under a thick flow of lava twenty years old. We hiked over lava by the sea. Slowly the plume grew larger as our distance from it diminished. It was late afternoon. The idea had been to be here as night fell. Laura, who wanted to take pictures in the afternoon light, walked ahead of us with Luca, who was helping her lug her equipment. My daughter kept up with them. As we scrambled up and down across the lava, the landscape slowly took us in, slowly revealed itself. I walked as fast as I could. I wanted to stay close to Livia to see her awe when she, for the first time, saw incandescent lava.

And suddenly it was there, a beautiful shock as we came in sight of a braided river of red lava flowing down a steep escarpment low on the side of the mountain. As lava moves, it forms tubes around itself and so for the most part flows unseen. On the escarpment, the tubes were leaking, to use the description favored by volcanologists. We sat down in the growing darkness and simply watched the red lava a good distance from the billowing steam where it entered the ocean. It spilled in a long, steep chain of fire that grew redder and brighter as daylight disappeared. Many other hikers had also arrived. Excitement may have been particularly acute in the aftermath of an event that had occurred a week before: in a "bench collapse," forty acres of the lava plain had fallen into the Pacific and slid down the volcano's submarine slope. Some people watching were hoping for another collapse. Some people included me. The plume of white steam turned to rose. We watched until the darkness was total, the red glow at its brightest.

We had flashlights, of course, as did the other hikers. Bobbing lights were all you could see as they departed or arrived, a procession of people with lights, like pilgrims enacting the stations of the cross. On our way back to the car, we stopped from time to time to turn and look again at the red lava. You could all but hear its crackling hiss, far away. We could not see one another well, but we were all there, all together, exhilarated pilgrims, vacationing on volcanoes.

Martha McPhee is the author of the novels Bright Angel Time, *a* New York Times *Notable Book in 1997, and* Gorgeous Lies, *nominated in 2002 for a National Book Award. Her short fiction and nonfiction have appeared in many publications including* The New York Times, Chicago Tribune, Harper's Bazaar, Vogue, Real Simple, Tin House, *and* Zoetrope. *She is the recipient of fellowships from the National Endowment for the Arts and the John Simon Guggenheim Memorial Foundation. She teaches creative writing at Hofstra University and lives in New York City.*

✃ ✃ ✃

Caramel et Miel

A virtual romance turns flesh-and-blood in France.

Does Laurent have my silver earring? Or is it lost in the dust of Vaison-la-Romaine—mingling with Roman ruins, feigning antiquity?

Laurent, such an improbable suspect. Willowy, lithe, with curly blond hair that seemed to bubble out of his head. "The skin on your stomach is like *caramel et miel*," I told him. Caramel and honey.

I was eight years older, but lied and made it four. Back when I thought we'd never meet.

It wasn't a romantic beginning. He ruthlessly corrected my French, lavish with mistakes, on an Internet bulletin board. "It's not proper to say *excusez-moi*," he wrote, "because you should not demand that the other person excuse you." *Je vous prie à m'excuser*, I responded with exquisite courtesy.

Pleasantries led to confidences. He called me *princesse* and said he liked spelunking. I called him *mon chevalier*, my knight, and confessed a fondness for balladeer Francis Cabrel. "Cabrel," he wrote back, *"Je t'aimais, je t'aime et je t'aimerais."*

"I loved you, I love you, I will love you," Cabrel sang, conjugating emotion.

Our flirtation floated on, like a high school romance, with 5,000 miles between the desks where we passed furtive notes. Only I played the teenage boy. I was forty years old, and yet I'd never felt so seductive. Released from a stifling relationship that should have been over long before, my desire was predatory.

I admit it. I was captivated by the idea of a French romance. I would tumble out of bed in the morning to find an e-mail waiting, sweet as a rose, in my mailbox. Our words were always beyond reproach, but passion lay in wait beneath the innocent *mots*.

I was taking my mother to France. It had been planned for months. I already had tickets, reservations. A wicked momentum was hurling me towards Laurent, to the very part of the country where he lived. "I am coming to Provence," I confessed.

Should we meet? Was it worth gambling our fantasy? The tension drifted back and forth between continents as we each privately mulled the prospect. Could I pass for thirty-six, I wondered? And what of his lies? He'd made no claims to be rich or handsome or famous. "I look too young to be a professor," he'd admitted, telling me he taught classes in technology.

We agreed to meet in Aix—my last day there. I was prepared for a clean get-away.

My mother has always been a superb travel companion. She needed to be. I mentioned I might meet up with an e-mail correspondent. She didn't raise an eyebrow.

The *rendezvous* was set for Aix train station. Wonderfully public. We would both arrive by car. Excellent escape potential.

As I climbed out of my little red Renault, I recognized him immediately. He was slighter than I'd imagined, not much taller than I. He wore a crisp, plaid shirt and sensible shoes. With his cloud of blond hair, a somewhat fussy, slightly nervous angel.

When he saw me, Laurent registered relief, and a flick of surprise. I was better than expected. Maybe I looked younger than thirty-six. We shook hands. I gave him a sweatshirt and he gave me a book. You see, we were quite proper.

We went for a walk, shy at first, waiting for our face-to-face life to reconcile with the ease of our e-mails.

I uncoiled my French. Not the tourist French I'd been prattling, but the French of *tu*, French murmured by those who can conjure up a past, lay it out with *imparfait*, then embroider it with *passé compose*, precise moments of history.

I decided to invite him to dinner, and he sat with my mother and me, eating *daub* in a tiny restaurant, while the chill Mistral rattled at the windows. "Your daughter speaks very good French—with a few little mistakes," Laurent teased. "I speak very good French," I translated to my mother, daring him to correct me.

We agreed to meet in Orange the next day. I still have the photos: Laurent and my mother at the Roman theater. Laurent smiling in front of the triumphal arch. But what I best remember is stopping at a little bar to warm our hands around mugs of hot chocolate. Red-faced working-men tossed back *pastis* and cognacs, shouting and laughing across the room, while we leaned close to hear each other amid the din, Laurent's hot breath on my cold left ear.

I folded back the side mirrors on our car and squeezed it through the streets of Vaison-la-Romaine to the doorstep of our bed and breakfast. After my mother was settled, I returned to the parking lot, where Laurent waited. I climbed in his car. Francis Cabrel was playing.

When the kiss came, it was long and sweet, born of late-night longings and words never spoken aloud.

"There is a hotel," he said.

What did my mother think when I told her? Was she shocked? Worried? Bewildered? Or secretly excited at my bold announcement? "I'll see you in the morning," she said, kissing me.

I drove with Laurent to a roadside chain hotel. The room was tiny, the furnishings molded out of plastic, the bathroom down the hall. "*Ça va?*" he asked. "It is what I can afford."

And so I made love with my intimate stranger, *caramel et miel*. The awkward wall of our physical presence melted away. "*Oui*," he whispered in my ear, "*Oui*."

In the morning, the thought of our audacity still startled us. "I didn't expect..." he began. "I know," I replied.

When I kissed him goodbye, I knew it would be the last time.

"You're missing an earring," my mother said at breakfast. And then, the perfect conspirator, "You know I can never tell your father."

There was an e-mail waiting when I arrived home. "*Princesse*," it said, "I guess you are my girlfriend now." I knew then, his fantasy had a different ending.

Je vous prie à m'excuser, Laurent. And I hope you have my earring.

❧ ❧ ❧

Gayle Keck has written for Gourmet, National Geographic Traveler, GQ, Islands, 360, Four Seasons, *and is a frequent contributor to the* Washington Post *and the* Los Angeles Times *travel sections. She also created the web site www.BeenThere AteThat.com, where foodies can post photos of their meals, search for restaurants, share opinions, and read her blog.*

✍ ✍ ✍

A Simple System

In her Korean apartment, an American decides
to take over her landlady's job.

I awoke thinking the mountain was on fire, confused
for a moment by the street lamp that transformed our
frosted window into a giant yellow nightlight. I could read
my watch by it: 4 A.M. Icy gusts rattled the windowpane,
the probable cause of my wakening. For the past week the
wind had blasted down the mountain, chilling us from the
ankles up. Our Korean apartment was heated by water
pipes embedded in the concrete floor. We would have
turned up the heat, but possessed neither thermostat nor
furnace room key.

Shivering, I realized the covers had slipped from our
sleeping mat. As I pulled the floor-warmed polyester comforter back onto the polyester sheets, static electricity crack-
led in the bedding, but Paul slept undisturbed. I ducked
under the covers to watch the sparks in the dark.

A hinge creaked. I held my breath listening, more curious than concerned; our door opened with a distinctive scrape. The creaking hinge probably belonged to the door of our furnace room on the landing. I wondered why anyone would be out there at 4 a.m., but was reluctant to leave my warm bed to find out. Metal clanked on metal. Curiosity won. I pulled on my robe and slippers and cracked open the front door. Our landing was sheltered from the wind, but the air was tear-freezing cold. The night smelled like woodsmoke and ice. Heat and light beckoned from the furnace room door a few feet away. I stepped across the landing for my first glimpse inside.

Engrossed in her task, her delicate profile lit by a bare bulb, our landlady, Mrs. Han, seemed unaware of my arrival. Somehow elegant in a black sweat suit, she stood in front of a cast-iron, waist-high furnace unlike any I'd ever seen. It had a solid front and sides, and three lids in a row on top. Hissing contentedly, it warmed me like a campfire, leaving my backside to freeze.

Mrs. Han gripped the handles of arm-length fire tongs with both hands, hooked the handle of the left lid and slid it aside. Then, with movements sure and graceful, she lowered the fire tongs straight down into the furnace, squeezed the handles together, and began to lift something straight up. What slowly emerged was a glowing red cylinder—a jumbo coal briquette, or "brique"—the size and shape of a gallon paint can. It had eight holes drilled in its top, for the tongs to grip and air to circulate.

Mrs. Han kept lifting it, until her arms extended straight up above her head, and the brique cleared the top of the furnace. Her face reflected red from the brique and glistened from the heat. She lowered the brique onto the concrete floor, where it sizzled a safe distance from her pink-plastic-slippered feet. Blue fire licked up the holes from deep within.

Gazing into the lambent flames, I savored the woodsy smell, realizing that burning coal, not wood, was the ever-present scent in the air.

I remembered the day we first saw our apartment, when my translator, Miss Yu, had told me, "Mrs. Han will start furnace." It hadn't occurred to me the furnace might be coal. I never dreamed that starting it meant maintaining it too. I had a strong feeling that if we were Mrs. Han's usual Korean tenants rather than Americans, she would not be stoking it for us. With a flash of guilt and dismay I realized Mrs. Han had been stoking it for two weeks, without any appreciation from us. She had her own furnace to tend. We shouldn't add to her burden. Paul worked long hours, but expatriate spouses weren't allowed to hold jobs, so I had practically nothing to do. The thought of making Mrs. Han's life easier warmed me inside, but more to the point—I wanted to play with the fire. I missed our fireplace in Colorado. And with me in charge of the heat, Paul and I could be warmer. Though my coal-stoking experience was limited to backyard barbeques, I figured, how hard could this be?

Mrs. Han guided the tongs down the hole in the furnace again, and this time lifted out a gray, burned-out brique of the same size and shape. She set it on the floor, gripped the still burning brique, and returned it to the furnace. Then she reached the tongs into the shadows behind her and retrieved a new brique, glossy black. She lowered it into the furnace, then slid closed the lid.

The simplicity of the system enchanted me. Before the top brique burned out it was switched to the bottom position, where it passed the torch to a new one above. A chain-reaction. Perpetual fire. Eternal flame.

Hoping not to startle Mrs. Han, I knocked softly on the doorframe. She turned and smiled up at me, as if she'd known I was there all along. A key dangled from her necklace made of twine. She bowed slightly, the tongs pressed between her palms like prayer sticks. When she straightened, I put my hand on the tong handles. With my other hand I pointed to myself and to the furnace, showing I wanted to take over. Smiling, she shook her head no.

I couldn't tell if her refusal was because stoking was a landlady's job, or because I was American and therefore presumed incompetent. I tried to reassure her and explain my intent at the same time by tugging slightly on the tongs, grinning determinedly. Still smiling, she kept hold. Smiling back, I began a steady pull.

Cocking an eyebrow at me in wonder or skepticism, she let go. I hugged the tongs to my chest and bowed to show I intended to take over for good. She shrugged a good-natured "O.K."

That settled, Mrs. Han became all business. She pointed to the pipes near the floor that led from the furnace to the water heater, and from the water heater into the wall of the house. I nodded my understanding; she'd given me a quick lesson on how the floors were heated. She pointed to the middle and right lids on the furnace, and mimed lifting briques in and out. I nodded; those still needed to be stoked. She pointed to three tiny air vents, the only openings on the front of the furnace, one near the floor below each lid. They were opened just a hair. I nodded; the vents could be adjusted to allow more air into the furnace. I knew that the more air, the hotter the furnace would burn—and the warmer my home would be.

She tapped her fingertip on the ten of her wristwatch. I nodded, though I wasn't sure if she meant stoke the furnace again at 10 A.M. or 10 P.M. 10 P.M. made more sense, as she could have stoked every night without our knowledge. But I'd check it at 10 A.M. to be safe. She lifted the necklace from her neck and, on tiptoe, placed it over my head. I closed my hand on the key. We bowed. She trotted down the concrete steps to her apartment.

The fire was all mine.

I switched off the bare bulb, too harsh for this soft hour, and took her place before the furnace. I listened to the contented *shhhhhhhhhh* as my eyes adjusted to the vents' faint orange glow. Then, with tongs more awkward than she'd made them look, I slid aside the center lid. Instantly I was mesmerized by the blue flames dancing in and around a glowing red brique sitting in a white-hot shaft. The furnace was made of fire brick sheathed in cast-iron, like a pottery kiln with three chambers. The chambers, or shafts, were barely wider in diameter than the brique.

My face tingled from the intense heat. I gripped the tong handles with both hands, aimed down the shaft, stabbed the burning brique through two of its holes, squeezed and began to lift what felt like a concrete block. It weighed much more than Mrs. Han's graceful movements had led me to believe. Raising it without knocking it against the shaft walls, then lowering it to the floor without dropping it or setting my robe on fire, took muscles I didn't know I had. I released it on the floor, far from the hem of my robe. Hearing the sizzle on the concrete, I smiled.

I lowered the tongs into the shaft again and removed the much lighter, burned-out brique. Gazing spellbound into the white-hot shaft, I spotted another dead brique at the bottom. Mrs. Han hadn't removed it, so neither did I. I placed the burning brique on top of it, set a new one on top of that and slid closed the lid. I repeated the procedure for the third and last shaft.

Then, to make our apartment warmer, I opened the vents to half way, about a quarter inch.

Reluctantly I left the warm furnace room, quickly locked the door, sprinted into the apartment, and spooned in beside Paul, my human furnace. I drifted into sleep, basking in the anticipated warmth of his appreciation.

I awoke shortly before the 7 A.M. alarm. The comforter had slipped off again. Paul's arm lay across my chest, his knee on my stomach. My teeth were chattering like the windowpane. I pulled the crackling comforter over us. But it was cold.

I placed my palm on the floor. Stone cold.

Watching our breath blow away like smoke, I wished I were dreaming.

I cancelled the alarm before it buzzed, disentangled myself from Paul without waking him and hustled outside. When I opened the furnace room door, no heat welcomed me. No reassuring hiss. I grabbed the tongs and shoved the lids aside. The shafts were dark. I lifted out each brique, hoping to find some spark of life. But they were dead. All dead.

Three hours after being entrusted with it, I had killed Mrs. Han's eternal flame.

Paul and I breakfasted in our hats and coats, the gas stove turned on high.

"My secretary speaks Korean," Paul said, "I'll ask her to call Mrs. Han."

"No! I mean, no need to trouble Mrs. Han. I'll ask Miss Yu how to start it."

Paul left for work. I phoned Miss Yu.

"You need fire starter," she said. "General store."

Of course; like a barbeque. I found "lighter fluid" in my Berlitz, practiced the Korean pronunciation, and set off for the little general store.

It seemed there was always a different family member keeping shop. Today's clerk looked about twelve.

"*Rah ee toh kee room?*" I said.

He looked blank. I showed him "lighter fluid" in my *Berlitz*. He held out a disposable cigarette lighter from the counter display. I shook my head "no," pointed to a plastic bucket full of fire tongs, then to "lighter fluid" again.

"Ah!" He laughed. "*Zoot!*"

"Zoot?"

From a plastic bucket next to the coal tongs, he retrieved what looked like a big hockey puck. Made of coal, it was the same diameter as a brique, with the same holes drilled through it. He took a match from his pocket, pretended to light it and touched it to the puck. "*Zoot!*" he laughed, and threw his hands in the air as if to say "problem solved."

I smiled with relief, and nodded my understanding. A *zoot* was similar to the wax and wood fire-starters I'd used in fireplaces, but made from coal and probably lighter fluid. It could be lit with a match and would burn long and steady enough to light a brique. I bought several. I also bought a plastic bucket, since he had no metal ones, to cart the dead briques down to the trash.

In the furnace room, I took up the tongs, stabbed a *zoot* through two of its holes, and rested it on the furnace while I thought about how to proceed. The shafts were about two feet deep. If I put the unlit *zoot* into the shaft, it would be difficult to reach down and light it without the match burning my fingers. But the tongs didn't close tight enough to hold a match. I decided to light the *zoot* first, then lower it into the shaft.

Holding a lit match at arm's length, I touched it to the *zoot*. With a split-second chain-reaction of sparks, "*zzzzzzzzZZZZOOT!!!*" it burst into flames. Black acrid smoke filled the room. I couldn't see, couldn't breathe, dropped the *zoot* and stumbled out the door.

Billowing smoke, the *zoot* wobbled out after me.

I dashed into the apartment and slammed the door, coughing, eyes watering, thankful the building was built of concrete.

When the smoke cleared and the *zoot* had calmed to a smolder, I retrieved it with the tongs. I placed it at the bottom of the first shaft. Recalling the buzzing sparks that had preceded its eruption, I theorized that *zoots* were impregnated with gun powder.

My next attempt went more smoothly. I placed an unlit *zoot* in the second shaft, tossed in a lit match, ran into the house and stayed there until the smoke dissipated. I repeated for the third and last shaft, then added new briques to each one. Nothing to it.

And once the briques were lit, getting the furnace hot again was simple as well. Knowing that the more air the fire got, the sooner our floors would warm, I opened the vents all the way (a half-inch) and fed the furnace every two hours, day and night, like a famished newborn. Meanwhile, Paul and I lived in our coats and soaked up the heat at the neighborhood bathhouse. After two nights I was exhausted from lack of sleep and the floors were only a tad less cold. Paul offered to help with the night feedings but I turned him down; he needed all his strength for his job. He asked if I wanted Mrs. Han to resume control, and again I refused. I broke it; I'd fix it. I couldn't let down America.

Four days after restarting the furnace, I lay spread-eagled on my tummy, hugging the warm floor in celebration. I had learned a lot that week. I'd learned that once my furnace was hot it took hours to heat the water tank, and once the water was hot, it took even longer for the pipes to heat the floor. I'd learned that briques were called *yontan,* where to find the closest *yontan* shop, that the minimum order was two hundred, and that luckily they only cost about a quarter each. I'd learned that if you don't wait long enough before putting dead *yontan* in the bucket, you melt the bucket.

But I hadn't learned my lesson.

With the vents reset at Mrs. Han's "just a hair," the furnace needed to be stoked every six hours—how she had tended it for two weeks without my knowledge was a mystery. And the frigid wind wouldn't cease. I wanted the furnace to burn faster during the day for more warmth, and slower at night so I could get eight hours of unbroken sleep. I figured it was simply a matter of fine-tuning the air vents. However, having learned from experience, I began my warming experiment by setting the vents a single hair's breadth beyond "just a hair," and kept close watch on the burning *yontan*.

As it turned out, any vent position other than "all the way" or "just a hair" made the burn rate unpredictable, put the shafts out of sync, and soon I was practically living in the furnace room, feeding each shaft at a different time like newborn triplets.

A few nights later, seriously sleep deprived, the truckload of new *yontan* stacked blackly behind me, I slumped against the furnace room wall. Gathering the strength to feed the hungry second shaft, I stared into the rambunctious flames of the first, noting the similarity to the fires of hell. Somehow I had to get these babies on a schedule.

I remembered Mrs. Han tapping her finger on the ten of her watch. I recalled finding her at 4 A.M., standing before the furnace as if it were an altar. The answer came to me: *Enough already with the Yankee "ingenuity."*

I sighed, took up the tongs, and started over. One by one, except for the dead one at the bottom of each shaft, I lifted all the *yontan*—all in various stages of fiery consumption— up and out of the furnace and, for lack of space, shuttled them out to the frigid landing. Next, still using the tongs, I lowered an unlit *zoot* into the first shaft—careful not to touch it to the white-hot sides and trigger a premature explosion—and noted the practicality of having a dead brique in the bottom to serve as a *zoot* platform. I placed a *zoot* in each of the other shafts. I lit three matches in close succession, tossed one into each shaft, leapt out the door and slammed it behind me just as I heard "*zzzzzzzzzzZZ-ZOOT! zzzzZZZOOT! zZZZOOT!*"

Sagging against the door, head bowed in exhaustion, I became aware of a gentle heat. I glanced up. At the end of the landing, the assorted *yontan* glowed and flickered in the dark like prayer candles. I meditated on them awhile.

Then, I turned around, took a deep breath, held it, and hid behind the furnace room door as I yanked it open. Black smoke roiled out and up like a demon into the sky.

When the furnace room cleared, I filled the shafts with new *yontan*.

I knelt before the furnace to adjust the vents to exactly "just a hair."

After cleansing myself of soot, I set the alarm for 4 A.M.

C. Lill Ahrens was a visual artist all her life until an isolated sojourn in Korea made her a writer. Award-winning excerpts from her memoir, Seoul Survivor—or—Where Are They Going with My Kitchen Sink? *(from which this story was excerpted), appear in literary journals and anthologies. Lill is a creative writing instructor and book doctor, a published cartoonist, and an editor for* Calyx: A Journal of Art and Writing by Women. *She lives in Corvallis, Oregon.*

❧ ❧ ❧

Bellodgia Caron

A daughter ponders the cost of not living.

*F*ear makes a debilitating travel companion. While my mother's parents could each move alone as teenagers to a new world thousands of miles and an ocean away, her longest and bravest solo adventure consisted of a weekly twenty-minute bus ride. Her journey began at the corner of our quiet street and ended at Kaufmann's department store in downtown Pittsburgh.

Nor could Mother be sanguine about my brother's or my own adventures, once we each grew old enough to have them. Every day, she reminded us, children drown in swimming pools, teenagers die in car crashes. We left home with the weight of those dead bodies on our backs.

When eventually our itineraries began with the airport, Mother's anxiety level soared with us. But now we were tapping something else deep in her and, almost until we were airborne, she told us of things she'd read about that we had to see—the real house of the seven gables in Salem; an inn built upon an inn where William the Conqueror stayed in 1066; Fortnum and Mason's, purveyors of the best of everything British; the Paris Ritz, Hemingway's favorite haunt during the war. She would wave us off with worry in her face, but then shadow our journeys in spirit like a Boswell, tucking our postcards, as they arrived, around the edges of the dining room mirror.

I required the security of her concern but hated her fears, her reticence, her lethal insecurities. They had cost her too much. I shared her weakness for dreams; but I was better at making them real. I moved hundreds of miles from home the first chance I got.

On my first trip to Europe, alone in Paris, I wept predictably before the Monets and Van Goghs, sought out Colette's windows, stared at the designs at Givenchy, and I bought trinkets I still find in my cupboards and a pair of dove-gray kid gloves that cost almost what I paid each month for my apartment in Cambridge. The gloves would be lost before the snows of that winter melted; but that cold January day in 1968, with my hands so finely encased, I walked across seas of pastel Aubusson carpets to enter the gilded dining room of the Hotel Ritz. It was six o'clock in the evening on my twenty-fourth birthday. For a year I had planned a solitary celebration at this legendary site.

Bellodgia Caron. As a child I stumbled over that name, saying it aloud, staring at it on my mother's dresser. There it lived in elegant print on a clear, rectangular bottle with faceted corners. The stopper supported a small glass plume of light. Inside the bottle, a pale golden perfume awaited the moment Mother would deem rare enough—worthy of this liquid and its application to her narrow wrists and long white throat.

The bottle, along with two pairs of silk stockings, arrived in our evenly spaced suburb in 1945, safe in the center of my uncle's army-green duffel bag. Silk stockings and fine perfume bought in Paris for my mother, Amelia, his oldest sister. Artifacts of survival to herald his safe return, made as if with Mother in mind.

Amelia was two when her first brother was born, five when this brother destined to shop in Paris appeared, thirteen when the parade of new siblings stopped.

Mother's story is commonly American. Every sixteen-year-old must have had anxious parents in 1929. Many had younger brothers and sisters to take care of—especially after the best bedrooms were filled with boarders, men who got hungry every day and wanted starched white shirts to wear while looking for work. Amelia was the lieutenant in their middle-class Cleveland household—the one whose church is discipline and who is held accountable when something goes wrong.

Amelia might once have had a sense of her own powers, independent of her mother's kitchen, her mother's rules, and her mother herself: a short and startlingly blue-eyed being, formidable, her hair knotted out of the way, whose mission was never to waste time, effort, or food. Apparently she often questioned her oldest child's commitment to these same ideals. If Amelia did once see herself as worth something outside her home, she learned to set that fragile concept aside, until it disappeared.

This busy girl maintained one ritual for herself alone. Every Friday afternoon after school she walked to the public library returning four books she had just read, to choose four more. It was rarely three or five; habitually four books a week, heavy or slight, every Friday afternoon.

Amelia's parents knew she deserved their effort to send her to college, and the first semester's tuition at a business school was counted out for her dollar by dollar on the dining room table. She conveyed to me, as she spoke of this event, my grandfather's pride and her own excitement and terror. She repaid the debt with A's. The next semester's tuition was again somehow swept up, dug out of the corners, and paid; but this time, on the first day of classes, a crowd of students including tall Amelia stood bewildered outside a padlocked door. The school administrators, chased by their debts, had fled with the students' money.

Mother had turned eighteen just days before. With no more tuition money to be had at the time, with guilt over this money wasted—money needed at home, thrown away—Amelia went looking for work. I see her going down the wooden porch stairs of her home that January 1930 in a thick coat over a cautious outfit—something like the white blouse and pearls chosen for her high school graduation photograph—a precise, pensive face in search of a future.

Her quest began officially as a cashier in the shoe department at Higbees. Eventually she bought herself something that felt like substance—later, when the money she earned didn't have to go straight home and she could buy a Schiaparelli dress or other designer clothing, hats and shoes on sale. Satin labels and expensive fabrics with French seams made her feel equal, at last, to others wearing ordinary clothes—at least while she was dressed. People still tell me how elegant she was, this thin, pale, young working woman with dark brown hair and blue-gray eyes.

An architect, a soft-spoken gentleman, had wanted to marry Mother. He might have built something grand for her. Later he built several of Cleveland's tall, important buildings. But it was my father—good-looking, smart, strong and cocky, raised on Pittsburgh's steel mills, sporting the nickname of a famous racecar driver—whom she later said "made me feel safe."

She didn't speak to me about money, but nonetheless conveyed her regret at not being subtly rich. She wouldn't have wanted show. Just freedom. Freedom to buy that pair of Stiffel lamps the minute she spotted them, without having to consult her instinctive calendar (February equaled furniture sales, May linens, June appliances). Freedom to book us into the Mayflower Hotel when we went to Washington occasionally, in pursuit of America for two or three smoldering summer days, instead of into the modest and tidy B&B she had found in a magazine.

The only thing ever built for Mother met the expectations she had learned to have for herself: three bedrooms, one bath, a dining room with an upright piano and a view of lilacs in a large, safe, grassy rectangle. But confined as this vista was, there was no containing the scope of pleasures in her magazines, *Look*, *LIFE*, and *Ladies' Home Journal* among them, where living rooms had fearlessly white chairs, precisely draped curtains in fabrics that matched the sofas, and porcelain bouquets at each end of the long mantelpiece; large, seductive pages where it was noted that Mrs. Averill Harriman—or someone else with a name like that—slept in a Paris hotel on Egyptian cotton sheets. High-class myth and luxury, quietly coveted from a simple green version of Pennsylvania.

Mother didn't tell me of her dreams. I simply inherited them from her, along with her nice eyes and ugly knees. But for me, the dream then wasn't of Paris, a place of a complexity and distance I was too young to see. For me, there arose simply possibilities—those that I, too, had learned to visualize: a tantalizing maelstrom of book-lined rooms and window seats in old mansions, Vogue pink suits and matching hats, more books (I knew that David

Copperfield's loneliness was mine), narrow tree-lined roads of promise, and grown-ups with deep voices and smiles of discovery in pursuit of—something. My girlhood contained, beneath its flat surface, a rich life after all—rich with imagined promise, such as that to be found in the evocative syllables of Bellodgia Caron.

On Mother's dresser the bottle and shiny liquid were reflected in a mirrored tray. Other bottles, many opaque or, like Chanel No. 5, entombed by indifferent black plastic, circled and formed a kind of court for the Bellodgia Caron. Flanking the tray stood crystal lamps with long, shimmering lusters that hung below stiff lace lampshades. The lusters remain my all-time grandest earrings. In my relentless games of dress-up, they hung almost to my shoulders—thick spears of crystal, faceted in scallops along the edges to a sharp point. To my reflection in the mirror, they gave a glimpse of splendor—diamonds, in fact—until my arms got tired of holding the lusters up to my ears. For a moment I had quit limitation and entered the soul and life of another girl; but now I was home again, my mother downstairs in the kitchen beating something in a bowl and listening to Don McNeil's breakfast club on the radio.

Parfum de Paris, the bottle itself proclaimed. Did that mean you had to go to Paris to wear it? Is that what Mother was waiting for? The bottle, now about five years old, had never been opened.

"What about this?" I asked her one day as she was dressing, trying one pair of earrings, then another, ignoring the possibilities of the crystal lusters. "Why don't you ever use this?" I pointed at the Bellodgia Caron, Mother watching me in the mirror. I don't think I touched the little glass stopper; and the thrilling day when Mother decided I was old enough to dust her vanity—requiring me to actually move the bottle—had not yet come.

Mother was wearing her silky black dress with a section of narrow pleats down the front and fancy buttons at one shoulder and the opposite hip. This dress, she had told me before, made her look thinner. "Uncle Nicky brought me that perfume. It's from Paris."

"I know," I said, loath to be told anything I already knew.

"It's very expensive," she continued. She picked up the dull black Chanel container and performed: a spray below each ear, at her wrists, and one broad sweep of scent above her head, to settle around her like a net. "It's for very special occasions."

We were going to a wedding. My father was wearing a black suit with shiny lapels, his collar had little wings; there would be a bride's dress and a cake with frosting flowers and garlands and tiny silvered balls and leaves. I wondered how much more special an occasion could get?

I'd never seen my father look like this before. Sometimes he wore a suit and a hat with a brim when he drove the Mercury. But most of the time he left home in a cap, plaid flannel shirt, khakis, and the Ford—to go operate his massive locomotive and make what was called "good money," or to rescue a nephew broken down on Route 19, or the priest whose prayers hadn't healed a leaky roof. His gutsy wisdom taught him how to run the meetings down at the union hall and at church, and how to fix any car, lawn mower, television—anything behaving badly. Indeed, he kept Mother "safe." But a realization of those ideals of hers, of the truly special occasion, lay beyond his powers. He bought her Chanel No. 5 every Christmas—and the talcum powder and creamy white oval soaps. Magazine ads implied that it ranked among the better perfumes. But he couldn't give her an occasion to reach for the perfume of Paris.

Mother dusted the unopened bottle of Bellodgia Caron every week of her quiet life, washed it during the compulsory spring and fall cleanings, buffed it to make it gleam. One day she moved it left of center on the mirrored tray, allowing it to be deposed permanently by a vase my brother chose for her in Greece. But never did she use it.

At the grand doorway of the dining room at the Paris Ritz I stood devastated by the news that it didn't open until seven o'clock. I couldn't wait an hour—I had a flight to Amsterdam at eight thirty—but my birthday had to be spent at the Ritz. Among the only facts of life Mother taught me, such dogma ranked high.

Yet she never would have entered this opulent salon alone; and here now, in my place, she would have fled to the first warmly lit bistro. "Only an American would expect to dine here at six o'clock," the maitre d's smirky face implied. But I had by then—while away at school, and later, living alone—found in me my father's nerve. I remained in the elegant archway, my eyes focused dismissively past this gatekeeper, exuding what I hoped resembled poise and refusing to let this taste go.

Soon I seemed to own a yellow silk Louis Seize chair in an alcove next to the dining room built not for the rank and file. I drank champagne and chose canapés and lemony petit fours from silver trays, served by the tuxedoed maitre d' and three or four of his twins. They liked my pluck and devotion to the Ritz and the opportunity to practice their English. The waiters were my age and all had that pale, slight, French look earned by living entirely indoors. Eventually the whole cadre escorted me to the checkroom to gather my bags—the gray American Tourister looking destitute in this context—and then out the front door and into a taxi I could no longer afford. They stood waving and I, peering through the back window, waved back, rich with champagne and exhilaration, as the taxi shot away, around the tall bronze column with Napoleon in command at the top, and out the far end of the Place Vendôme. I've bought moments of pretense like that in lots of places. I know that, in part, this is what money is for—money and the will to live now.

During a visit home, I noticed that the Bellodgia Caron bottle no longer looked full. A faint line on the glass marked the original level of the liquid. Below it a discoloration recorded the passage of time—the weddings and funerals my parents attended, the birthday and anniversary parties, the graduations, mother's bus ride to Kaufmann's—as the perfume evaporated, awaiting its moment. The seal around the stopper looked cracked like old, dried Scotch tape; but it had never actually been broken.

Eventually, after long decades, all of the *parfum de Paris* disappeared, leaving the bottle empty and clouded, dull as the black plastic Chanel. While on a later visit, some time after I moved to California, I noticed that the bottle itself was gone from the dresser, replaced by a blue Wedgwood box I had sent her from Harrod's.

"It's in the dresser. One of the drawers," Mother said, when I asked her about the bottle. Knowing her, I knew also that it was safe, wrapped in layers of tissue paper and satin or velvet jewelry rolls held in place by rubber bands. Later, that is precisely how I found it—the velvet and rubber band treatment—when the time came for me to go through Mother's things. It sits now on my own dresser. Empty, nearly opaque, reminding me every day of the cost of a life not fully lived and of the need to embrace Hemingway's famous dictum: to live life "all the way up."

❧ ❧ ❧

Millicent Susens is a playwright, essayist, and writing coach living in San Francisco. Previous essays have appeared in regional publications. A former high school English teacher, she writes, edits the work of others, and substitute teaches at an all girls' high school in order to be inspired by young ideas and to be free to travel when she chooses.

≈ ≈ ≈

Rejoneadora

Danger beckons.

$\mathcal{I}$n southern Spain, among the rich at least, no one takes things too seriously. Omnipresent business deals and the state of one's testicles are matters to be approached fairly casually and not allowed to seriously impinge on eating, drinking, and generally enjoying life. Or maybe what the Spanish have really mastered is how to mix it all up together and make life continually sweet.

By contrast, everything that I did at that time when I lived in Spain had an intensity and fervor to it that had to be exhausting to my family—particularly my riding. Horses occupied first place in my priorities. I was a zealot, practicing hour after hour, until the midday sun pressed its own not-to-be ignored intensity on the land. Then hot, dusty, and often ragged with frustration, I'd head home and drop into exhausted sleep.

Somewhere in those years I had become obsessed with the need to confront my own mortality, test my courage, look death in the eye and laugh. Walking at dawn to the stables, I had whispered a prayer, or maybe it was just a fervent plea to the empty streets: "Please help me to face this test with dignity and calm, no matter what." Now the day I had been preparing for was galloping toward me at full speed through the dust.

The months of preparation were over. The many nights fading into headachy dawns of too much *Tio Pepe* and *La Ina*, the pale sherries of southern Spain. Nights of too much laughter and camaraderie, endless cigarettes, till my throat and nostrils were numb. My continual smile, and the strain it required to maintain it, had taken a toll. I am by nature serious, and in the fun-loving crowd of Spanish men with whom my husband Malcolm and I hung out, serious was not allowed. In countless bars around town, a thick carpet of prawn and lobster shells lay crunched under the heels of countless handmade boots. This expensive detritus paid homage to my companions and backers, these sated princes of Andalucía. To them I represented novelty and a curious mixture of intensity, machismo, and femininity. And I, a young wife and mother of four, wanted to live as carefree and robustly as they did. They were giving me an unusual chance for a woman and a foreigner: the chance to test my courage and skill in the *rejoneo*, the artful bullfight from horseback. In this centuries-old sport of the royalty of Spain and Portugal, finely trained horses of great beauty and speed wear no protective padding; their safety depends entirely on their rider's skill. Yet I was so intent on proving myself to myself that I didn't even notice the double-edged quality of their gift: my test, their entertainment. Pride and arrogance, like the viscous sweet Malaga wine, had gone to my head. We would use each other well.

Outside the bullring, dark Mercedes disgorge rotund bankers, ranchers in suits and gentlemen playboys from as far west as the perpetually foggy province of Cadiz. Today's spectacle will be presided over by patriarch Don José Quesada, who, in honor of the occasion, has donated three-year-old fighting bulls from his breeding ranch. Wide brimmed *sombrero Cordobeses*—the elegant, flat-brimmed hats of the region— bob above long, expensive, *Monte Cristo* Cuban cigars, and make their way in a crush to their seats. Two of Spain's top matadors will be with me in the ring—just in case. A mammoth fig tree provides dappled shade. Wine and tapas flow—tulip-shaped glasses of sherry, plates of grilled pork loin, *manchego* cheese, and green olives—all to whet the appetite for the spectacle to come.

My boots are new, hand made, and rub lightly on my inner calf. This morning, after I had dressed, I had been pleased and proud of my reflection in the dimpled old glass of the doors to our patio. Blond hair tied back with a black velvet ribbon, setting off my short black jacket with its velvet collar; the white lace front of my shirt and cuffs, starched and stiff. Pinstriped, body-hugging trousers rise high at my waist. They're a little slack now, since the kilos have melted away in the course of preparing for today. My leather chaps— *zahones*—are hand sewn with white catgut, with my initials at the wide band at my waist. These supple *zahones* will protect my legs from a dangerous slice by the bull's razor sharp horns. The horses have no protection other than my skill. All these trappings had mattered this morning as I carefully placed my pale-gray *sombrero Cordobes* on my head. None of it matters now. What matters now is the safety of the horses, managing their fear and my own and the bull. No amount of imagining has prepared me for facing a *toro bravo*, but no matter what happens, I must not falter in fear.

A big van with the horses arrived an hour ago—$20,000 of sleek Spanish stallions, hauled in an open produce truck. Favorito, my big white steed with his majestic head and noble heart, stands saddled and bridled. His mane is braided with red and yellow satin ribbons, the colors of the Spanish flag. He is impatient and restlessly paws the ground with one front hoof. Pepe the Horse, his trainer, hisses a threat *"caballooo,"* drawing out the long vowel. The pawing stops obediently. After Favorito I will ride Cancionero, a dappled-gray I know less well. Because of the terrible tension the horses experience with a charging bull, they tire easily and must be changed often. Eighteen-year-old Diablo, quick to throw any rider who dares to tug on his mouth, glows bronze red in the sunlight. On these three my life may depend, and their safety and security rests in my hands; a delicate, fragile thread of trust runs between us.

Now I stand on a whitewashed wall, looking down into dark, expressionless eyes, noting the smooth muscled shoulders and the almost perfect crescent curves of horn. And despite the brilliant sun on my back, I feel a cold quiet descend over my body and mind, feel myself move to another arena where I cannot be touched.

Up into the saddle, the gates of the ring swing open; Don Antonio Albion, my trainer and a skilled *rejoneador*, leads the way. I sit tall and firmly rooted to Favorito as we canter into the ring. I catch a glimpse of red capes and the matadors standing along the barriers at the ready. Suddenly a sledgehammer starts pounding in my chest, obstructing my breath. I can't remember which leg to press against Favorito to swerve him left, out of the way of those deadly horns. Through thick cotton I hear Pepe's voice yelling instructions.... *"Doña Diana, muevese a la izquierda, aprieta las piernas...."* It's a language I don't understand.

Why can't I think? Despite so much practice I remember nothing. Is it possible that one heavy, black *toro bravo* can cover the distance across the ring in the blink of an eye? Yet here he is!

For one moment that lasts an eternity, my heart stops, as Favorito receives the full force of the bull on his right flank. Other than that awful mishap, and the fact that my head emptied of all the moves that I thought I knew how to do, we survive. We canter in wide turns around the bull but cautiously, keeping our distance, as I now know the speed with which he can move. Favorito, who so willingly carried me into battle, will take many weeks to recover his spirit and health. I have ruptured our fragile thread of trust with the horse I love best!

Lunch is a celebration. Long tables have been laid with white linens on the terrace above the plaza. Bread, olives, almost transparent slices of *jamon Serrano*, platters of green salad glistening with olive oil…a celebration and a feast! White-jacketed waiters carry in the main course: huge pans of golden-hued paella, a seafood and rice regional specialty. One of the promoters has brought along all the cooks and waiters from his hotel along the seafront. I eat almost nothing but gulp down cold white wine to celebrate still being alive. And the *vino* flows, then coffee and cognac and, of course, more Havana cigars.

Now the second half of the day unfolds: taking up the heavy crimson cape and meeting another bull, this time on foot. The dust in the ring is thick and deep. One needs to be light of foot to even move in it. All the hours spent with the cape to strengthen my wrist, and all the passes I have practiced over and over again, I need now. With my head floating from too much wine and too little food, I stand in the ring, cape in hand, tall, erect, alone, calling the bull to me. "*Heh heh Toro.*" My voice comes out sure and steady. And he comes. So fast, so direct, that I have no time to move. Luckily he mows me down. I say luckily, because it might have been otherwise. It might have been his horn in my gut. Temporarily drawn off by the matadors, the bull's attention is deflected and I scramble to my feet without the good sense to be shaking. I grab the dusty cape, and with legs firmly rooted to the sand, call him to me with all the arrogance I can muster. But my feet are clumsy and leaden, and I can't seem to move them. Twice I get up for more until on the third try, I can see his eyes looking not at the cape, but dead center at my torso. This time he not only tosses me but catches my head with one of his hoofs and I go down for the count. I recall little more than lashing out with one spurred boot in furious frustration. The next thing I remember is being carried from the ring protesting, and having cold water sloshed unceremoniously over my head, without regard for the velvet collar. Perhaps the fun has gone too far.

It was only sometime later that I learned that I should have been warned to take off my spurs as they impeded my quick movements in the deep dust. The rest is a blur. I vaguely recall the offer of another fight, then home and bed. Weeks would follow when I'd jolt awake from a deep sleep seeing the piercing, intelligent eyes of that bull focused squarely on my body. I had come to know fear intimately.

I only dimly remember the details of returning to the ring for another, less feted, attempt. But it was about this time that I began having a recurring nightmare of a riderless white stallion about to be gored in the bullring. Always it was the same white stallion—Favorito—always facing death. I would wake sobbing, the tears soaking my pillow. That dream horse about to die has haunted me all these years. I learned I didn't want to kill bulls, didn't want to snuff out their magnificent power.

We all test our courage in different ways. I did what I did at the moment because it was offered. Carpe diem. That's the way I have always lived. But didn't I realize that long ago morning, as I sent my children off to school, that by risking my life with the bulls, they could lose their mother? Did I really not see the risk of dealing them such a terrible loss? I think we simply cannot know what we yet don't know.

Pushkin said something like everything that frightens us and brings peril close promises some uncanny felicity which may be an inkling of our immortality. It is certainly true that when death is close life is more intense. Is that what this was all about? All these many years later I still don't know.

Diana Cohen lived for many years in southern Spain, working as a potter, riding beautiful horses, and studying the rejoneo, *the art of the bullfight from horseback. She wrote for* Lookout, *an English language magazine published in Spain, about the Romeria del Rocio (a pilgrimage). A graduate of Mills College and a 1983 Coro Fellow in Public Affairs, she lives in San Francisco and is finishing a memoir on raising a family in Franco's Spain.*

True Stories

In solitude, she found a voice.

For many years I was alone and I found that—but I am already putting it in past tense, please note. So, for many years I've been alone and I find, what? Find that it doesn't get any easier? Find that I'm writing my way right into another cliché? Let's try again. As follows: For many years she lived alone. For many years she will live alone. She. Alone. A woman. Many women alone. Always alone. And it is here the true stories begin.

When did we start thinking it would be otherwise? Men have always left, or died. Or worse still, stayed with us, half-dead. Children have come from our bodies, grown up and left.

A woman wakes alone on the prairie—North Dakota, say—in 1850. Her bed is faintly warm, around her body only. The wind coming in through the chinks howls in a way that can only carry snow in its sound. She lies there in the half-light, trying to remember what it was like once to fit her body around another's. A child cries out in its sleep beside her, then subsides. She is tired already, thinking of the cold, the snow between her and the animals out in the shed, the work to be done of getting a stove going. Where is the man in this picture? Out exploring America somewhere?

Or perhaps she has outlived him. Strong, quiet, she rocks on a front porch of a white house in a small town in upstate New York. "She'll never get over his death," we say. 1911, she stokes the stove, clawed like a large green cat in the kitchen. She rocks and rocks. "Mama really came into her own after Poppa died," we say. She never talks of him, never speaks of her loneliness, those long gray nights, when she reads and rereads the *Lewis Tribune*, spreading the clumsy newsprint sheets on her own embroidered sheets. They were a wedding gift to herself once, cross-stitched, initialed in careful chain stitch with her name. The trousseau. The wish chest. The Despair Barrel, as we single girls used to call it, sitting together, embroidering.

When my husband left, I took my two babies and... there. Put it right out on the page. Squarely. "When my husband left." Simple fact. Try to put it down on the page without emotion. "No Blame" as the *I Ching* says. It also says "Persistence Furthers." But quite often that is untrue. A whole profession has been built on False Assurances. Fortune Tellers, Oracles, Marriage Counselors, Dermatologists, the Church. Well anyhow, my husband left.

There is a bluish hush around that sort of event. Everyone stops. The children stop growing, fixed at that awful point in their lives. A woman stops laughing and singing. People don't want to talk, yet do talk, about it. But there is an ozone hum around the conversation as if real things are avoided. It is like heat.

"Don't talk to Margaret about it." That sort of thing. In a dining room in semi-rural South, chairs being pushed back, ice water, misting the half-empty glasses. 1937, a fan going round and round. Margaret has already left the table, hurriedly, before the apple pie course, a lace handkerchief delicately pressed to her mouth. Her chair, scraping the warm night as she left, is the only sound for a while. The family looks at one another. "Poor Margaret."

And Margaret is sitting alone upstairs on her bed, staring out into the pregnant night, wondering how she is going to cope with a string of these nights, these strained supper conversations. A lifetime of abandonment. Oh, the shame of being a woman left.

So when my husband left, I also left.

It was not going to be him leaving me—I also had places to go. The children were six months old, and a year and a half, the biggest boy. And I took a job as caretaker of a wildlife conservation area on the Cape Cod Canal on the New England coast. For if I were going to be alone, I would be fully alone.

Finally, fully alone, but removed from the eyes of other pitying humans.

We were to live there for six months, the children and I, in a little stone cabin on a cliff overlooking the ocean. Below, my small sailboat floated at anchor. No electricity. An outdoor toilet. No phone. Outwardly, the setting was idyllic.

At night I tossed and turned, exhausted by the care of two babies and my emotions and the strange sounds. Blue herons croaked as they settled at night in the large tree outside the cabin. They shrieked again as, at dawn, they flew back into the marshes. I was awake to hear them then, too.

The children kept me busy by day. There was a sink with cold running water. There was a stove that ran on bottled gas. A large pot of water steamed in the cabin, heating.

I planted a garden. I fished. I carried the children up and down the cliffs with me—the hardest physical part of the whole endeavor. At night I would cast into the darkness, set the rod, and go back up the cliff to check on the children, then down again to test the rod and line. Sometimes I caught a large-jawed Something. A big bluefish, thrashing and snapping. A new problem—how to unhook the thing. My oldest, now almost two, tried to help me hit the fish with pliers. I learned to take a rock to a fish, to stun or kill quickly, avoiding its teeth.

The garden produced snow peas and even a few tomatoes. Each "Organic Tomato" costs $9.50 apiece to grow, I read somewhere. I made an insect spray of oil, garlic, and cayenne pepper and sprayed the garden. The tomato worms fell off and died, but downwind there was a whiff of salad dressing coming already off the plants. If I had been less cynical, I would have worn a long dress and granny glasses.

When I put the children in the sailboat to take them across the bay to the grocery store they clawed my knees in terror. The boat rocked and yawed, but it was a good, sturdy, beamy wooden catboat, the kind you see in the Winslow Homer paintings, and nothing could tip it. The boat heeled, the babies quieted down. My heart was pounding with their fear, but they were in lifejackets, I reasoned. There was an outgoing current and if I caught the tide or wind wrong, the boat could not get back to our landing. Not enough sail power and we did not have a motor.

The children learned to wave their diapers over their heads at passing motorboats or the Coast Guard for a tow. And many times we were towed back across the channel.

But the loneliness. Still, the loneliness. There was no one over the age of two years old to talk to. Silence and solitude and rural beauty can be soothing—but after about two days of it all nature starts to shriek. The mosquitoes mock me. Birds fly in pairs. Each wave dashing against the rocks below one's gaze echoes the solitary heartbeat, the chest pounding with hurt. Try as I could, under that beautiful changing sky, the long line of horizon and the line of shore, I could not feel serene. With my babies I could be for a time complete, or doing some physical chore like clearing brush. But activity stopped; the children slept, I tried to rest—which I desperately needed—and it was then that the real restlessness set in. Even flowers made me sad.

Sometimes I would flash outside of myself—watching myself maneuver the boat, for instance, or changing diapers or weeding. Kathleen the heroine—and pride in my growing competence was forming. But the other side was—over-compensation—a woman rejected who didn't know where to turn. And sometimes the beauty of the little harbor as I brought the boat in, my two curly-haired babies with me, made me ache.

It was then that I turned to writing stories. For I needed someone to talk to, and the page had always provided some solace. At night, by the feeble kerosene lantern, I started scribbling on yellow lined pads. Mercifully, the light was so dim and my handwriting so bad that I could not read back what I was writing. Self-censorship had always stood in the way of longer writing. Before, I would start a paragraph and exclaim, "Yuck!" before the second sentence. However, in the half dark, with only a small bit of time to write before a child woke, there was no place for the groans and sighs of disgust. I decided to try and write some little stories about women's lives—a subject I was finally, after years of struggling with and against, beginning to know. I wrote thirty of them. By the twentieth, I started to understand the form, or rather, to understand what my writing lacked.

The stories at first were simple, flat when I looked back on them. But they described situations of women, struggling. A rape I had never fully overcome became a too flowery story of a woman afraid. My husband's infidelities when I had my second baby became the subject of a humorous, wry, ironic little fiction. It took me twenty or thirty tries before I understood how hard it is to find one's "voice" in fiction. But meanwhile I was talking to my characters on the page and they were talking to each other and to me and doing surprising things. Alone with the pad of paper in the middle of the breathing night I found myself laughing out loud. And when, exhausted, I put down the pen I slept soundly.

Suddenly there was a meaning to my chosen solitude, beyond proving that physically and emotionally, "I could do it." "Voice" in writing, that most simple and direct expression of thought, is the most difficult to locate. I didn't have it yet, but there were stories to tell.

And after the first thirty stories, I began to be able to write more deeply, exploring relations with parents, the culture, and taking on deeper subjects.

The little cabin became a ship under the stars, and the children slept as I piloted among fictional adventures. Sunrise became beautiful to me again, and the gardening, sailing, fishing, and time with the children a part of a larger rhythm.

I wish I could write deeply for all women, or that they would write for me. Which is not to say that I don't still avidly read the writing of men. But I cannot write nor see from a man's point of view.

And I wish I could tell you that I returned, after six months of isolation, to my life in the city fully healed. But no, it was as difficult as ever to enter a room full of strangers and nights were as long and lonely as before. But I was stronger, in my bond with my children, my faith in our survival, and my competence to do it with grace. What were the achievements of that six months totally alone, beyond being able to stand it? My now-two-year-old was toilet trained. I was a better sailor. And I had written some thirty-odd stories, as well as scores of poems. And some of them were not bad.

"I hope you're not planning to support your family on fiction," a novelist friend muttered, aghast. I admit I had harbored that private plan. "Fiction is even harder to publish than poetry," she continued. And of course she was right. But some of the stories were published and for some I got paid—well—so it was not a total loss. And I knew now what I had to learn about writing, so I resolved to write two stories a month in the next year. That, a teaching job, and the children kept me busy. Before I knew it, we were, you might say, almost happy.

Kathleen Spivack is the author of Moments of Past Happiness; The Beds We Lie In *(nominated for a Pulitzer Prize);* The Honeymoon; Swimmer in the Spreading Dawn; The Jane Poems; Flying Inland; Robert Lowell, A Personal Memoir *(forthcoming). Published in over 300 magazines and anthologies, her work has also been translated into French. In Boston, Kathleen directs the Advanced Writing Workshop, an intensive coaching program for advanced writers. She is Visiting Professor of Creative Writing/American Literature (one semester a year) in Paris.*

ALEXIS WOLFF

❧ ❧ ❧

Silver Dust

She makes a journey into the ancient ways.

Several weeks into my four-month stay in Niger, I walked through the gates of le Musée National in search of Mamadou Abdou, the Tuareg silversmith who was expecting me.

To get there from my apartment I'd wandered down the dusty Rue de Martin Luther King, often leaping over deep ruts and accidentally stepping in thick brown puddles. Niger had no sewage system or official means of disposing waste, so everywhere sat piles of excrement and waste ridden with infectious diseases. I turned onto Avenue de Gountou Yena, where, in a country whose average temperature hovered in the 90s, I fought goats and camels for occasional patches of shade. Then I took a shortcut through Djamadjé, referred to by my expatriate friends as "the smelly market," where I passed piles of unrecognizable spices, heaps of tomatoes teeming with flies, and slabs of meat baking in the sun, hairy tails still attached. I jetted across Avenue de la Mairie's traffic—Peugeots and Citroens plucked from French junkyards to be reborn as Nigerien taxis—and headed down Rue de Musée, stepping over polio-mangled bodies crawling awkwardly down the street, their gnarled hands outstretched to ask for a little change.

This wasn't my first jaunt in the developing world. I'd traveled in Haiti, Nicaragua, and southern Africa, but I'd decided to spend a semester in Niger—the West African nation that was the second poorest country in the world at the time, and projected to be the poorest again as soon as Sierra Leone recovered from its civil war—to prove that I could hack a career in humanitarian work after graduation. Niger, however, was worse than I'd expected—poverty on steroids, as I'd begun to say—and I was beginning to question whether I could handle such a life after all. This doubt beleaguered me during my sociology classes and my work at a nonprofit fighting guinea worm, and I traveled to the *musée* seeking a mindless distraction.

Inside the *musée*, I followed a maze of stone paths that wove me past cages of scrappy-looking animals and one-room buildings with eclectic glass-cased displays. I traveled over a small bridge and then looked up and saw it—the artists' hangar, an open-front structure in which leather-workers, woodworkers, and metalworkers toiled away at their trades.

As I approached I saw that half the hanger was occupied by several dozen silversmiths working on straw mats, each man sitting with one leg on the ground in Indian-style and the other bent up into his chest. A flat-headed anvil was jammed deep into the sand in front of him, and it was on this anvil that he worked, holding his silver steady against it with pliers as he hammered, engraved, or filed.

A square leather mat, a jagged hole ripped out its middle, surrounded the anvil to collect the falling slivers of silver. Behind him was a metal lockbox with his tools, and in front of him was a short display table draped with red or black velvet that showed off shiny finished pieces—knives, letter openers, barrettes, bracelets—all arranged by object in straight, neat lines. As I got closer still I heard a handful of languages, not only the silversmiths' native Tamashek, but also Hausa, Zarma, and French, mixing with the *cling cling cling* of the metal hammers hitting silver.

"*Bonjour!*" an older man called to me. The Nigerian friend who had arranged my apprenticeship had told him I would be coming.

He was tall and thin, and his skin was wrinkled and worn like that of a well-loved football. His face was small and his top lip protruded further than his forehead, making him look a little like a turtle. With a smile that exposed his crooked teeth, he jumped up from his mat and extended his hand in greeting. He introduced himself to me as Mamadou, then introduced me to nearby silversmiths as his American. I smiled. He would be my Tuareg.

By this point in my stay I'd interacted with members of most of Niger's major ethnic groups—the Hausa guards of my apartment complex, the Zarma men who washed my laundry, the Fulani children in my neighborhood—but not yet a Tuareg. Although hunger and modernity had recently brought some of the nomadic group to the capital, most of Niger's 700,000 Tuareg still traveled by camel caravan through the Sahara Desert.

"You'll make the cross of Agadez," my Tuareg told me in French, pointing to a pendant on a nearby display table.

Tuareg silversmiths, I knew, were renowned for their crosses. Although early missionaries assumed the crosses proved a Christian presence, they're in fact secular: the Tuareg attribute crosses to towns and encampments in addition to names. The most famous is the cross of Agadez, which represents the city in central Niger that was once a bustling trading post and the largest Tuareg settlement.

I appreciated the cultural significance of Mamadou's proposed project, but the cross wasn't my style. A hollowed circle sits at its top, connected below to a diamond with sharp arrows on the side and bottom points. It looks like something goth high schoolers would wear.

My eyes wandered to other pieces of Tuareg jewelry. I spotted dangling earrings I had to have and a chunky chime bracelet I wanted to make. But that I could do later. For now, I'd acquiesce to my Tuareg.

My arrangement with Mamadou was casual: he would be working under the hangar Monday through Friday, and I could join him as frequently or as infrequently as I wanted. Several days after my first visit I returned, plopping down on the space Mamadou cleared for me on his mat and watching him eagerly as he put away his crosses.

Because my language skills were elementary, we communicated mostly through gestures and movements. He motioned for me to follow him to an area in the front center of the hangar where a few rocks glowed with heat, and instructed me to feed the fire by pumping gusts of dry air with an organ-like device, likely made by the leatherworkers nearby. He held a ball of hard yellow wax over the rocks, and I pumped for several minutes until he gestured for me to stop. The wax was sufficiently warm.

Back on Mamadou's mat he handed me a wooden board, a sharp metal tool, and the ball of warm yellow wax. I followed his lead, shaping and sculpting the wax into three rough replicas of the cross before me.

I peeled the three yellow crosses from the board, set them in my palm, and nudged Mamadou to signal that I was done. Grinning, he took my other hand and led me into the sunlight. I walked palm up, carefully, as if carrying a tray of champagne glasses. He grabbed the crosses and plopped them carelessly—my heart skipping a beat—on a cement block in the dirt, then sent me home for the day.

I was lounging in the shade of a baobab tree near my apartment one afternoon during the mini hot season, a few weeks in October and November when temperatures hover around 100 degrees. It hardly compared to the regular hot season, which plagues the month of April with temperatures nearing 120 degrees, but the mini hot season affects the country profoundly because it typically overlaps with Ramadan, the Muslim month of ritual fasting. Between the heat and the hunger, Niger's already slow-paced life wanes practically to a halt. Although I fasted only half-heartedly, it was enough. The tedious tasks of everyday living—bathing, getting food from the market, washing dishes—proved grueling. I took a break from silversmithing.

That afternoon I pumped my t-shirt in and out and scratched the pink spots that dotted my ankles. My hair, washed only an hour before, was already wet with sweat and oil. I was tired. I'd lain sleepless in a pool of my own sweat the night before, using my hairbrush to scratch bites from the countless mosquitoes that somehow found a way under my net. I eventually admitted defeat and jumped fully clothed into the cold shower. Wet and cool, I finally fell asleep only to awake an hour later squirming in my sweat again.

In the morning the bright sun stole the small amount of energy that survived the night, and now I sat wondering how I'd survive until my return flight in December—and what I was going to do with my life then—when suddenly the space around me turned dark.

I ran out from under the tree for a better look at the sky. I didn't understand what could have happened to the sun. There were no hills for it to tuck behind, no clouds to obstruct its bright rays. But the sky was now orange, and as I stood staring at it, my t-shirt and long skirt flapped like a flag in the wind. I held out my arms and closed my eyes. Sand and dirt crashed into my skin. It hurt, but it was a good hurt... tingling, sparkling, and then itching as it stuck to my sweat.

Then rain poured down and washed the sand away. I smiled and danced in circles, delighted that I'd outsmarted the weather. I thought the sun would come back and my drenched clothes would keep me comfortably cool, at least for a while. Instead, the cold air stayed longer than the rain, and so on the same day sweat dripped from my body, goose bumps popped out from my sunburnt skin.

It was typical of Niger, where all of my expectations were being negated.

When I returned to the *musée* a week later, after the heat began to calm, Mamadou's eyes lit up. He put aside his work to stand and shake my hand, slipping on his blue plastic flip-flops and leading me out to the cement block to pick up my yellow crosses, which were now hard.

I followed Mamadou back under the hangar, where we wrapped the yellow cross with a cement mixture and then piled the cement-covered crosses atop one another and added another layer of cement. Mamadou was careful to keep the very top of each cross visible, a yellow dot poking out from gray. Then he led me back to the sunny spot in the dirt, where I again watched him drop my creation.

After fetching my baked cement the next time I returned, I followed Mamadou to a metal table piled with coals. I turned a crank attached to the back of the table, as Mamadou told me to do, and flames rose from the cracks between coals.

Mamadou threw the cement creation into the fire, and after poking it a few times with a metal rod, he reached in his pocket and pulled out a clear bag filled in one corner with silver chips. He dumped the chips into a shot-glass-sized cup made of blackened cement and then placed that in the fire as well. As I watched the glowing silver turn to liquid, Mamadou explained that the wax inside the cement had melted. It occurred to me only then that I'd made a mold. We watched the fire for several minutes before Mamadou instructed me to pour the melted silver into my cement mold, filling the space where the yellow wax had been.

A few days later I cracked the baked cement with a hammer and found three rustic crosses of Agadez inside. I smiled, assuming that I was done, but as it turned out my creations were only rough approximations. Not only did I have to smooth away the grooves and textures left from the cement with sandpaper, but I also had to file each cross into the exact right shape. What was more, I had to do this with a tool that resembled a metal nail file. I pressed as hard as I could, but progress came slowly. Day after day I filed and filed my crosses—crosses that I knew I'd never wear—until my hands ached.

I didn't feel like much of a silversmith, not that I should have after a few months of my part-time apprenticeship. Traditionally prospective smiths work first with wood, then clay, and then only the cheapest metals before finally being entrusted with silver. Most apprenticeships last a decade, and not all those who enter apprenticeships become smiths. Tuareg silversmiths, moreover, are all male—a fact of which Mamadou reminded me once when I imprudently showed up to work in a skirt. He sent me home.

Given my gender and skin color, being allowed to mingle with the silversmiths at all was unusual, and actually studying under one was an extraordinary privilege (one I was probably only afforded because my study abroad program paid Mamadou a small stipend). But it was difficult to remember how lucky I was as I struggled to finish my crosses beside Mamadou, who threw aside perfect pendant after perfect pendant. I couldn't help but feel like a failure.

Silversmithing hadn't turned out to be the escape from my worries that I'd intended. Instead it had become an embodiment of them.

Weeks and many visits to the hangar later, the silver on my three crosses was finally smooth. It was time to carve designs onto the pendants. Studying Mamadou's work, I noticed that circles and series of short parallel lines appeared occasionally, but triangles appeared most often. The triangle, Mamadou explained, is a common theme in Tuareg design. It's thought to protect against evil.

Mamadou got out his tools: two stamps (a triangle and a circle), a hammer, and a flathead screwdriver. I placed the stamp atop my silver cross and hammered down lightly to leave an impression. It was simple, even for me, but using the screwdriver was another story.

I'd seen Mamadou use it to carve both borders and intricate patterns of lines. Holding the screwdriver against the silver with just the right amount of pressure, he rotated his wrist back and forth quickly but slightly, pushing forward, digging a small, straight canal.

Mamadou told me to carve a border just inside the edge of the diamond section of my cross, and I tried, but several millimeters into the task I pushed too hard and rotated my wrist too quickly, slipping off track and carving an awkward line across the diamond. I dropped my pendant on the mat, closed my eyes, and took a deep breath. I went home for the day.

"At last, my American Tuareg has arrived," Mamadou greeted me in French a few days later when I finally returned.

As I lowered myself to the mat, I grinned and continued what had become our ongoing joke, insisting that I was completely Tuareg, no part American—even though I felt anything but. I shook my head when Mamadou tried to hand me a file. Today I just wanted to watch.

Soon an American tourist approached Mamadou hoping to buy a necklace for his wife. He ran his fingers up and down a larger piece Mamadou had pulled from his lockbox. The pendant required a lot of silver and a lot of work, and it usually sold for about 25,000 CFA, roughly equivalent to U.S. $40. I drew circles in the silver dust in front of me as Mamadou attended to the American, engaging in the standard bargaining ritual.

After a few minutes the frustrated tourist turned to me. "He says thirty-five thou.... Is he ripping me off?"

I sat up, folded my hands in my lap, and lied, "Oh no, not at all. They usually go for twice that."

Mamadou wrapped the American's necklace in recycled scraps of an outdated U.N. Development Report, and I returned my attention to the silver dust, pressing my hands palms down on the mat and then lifting them to eye level, turning them this way and then that way so the silver dust sparkled.

As I watched my glimmering hands I forgot everything—my ineptitude at silversmithing (and everything else Nigerien), the burgeoning realization that when Air France flight 731 jetted me back to the land of flush toilets and garbage trucks I'd have to redraft my life's plan, and most of all, the disappointment that the person I wished I were, a fledgling humanitarian, wasn't who I actually was.

When I looked up the tourist was gone. Mamadou was watching me, waiting. He showed me that he had finished my crosses and told me it was time for me to start a new project. He said I could make anything I wanted.

I strolled the aisles of the hangar studying the displayed jewelry before settling on the pair of dangling earrings I'd been admiring for months.

"*Ceci,*" I said in my rusty French. "*Je veux ceci.*"

Mamadou handed me some yellow wax and sent me over to the fire to warm it. As I pumped I wondered how I'd make my earrings. I'd thought only crosses required wax molds.

When the wax felt warm in my hand I headed back to Mamadou's mat, arranging my limbs in that uncomfortable Tuareg position—one leg on the ground Indian-style, and one leg bent up into my chest. I looked at Mamadou with wide eyes and smiled, letting him know that I was ready. He rustled around in his lockbox for a few minutes, his hands eventually emerging holding two metal crosses.

"Copy," he said in French, throwing them down in front of me and gesturing toward my warm wax.

I stared at the crosses. They weren't crosses of Agadez (they were crosses of Tahoua and Iferouane, I'd later learn), but they certainly weren't my dangling earrings.

I shifted my stare to Mamadou, waiting for him to laugh, but he had already returned to his own work. Maybe my request to make the dangling earrings had been lost in translation, or maybe he thought that since so much about me wasn't typical of a Tuareg silversmith, the least I could do was stick to traditional projects.

Wondering what had just happened, I watched Mamadou for a while. Finally, the laugh came—but it came from me.

Maybe nothing works out quite as planned, I thought as I ran my finger through the silver dust on Mamadou's leather mat one last time before picking up my yellow wax, *and maybe that's okay.*

Alexis Wolff earned a BA in African Studies from Yale University and an MFA in Nonfiction Writing from Columbia University. She lives in New York City.

❧ ❧ ❧

Paradise—Lost

The author remembers the Afghanistan that
once was—and the nightmare it became.

I was born in Khandahar, Afghanistan, where I lived
with five sisters and four brothers. None of us ever
attended school until we left Afghanistan. Even though my
parents have lived in the United States for over ten years,
they are still illiterate in English. In Afghanistan where
a craftsman earns more than a doctor, education was not
considered necessary for a good quality of life. But there
were other reasons as well why we never went to school
when we were young: my parents were afraid to let us spend
our days away from home. There was always war or the
threat of war. Every mother had either lost a child or seen
one horribly crippled.

But I have pictures in my memory of a country so beautiful that it is painful. My mother keeps the pictures alive.
She always calls Afghanistan "my beloved country." And

she remembers something I don't remember. She remembers the time "before the wars."

She speaks now as she has always spoken: "Afghanistan was a paradise. Kabul was a great jewel of a city, the exotic destination for people from all over the world. It was the vacation place for both hippies and archaeologists. The museums were filled with the most beautiful and rarest arts. Collectors from around the world came to purchase antiques and fine Persian carpets. We were proud of our country and of our history."

But it's not just what mother says. I remember things as well. I was a small child, but I remember our house vividly. Like so many houses in Khandahar, our house was beautiful and far larger than Westerners might imagine. It was built in a rectangular shape and had a roofless center garden with many rooms radiating around it. In the summer some of us would sleep in the garden and some would sleep on the roofs of their rooms. We had a magnificent house that had ten rooms and a balcony. Even with such a large family, we had our own rooms, each filled with colorful handmade rugs and accessories that matched them.

Fruit trees and grape vines surrounded our center garden. Flowers grew everywhere. And in the garden itself we had cucumbers and tomatoes, eggplants and hot chili peppers. In the evenings, tired and exhausted from the warm weather and the hard work, my family would spread the garden mattress on the ground under the shady grape vines. We sipped black or green tea until it was time for dinner.

On one side of our garden, near the kitchen, there was a well of drinking water. In the middle of the courtyard there was a duck pond. On the other side of the garden my father had built me a small dollhouse out of mud bricks.

In the dollhouse, I had my little puppets, together with the beds and carpets and clay pots that my mother had made for them. Right across the street from our house was a river where the children and the men used to swim. Most afternoons, I would get myself wet and enjoy my time with my friends.

Every morning before sunrise, the mullah—prayer leader—woke people by calling out the Morning Prayer. Sometimes the crowing roosters would wake us even earlier, but then too we were awakened to prayer. Children over ten years old would get up and pray with the adults. I was younger. But I still prayed with my family and enjoyed the early morning breeze. Afghanistan had glorious mornings like mornings nowhere else in the world. I remember vividly the smell of fresh dew on our dirt ground. It is the smell of home, the smell of the world as it is supposed to be.

After morning prayers my father would send out one of my brothers to bring fresh creamy milk and bread for breakfast. When my brother came back, my mother spread a long tablecloth on the ground and we all sat in a circle around the cloth and ate our breakfast.

Afterwards, the men and boys headed to work till late evening. The women in the house would perform the household chores, sweeping the rooms and the courtyard, preparing meals, sewing dresses or hats. My mother sold the clothes they made and saved the money for emergencies. Life was filled with happiness, friends, and play. If I grew tired, I slept. If I was hungry, I ate.

In Afghanistan, Friday was always special, the holy day of the week. Every Friday, the midday call for prayer could be heard throughout the city. Businesses closed their doors once the call for prayer was heard. People congregated and prayed side by side in the mosque. Others spread their prayer rugs in the back of their dusty stores and prayed there. At all other times everyone was rushing and running around. Noises came from factories and cars and playing children. But on midday Friday the world fell silent. Everyone stopped what they were doing and turned to Allah. In the peace of that great silence, the greatest prayer was the prayer of thanksgiving. Life was beautiful.

The downtown streets in Khandahar were crowded with traffic. Buses were packed with passengers. There were pickup trucks, cars and horse-drawn carts. Vendors shouted the names of the wares they were selling. People on foot kept the streets clogged. Children and men carried heavy loads on their backs and heads, making a living as transporters. In isolated pockets, beggars pleaded for food or money. The sides of the street were covered with repair stands, welding shops, carpet and retail stores, butcheries, and food-sellers. Women covered in *hijabs* kept one hand on the shopping basket while the other clung to their children. Everyone and everything was rushing in all directions.

Sensuous music could be heard from fabric stores that were filled with piles and piles of colorful fabrics. Everything was colorful. Life was overflowing. There was no sign of struggle, no blood stains on the walls, no heaps of dead bodies, no shattered buildings, no agonized screaming, no wild animals digging out the graves to feast on the flesh and bones of the dead. Instead, everyone went about their business. They slept in peace and they walked in peace. They did not kiss their children each night as if they would never see them again.

Then the bombs came. With the bombs, images were seared on my mind that scarred me for the rest of my life. The paradise of Khandahar became remote and far away, like a beautiful dream hovering behind endless layers of nightmare apparitions.

To bear the scars of war is to feel terror behind every wakeful moment. Images of people crying and screaming in confusion always remain alive within you. No one wants to understand this. Everyone asks, "How do you like being in America?" They want to hear how grateful I am that the nightmare is over. They do not want to hear that the nightmare is still alive in me. They want to hear how thankful I am that I have been allowed to enter paradise. They do not want to hear that the real paradise is one I left behind, one swallowed up by war, confusion, and pain.

Part of me does want to say, "I am grateful for being in America. I am grateful for the education I have received; grateful for the many opportunities I have been granted." But another part of me wants to reply, "I am so sad to be in America." Because I have such difficulty forming a satisfactory answer to the question about how I find life in America, I find myself constantly afraid that the question will be asked yet again. I know I am supposed to be grateful. I know that no one is supposed to be sad in America. But often I am sad.

The effect of war has left me with a mixed and confused identity. I find it hard to tell what is real and what is unreal. I don't even know whether I hate or love war. I don't know whether I hate or love my homeland. When I am unhappy, I know that I want to be happy. The problem, however, is that when I am happy, I find myself wanting to remember—and remembering is what makes me unhappy. A victim of war, I am locked in war forever. I want to be out of it, yet how could I? It has become who I am.

Many times I feel a burning inside of me and I shiver with anger. I try to breathe steadily and keep my face normal: smile and be happy, just like everyone else. But I know deep inside that I can never be like everyone else. I know that I can never forget my sister's death, my wounded friends, and our shattered house: my lost paradise. I will be carrying the burden of my childhood experiences for the rest of my life. The burning will never really go away.

When I recall the horrific memories of my childhood to some of my friends, they ask, "How can you remember everything that happened so vividly?" Well, I don't remember everything. I don't even know when I was born. As a matter of fact, no one in my family knows when they were born. Most families in Afghanistan don't keep track of birthdays. I know that I was a child—and I know that the person I am today experienced utter horror. Unfortunately, my childhood experiences have become my vision day and night.

At night when everyone is sleeping in peace, I am still lying in bed fighting hard to shut out memories of machine-gun fire and the cries of parents for their wounded children. I fight *it* until I sink once again into my nightmares.

Tonight is such a night. I am lying restlessly in my college dormitory, struggling with every bit of energy left in me, to overcome *it* and fall asleep. My day was long and tiring. Studies and exams have worn me out. I do not have the strength to continue being awake. I just want to sleep. I have more papers to finish before I go home for my break. But I cannot fall asleep. The tortured screams of wounded children, the agonized cries of their mothers and fathers are keeping me awake.

Then, I feel a sudden tickling sensation. I am overwhelmed with chills. It has been too long since I last saw her. I wonder if I will ever see her again. She haunts my dreams, but only as a shadowy figure: no, as a heap of shadows. Bodies are piled silently and motionlessly on the dirt ground of our courtyard. Within the tangle of the shadows, I see my sister. I see friends, neighbors and strangers all mingled with each other. I am confused and lost.

My heart begins to pound. It is getting louder and louder. The ringing in my ears feels as if someone just popped a balloon right next to my head. My heart is so loud, I am afraid it will wake up my roommate. I look from the corner of my eyes to see if the sound has awakened her. No, she is *peacefully* sleeping while I am crying out to God, "I need to do well on my exams; I need to sleep in peace." The dim light of the lamppost across from my window is reflected on the bare wall of my room, forming a spider with numerous missing parts of his body. The spider is immobile. As I stare at the reflection, I wipe tears off my cheeks. Then I sit on my bed. With my head leaned back against the wall, I close my eyes and surrender myself to the inevitable memories...

The day is ominous. I am sitting under a broad sky that is dark and unpleasant. Everything feels creepy and mournful. I am anxious, as if something is going to happen. This morning the warning came that "Khandahar will be under attack by the Soviets." Even so, everyone has gone off. My father and my brothers went to work. My mother is also gone. She spent the entire night in the hospital, caring for my oldest sister who is sick. Although it is now late afternoon, she is still there. My baby sister and I are alone with Gul Makia, my second oldest sister.

I almost see her, but then awaken with eyes wide open, staring into the dark. Annoyed, I toss and turn to return to sleep, but I can't. No, *it* won't leave me in peace. So I start to count: 1, 2, 3, 4, 5...100. But *it* won't permit me to rest. It is 4 A.M.; I am still awake. I struggle and struggle to escape, but *it* draws me down further and further...

Gul Makia is stepping fresh and clean from out of the showers. She walks toward me and finds me covered with mud, playing in a muddy pond formed from the heavy rain. I then see her heading toward my baby sister who is crying in a metal crib that my father had made. She picks my baby sister up from the crib and starts singing as she makes repetitive circles around the duck pool in our courtyard. I then find my tender legs racing, with no direction in mind. Holding my baby sister in her arms, Gul Makia is running toward the door that leads out of the courtyard and out of the house. I run after her.

Suddenly, I hear a multitude of anguished voices from the neighbors next door. With one arm over her head and the other arm holding my baby sister tightly to her chest, Gul Makia is running toward the door. Bullets are piercing the muddy walls of our courtyard and the doors of our rooms. The windows of the rooms surrounding our rectangular courtyard are all shattered. Broken glass covers the ground that had been covered with mud. I hide under a tree, shrunk to the size of an ant, crying for my mother as the breeze from the bullets and shrapnel sideswipes my shoulders. The enormous courtyard has shrunk to the size of a small box. I am pinned inside, buried alive in my grave.

Clouds of dust rise upward from the neighbor's courtyard. As my hearing returns, I am lost in the screaming and feeble wailing. A missile has crashed into our neighbor's house. The screams frighten me. I want to get up and run toward my sister who is worriedly peeking out of the door, looking for my parents. I try to stand up and run toward her, but I cannot move. Each time I get up I fall to the ground; I feel weakness in my knees. So I hide under the tree and listen to the hopeless cries.

A roaring sound comes from nowhere. Through the dark clouds of smoke I peer upward and see a gigantic jet just above my head. Leaves and apples and grapes and rose blossoms are scattered and fall dead on the ground. The gigantic jet circles over our courtyard again, roaring around the house like a lion circling its hopeless prey.

My roommate's coffee pot is boiling and wakes me up. I look around the room, but she is not there. I slowly get out of bed. Lightheaded, with ringing in my ears and a sharp pain running down my fingers and wrists, I walk toward the phone to call my mother. With the rest of my family, she is in Portland, Maine. We have lived there since we moved to the U.S. in January 1993. I dial the number to my house. "Salaam, Najla. How are you?" Najla, my youngest sister, says she is doing fine. "Is Mother home?" I ask.

"No, mother went to take little brother to school."

Najla asks worriedly if I am O.K. "Yes," I say, "but I am out of my heartburn medication. The acid is burning me up. Could you have Mother refill my prescription and mail it to me as soon as she gets the chance?" The acid keeps getting worse.

"I'll tell mother as soon as she returns," Najla assures me. I thank her and put the receiver back on the phone. I head back to the bed, where I rub my knees to release the intense pain in my joints. Then, I get up to get the heating pad from my closet. Once I stand up again, I feel a sharp pain in my wrists and lower back. I walk slowly toward the bathroom, gritting my teeth in pain and trying not to disturb my roommate, who has returned. I close the bathroom door and sit on the bare floor, tearfully massaging my wrists and my knees. After a while, I walk toward my bed to heat my back. I can't tell anyone how awful I feel. They've heard it all before and don't want to hear it anymore. So I stay in my room and once again fall into the same dream, the one that never changes...

The gigantic jet is flying away. I have once again lost my hearing. I can't even hear the cries of my baby sister. Clouds of dark smoke rush upward, the walls of our courtyard collapse around me. More thick, dark smoke and dust, and I am lost in black-

ness. The silence is complete. I try to run, but I still cannot move my legs. I want to hold on to the smoke until my mother gets home, but I cannot move.

I sit in pain, staring at the pieces of the courtyard's metal door. Now there is no door to separate the courtyard from the outside. I sit there staring at the gaping hole where the door should be. As the dust and smoke gradually settle, I notice my sister's scarf with ashy holes in it. Her shoes are half melted in the middle of our courtyard. Something has gone horribly wrong.

Once again I am awakened, this time by the ringing from my cell phone. "Salaam, mother, how are you?"

"I am O.K., what is going on with you again?" my mother worriedly asks.

"I don't know, mother. I am having a lot of acid and joint pain all over, not just in my wrists, but all the way down into my knees and ankles."

"I don't know what is going on with you. What do the doctors say?" My mother sounds so tired and helpless.

"I called them several times, but all they do is give me more medication. I take too much medication."

"I don't know, I wish I could do something, I don't even know the language well enough to talk with your doctor. I wish I could help, I am sorry. I am going to mail your medication this afternoon."

"O.K. mother, but don't worry about me, everything will be all right." I hang up. I walk out of the room and out onto the campus. After a couple minutes of walking, I feel lightheaded and shaky. So, I return to my room and sink back into the nightmare...

There she is again, lying face down on the ground, near the doorway: motionless and innocent. Arms outstretched, her light brown hair is coated with dust and blood. Her torn scarf and shoes have been thrown far away from her. The baby girl, fallen from her arms, is crying next to her immobile body. Drenched in her own blood and pain that came suddenly from nowhere, my baby sister is crying, hoping for someone to lift her up again.

Gagging from the smell of burnt flesh, I cover my nose with my hands and tearfully watch where Gul Makia is lying, face down on the dirt ground near the doorstep. My little sister lies beside her, covered with blood and dust. She is screaming in pain, her little feet planted against her big sister's silent body. I see brains gushing out of the huge gash in our sister's skull. Blood still boiling from the heat of the shrapnel is squirting everywhere around her, forming a steamy bath for her silent body.

My body aches, as I sit there waiting for my mother to come home. Everything seems red, even the color of the sky has changed to deep blood-red. The smoke is slowly rising upward, making my sister's body more visible. Terrified, I look around the house. The brick walls of our courtyard are now flattened and have become one with the dirt ground. The glass windows are shattered on the dirt ground, doors are blown apart, the ducks in the duck pond lie buried under dirt and bricks. Chunks of shrapnel are scattered around the courtyard.

I gaze up at too much sky, for there is no roof left at all. The sound of explosions and gunfire still can be heard. My ears are hurting. The sound is painful to my ears. My baby sister is crying. I am crying. I hear more artillery fire. From the distance, I hear the roaring sound. Then I hear another familiar sound: my mother is screaming. I cry harder. I hear everything, yet I hear nothing. I am lost as to what is happening.

My mother rushes toward my sister's body. She keeps falling on the ground with waves of tears streaming down her face. As she finally manages to reach my sister's silent body, she drops on her knees, feet lunged forward next to my sister's silent body; she watches her closely and quietly and lets her tears pour over her daughter's body like a waterfall. I cry harder and harder; my mother ignores me. Then I scream and my mother still ignores me. My mother is placing her hand over my sister's wounded head. Then she moves her hands from the wound and brings them close to her face. She stares at her hands as the blood drips to the ground. She remains as silent as my fallen sister.

One after another my extended family members rush into the house. Women reach for my mother, while men hurry to help my father and brothers who are cleansing the wounds on my sister. Weeping is flowing over the walls of our house. The screams of babies and children swell the air around me. My sister drowns in her bath of blood. The sound of gunfire has not stopped.

I watch her in horror. My father and brother turn her face upward. They say that there is still breath in her mangled body. I see only the ghastly face. I scream and run toward my mother, but then turn back to my place under the tree. My sister is not my sister. She is scary looking. She has a huge hole in her face that resembles the numerous holes on our wooden doors. She looks like a ghost. My father and brothers carry her body to the faucet near the well in the courtyard. They wash her wounds as the blood pours down from her nose and ears to the dirt ground. Her eyeballs are popping out and her lips are swollen like a red balloon. Kneeling by the tree and hands drawn close to my chest, I watch her as the blood keeps pouring from the huge hole in her forehead.

I whirl around the house, when I see my mother sitting in the corner of the courtyard, head down, staring at the dirt ground. Except for the tears that are running down her eyes onto the dirt ground, she looks almost peaceful. I cannot understand why she is quiet and still, while everyone else is running around the courtyard screaming.

A swirling black cloud covers the sun. Tanks and artillery rumble by. I can feel the vibration deep in my chest. The bones of our neighbors are being crushed under those tanks, they are being crushed into my chest, they are being crushed into me where I can never let them go. Unlike other mornings, this morning no birds sang, no wind blew through our courtyard trees and rosebushes. It seems like the whole world just stopped breathing.

I sit up in bed, awakened by my own screams. I am cold and wet and my heart is wildly racing. My head aches, so I tightly press the sides of my head with my hands as I take a deep sigh. I get up and walk out of my dorm room, trying to escape my memories, trying to escape who I am. But something in me tells me not to walk away. A feeling of guilt overwhelms me. I stare up at the sky and mumble: "Why, oh God, do I love *it* even though I hate *it* more than anything in the world?" I return to my dorm and write: "Why do I live in memories that I hate? Why is it that what I most hate is what I seem to love? Why do I keep revisiting that awful *thing* that brings me so much pain and misery? Dear God in heaven, I feel nothing but shame for wanting to be back in that moment, to feel that pain. I want to leave it behind as far as I can. Escape to a place where there are no sounds of gun shot or of the screaming of mothers. I feel lost and confused, full of guilt and shame. I am doing this to myself. I look at what I should not look at. But I am only looking at myself. How could God have done this to me?"

My dreams never take me beyond the shattered courtyard. It is as if I am stuck in one dream, the repetition of one utterly awful day that I am condemned to return to forever. But there are other things I remember. I was young when it all happened so my parents say I must be remembering stories I have heard them tell. Wherever the images come from, I cannot get them out of my mind.

Gul Makia, who in my dreams was already made into a ghost, lingered in tortured pain for many long days after the bomb fell. My father and brothers had taken her immediately to the hospital, and later that day my mother joined them in the company of a number of our relatives.

My mother practically lived at the hospital. Once, while she was away, the sky again exploded into flames. We hid from the hungry bomb inside of our dark cellar. We wrapped ourselves in each other's arms, no one spoke or cried. Mouths dry, eyes wide open, ears erect, we listened in horror to the sounds of renewed warfare.

At some point, my oldest sister went out to see if everything was safe. She let us enter the remains of our courtyard, where we stood staring up at the sky. The night was completely silent. Suddenly we heard screaming and wailing. My sister held the baby, while I clung to the two of them. I was told to turn back, but I refused and followed where she was led by her own curiosity. I saw a pale and sickly looking man running by our house, carrying a girl of four or five. I saw her lifeless tiny arms and legs outstretched, flying in the air as the man hurried by. I saw her face. I saw her gasping for air. I saw the blood pouring out of her onto the man's clothes, arms and chest and then down to the ground below, where it left its trail.

Tormented shrieking caused me to turn in another direction, where I saw a feeble old man, with a white beard, bare feet and a hump on his back. He too carried a screaming young girl. He too was coated with blood. The bomb had torn off her left leg. The bloody flesh swung from her meaty bones, causing the hair on my body to stand up. I wanted to throw up.

But I stood there covering my nose with my hands and watched men, women, and children running endlessly in different directions. I watched until my mother returned home, afraid that this new bomb might have injured one of us. She looked as if she was wearing a mask, black circles painted grotesquely around her eyes.

Afraid now that the hospital could be bombed as well, we all insisted that our mother take us to see Gul Makia. We did not have a car, so we walked the whole way. My mother said we must keep our heads down and not look at the world around us. She held one of my hands and my oldest sister held the other. Another one of my sister's held my mother's free shoulder. We walked the streets, listening to the agonized wailing of mothers. We could smell the blood and the burnt human flesh. We saw the dead bodies. We saw living men, soaked with blood, mourning their lost legs, arms, and fingers. We saw and we saw and we saw.

The streets of Khandahar were covered with the blood of people so innocent that they did not realize who might be fighting or what they might be fighting over. I remember all of this. What I cannot remember is arriving at the hospital. I cannot remember seeing Gul Makia that day.

I do know that things calmed down and the city came back to life. I remember when my mother was once again cooking and humming in the kitchen, preparing for Gul Makia's return home from the hospital. Perhaps I remember the day she came home. Perhaps I do not. But I know that her return brought only more sorrow. I remember how she screamed. I remember her words: "Mother, I cannot see anything. Mother, everything is dark; please, mother, help me. Something is moving in my head."

The doctors had closed the hole in my sister's head without removing the shrapnel. Because they were too busy with the other wounded patients, they had simply sent her home. They had no time to perform an operation on my sister again. They left her for mother, who was always crying. And for father, squatted next to my sister's bed, his head hanging down hopelessly.

The doctors had told my father that he could flee to Pakistan and seek help there for my sister. At the same time, however, they warned my father that the bumpy roads might cause the shrapnel in her head to deepen the wound, resulting in her death.

But what else could my father do? We made the long trip and found our way to the strange dark house in a foreign land. And that is where I watched my dying sister through the holes on our wooden door. I watched her waste away and listened to her awful moaning. I planted my eyes in the holes on the door. They let me see my mother and sister, even when I could not possibly have entered the room they were in. After seven black days, my sister finally died.

Back in my dorm, so many years later, I relive the memory. Eyes wide open, heart palpitating, throat knotted with screams, small droplets of sweat drip from my temples to the side of my pillow. I lie in my bed panting loudly. The longer I lie there, the louder become the screams and the gunshots and the awful anguish that fill my mind.

Ever since the war between the Soviet Union and Afghanistan, new wars have erupted there. Thousands and thousands of bombs have left my people with shattered lives. Paradise has been destroyed. Afghanis breathe, yet deep inside they feel lifeless. The big powers toy with the people of innocence.

But somewhere in that earth, beauty is still buried, just as my sister is buried. I know that there is still the smell of the dirt after the rain, the smell of grass and flowers. I know that the beautiful clear sky is still there at night and that the Afghan people walk about their courtyards trying to wake up from their nightmare. That is where my paradise and my peace are to be found. Underneath the devastation, beauty still slumbers.

Momena Sayed lived in Khandahar, Afghanistan until the age of ten, when she and her family immigrated to the United States. A recent graduate of the College of the Holy Cross in Worcester, Massachusetts, she is currently writing a memoir, and hopes to begin law school soon.

ɕɕ ɕɕ ɕɕ

The Train to Florence

A mother and daughter navigate the borders
between Spain, France, and Italy.

One January a few years ago, my twenty-four-year-old
daughter arrived in the village where I live in Spain
to spend two weeks with me. She had the romantic idea of
taking the train from Málaga all the way to Florence. From
Málaga we would go to Córdoba, where we would board
a night train to Barcelona; there we would change again
and cross into France, then change once more and head for
Nice, Milan, and then on to our final destination, arriving in
Florence, Ana had planned, the night before my birthday.

We packed as sensibly as we could, drove my old Citröen
into Málaga, where I found a parking place on a side street
near the train station, hoping the car would still be there
when we returned a week later, and went in to confirm our
schedule with the man who specialized in Eurail passes.
He confirmed nothing! He told us emphatically, in the

typically dramatic way of southern Spanish bureaucrats, that all the times that Ana had researched and written down were wrong. We wrote down new times for connections and went out to board the train to Córdoba, hoping that the connections would smooth out as we went along. I hadn't ridden a train in twenty years and neither Ana nor I had ever gone such a long way by train. This trip was said to be thirty hours, if, that is, the connections worked out. I had never been to Tuscany, never seen Nice, and I was geared up for the notable sights of Florence.

Changing trains in Córdoba, we crammed ourselves and luggage into the four-person couchette for the overnight run to Barcelona, sharing the space with an older Spanish woman and her daughter. The older woman coughed all night, so we didn't get much sleep. At some point in the night I noticed that the train had stopped somewhere in total darkness. The next morning it became apparent that we would be late coming into Barcelona, and, in fact, we did miss our connection across the border, which made us late arriving in Montpelier, where we had to wait for a later train to Nice. My daughter was upset, thinking we would not make Florence by my birthday, but I told her we would get as close as we could and see what happened, spending the night in Nice if necessary.

As we embarked from Montpelier I sat in the coach across from Ana peeling an orange with a huge knife she had brought along. The journey along the Mediterranean coast was lovely—the sea a deep, intense blue. The train rolled through town after town of brightly painted villas and markets full of people. In one a band was playing in the town square. We arrived at the dreary station in Nice after dark, disembarked with our backpacks and duffle bags and set out to find an inexpensive hotel nearby. Ana waited with the bags on a corner while I went scouting.

The first places looked grim and dark. In one a few surly-looking men stared at me as I asked about prices. Finally, I found a hotel where the lights were at least bright. I went back for Ana and the luggage and we checked in. The hotelier, a youngish man, offered to make us a cup of coffee, for nothing appeared to be open in this area of town. This was not how I had imagined Nice.

In fact, throughout the entire trip, only the French gave us any trouble. They were surly and usually unhelpful. Did they actively dislike travelers? Were they depressed? We had to pay to use any station bathroom and on one train the conductor yelled at us for not stamping our tickets properly in the machine before getting on. He fined us twenty dollars, trying to make us believe that we were getting a bargain because he could legally have charged us forty. I told him we were traveling from Málaga and that nowhere else did we have to stamp our tickets in a machine. This is not Spain! he shouted. Well no, I thought, it certainly isn't. Nor, we would find later, was it Italy, where everyone we dealt with seemed sophisticated, clever, charming.

The next day we traveled to Milan and then on to Florence, passing through the Tuscan countryside, which I had only seen before in films and paintings: dark or honey-colored stone, cypresses pointing to the sky, golden light deepening to blue-black as evening came. The atmosphere felt secretive and intensely old.

We arrived in Florence under a full blue moon—my birthday moon—and after checking into a hotel not far from the station we walked out, and walked, and walked, soaking up the atmosphere through our skin and eyes. We had our first Italian meal—a tasty risotto—and walked again in a kind of rapture, coming upon the enormous Duomo, the Cathedral of Santa Maria del Fiore, glowing in the moonlight. Not until morning would we be struck full-on by the colors and patterns of the marble. Finally that night, through a series of turning streets, we eventually found ourselves in the Piazza della Signoria, where the statues of David, Neptune, and others stood silent and bewitched in the moonlight.

Throughout our few days in Florence I felt overwhelmed. I became quite emotional. So much beauty. Such a highly wrought and conscious beauty. So strong the atmosphere created by the buildings, the overlaying of cultures and styles, the marble, tiles, statues, and paintings, the food displayed artistically in the shops, the sandwiches laid out like lovely fresh fishes, colors glowing, the chocolates and pastries like enameled jewels, the elegant Florentine women in their fur hats and padded coats and boots. The extraordinary riches of the Uffizi and the Arno River and all its bridges. The city and its surroundings were a dance in constant motion, and the dance could not change; it must always be the same dance, moving through patterns laid down long ago. Everything in Florence is a "work of art." Even the people, who, highly conscious of the richness of their city and its surroundings, struck me also as finely made, canny and deep, sardonic and world-knowing. That same aura of something deeply secretive and intensely old lit and shadowed their eyes, which looked as if they had seen everything, as if they had always seen everything. They looked as if there could never be anything they had not seen.

On the return trip, in Nice again, where we arrived at 8:30 P.M. with a two-hour wait for the overnight train to Port Bou just across the Spanish border, I asked two men behind a glassed-in enclosure where the restroom was. All locked up now, they said, pointing to their watches. Outside, the public toilets were also bolted—against drug dealers and worse, I guess. I had to go somewhere and was seriously thinking about doing it on the tracks, but figured

I'd for sure be run over. So I waited, uncomfortably, for the train to pull in. We sat there in the station with other tired travelers, on hard benches, not enough of them to go around, and nothing open at all, not even for coffee. Meanwhile a drugged-out, shaggy-looking character wanting money, cigarettes, etc., proceeded to make a nuisance of himself. No French police or station personnel (present but resolutely remaining in their glass cages) did anything with this person, who shouted and aggressively strode about intimidating people. We waited, practically sitting on our luggage to protect it, and finally the train came in.

Thinking later of our experience in Nice, I realized that because it is primarily a resort destination for people seeking sun, surf, and relaxation, lacking the extraordinarily rich artistic ambience and labyrinthine political history that Florence is steeped in, the inhabitants perhaps have grown jaded in their dealings with visitors. I also realized that probably the more fashionable travelers, those with money, come by car and airplane, no longer by train, so that the part of the city we entered had become neglected.

As we moved through the night, happy to leave Nice behind, the moon was a golden apple thrown up over the sea—this cradle of so many civilizations, scene of so many battles, piracies, and shipwrecks, of so much trading in spices, timber, cloth, and slaves. We carried with us what we had seen in Florence and been barely able to absorb, and I thought again, with renewed understanding, how much the spirit of a place, created by all that has happened there, creates within its inhabitants the same spirit, so that the people of a place mirror and reflect it.

ℬ℘ ℬ℘ ℬ℘

Sharon Balentine's poetry has appeared in journals such as
Plum Blossom, Balcones Review, Borderlands: Texas Poetry
Review, Stone Drum, Poesia y Calle, West Wind Review,
and Timber Creek Review, *as well as in her two chapbooks of*
*poetry (*Isis *and* Spellbound*). Her poetry has been nominated for*
the Pushcart Prize, and included in the anthology Terra Firma.
Her nonfiction has appeared in four Travelers' Tales *anthologies:*
Women in the Wild; A Woman's Path; *and* Best Women's
Travel Writing 2005 *and* 2006. *Short stories have appeared in*
The Missouri Review, The Tulane Review, Rosebud, Pangolin
Papers, *and* StoryQuarterly39, *among others.*

MEI-LING MCNAMARA

🌊 🌊 🌊

Between the Devil and the Deep Blue Sea

A development worker in Madagascar confronts one
question: What is she actually doing there?

*I*t is the month of October. The children are all arms
and legs and bloated bellies, dipped in melted chocolate and hardened by the sun. I have become another kind of
mineral, a burnt laterite face floating in a sea of black obsid-
ian. I can feel the corrosive elements eating into my bones
the way the salt and the sea air have wormed their way
into the wood. Millennia could pass before anyone would
discover this body.

This small coastal town in Madagascar shows three
faces to the ocean. Each spring, the whales make their
migratory course past the peninsula, breaching their bodies over swells of sea foam. Cargo ships carrying tonnage
of Pakistani rice bring the dark faces of men running to

the docks. Runnels of gray-green earth flow past the corrugated huts, where the whites of eyes float like miniature moons in the beetle-black darkness.

Two months in this outpost turned into four turned into sixteen. A square root of a life. I look up from my bluff overlooking the ocean and watch the planes as they roar their arrival, turning their downward trajectory toward the sea-stung airport.

Every day, every month, the earnest scientists from England, the gamin researchers from America, the coarse-talking miners from South Africa, step down onto the runway. Each one speculates on how to pull this place out of the mire and filth. After a few months, they stop speculating, and become merely spectators, plied into their first row seats of a play in which the Malagasy dismantle themselves—only to rebuild their small, clay worlds up again.

On the surface, nothing changes here—the grinning woman who sells blackened fried fish in the market, the gravel-voiced spear seller who sniffs out tourists on the beach, the tight-waisted fishermen who push the dugouts out from shore. These people have become fixtures here, tenured characters in their own infinite tragedy. I sometimes wonder if I have become one, too.

I didn't use to be like this—so certain of the inviolability of the Malagasy way. Their passive resistance to change, their inscrutable approach to the new, their idle submission to destiny. I didn't judge, at least not in the beginning. I didn't keep my distance. Maybe pain and the avoidance of pain does that.

I can recall the first scent I had of Madagascar, that spicy scent of clove and vanilla mixed with the thick sea air—and later, much later—of felled eucalyptus and hospital rooms and burnt earth. But with that first breath of arrival I had warmed my bones, set ablaze my cold-country cheeks.

The beginning of a life starts like this. Smells so strong and hues so vivid that they manage to eclipse the past, crush it like calcified stone. One carves a new face and a new name in the rock, and begins their life again. And as banal as it seemed, Madagascar felt like a fresh dawning. I was deluded of course, and I was vaguely conscious of that delusion. Yet I was certain that I saw a rose instead of a weed, a smile instead of a scowl. I devoured those first subtle effects of sky and earth; put the soft filter on a harsh lens that would otherwise obscure my view.

But before then, before I knew the price of this life, where your one choice excludes all others, I lived in a state of suspended happiness. Bantering with the garrulous taxi-drivers, haggling with women over five cent market greens. Even the music evoked a kind of carefree cadence. It rolled like a long taxi bush ride, where copper-eyed women hummed the hymns of their mothers and their mothers before them. All seemed unadulterated light and color then—pure, untainted topaz and vermilion, setting over a lapis sea. With these pure elements in my hand, there existed a joyful expectation—a tension before the brush is touched to canvas.

Everything on the island was accepted and embraced like a new lover. I rode on the back of trucks down eroded roads through barren desert landscapes. I swam with children on shipwrecked beaches pounded by waves. I shivered under thin, cosseted *lambas* while squatting women stirred earthen pots of smoking cassava. I patronized local eateries, where insolent young girls spooned out thin goat gruel over red rice.

For the last year, I shared a ramshackle house in the Antanosy outpost of Fort Dauphin, with a young British development worker. Owen had become my confidante and colleague, and occasional sparring partner, debating the pros and cons of development work.

My borrowed time living as a volunteer in Madagascar had come to a crossroads: where I had to decide between continuing work in development or pursuing a more straightforward path—without the nagging fear that I was disrupting the delicate balance of others' lives. It was a dilemma that left me feeling purposeful at times, redundant at others.

"You know what your problem is," Owen said to me one day, biting into a swollen mango, pointing one dripping finger in my direction, "You're a jack of all trades. You need to specialize if you want a future in development. Otherwise," he spit out a piece of green skin, "you'll end up being a master of none."

I looked up at him, tanned and green-eyed, his pale shirt gathering loose strings at the frayed edges. He sat with his back against the linoleum counter, his frame outlined by the blue bright day outside, all the while speaking with a kind of fatherly affection.

I sat on a chair, my frame swathed in a printed cloth, maroon and golden with the edges framing a Malagasy saying: *Mamy ny tantely mamy ny fantianavana*. I ran my fingers across the border: Honey is sweet and so is family. Yes, I suppose, through our self-exiled commiseration, we had, in a way, become like family. Two unlikely surrogate siblings, thrown together in a development dystopia, high atop a peninsula in the middle of the Indian Ocean. In the past sixteen months that we had lived together, I had become Owen's sounding board about duplicitous colleagues and post-colonial bureaucracies. And he had, in turn, become a kind ear, an indispensable friend helping to turn my tides of disillusionment. In short, he was my kindred spirit, floating just like me, working in a region of Madagascar people aptly titled "the graveyard of development projects."

I was thinking now about Owen's words. My hand absentmindedly picked up a lychee from a bowl and peeled it—slowly, thoughtfully. A fruit fly rose drunkenly out of the candied bunch, gliding away. The clear juice burst out of its reptilian skin and I caught the flesh between my teeth.

"The other thing is," Owen said, finishing off his mango with a breezy relish, "you need to figure out what you want to get from being out here." He threw away the stripped pit and hoisted himself upon the kitchen counter. Reaching for a banana from a hanging basket, he began to peel it pensively. I watched his eyes flash briefly as he punctuated a thought. "A lot of people never really ask themselves that question, you know, looking for all sorts of reasons to justify their existence in this place—in development in general." He bit into the bruised flesh, "I mean really, what's keeping you out here? Is it the lifestyle, the weather, the adventure? He tossed the skin into the bin, crossed his arms, and looked at me. "Everyone has similar reasons for coming here, Mei-Ling. But sometimes, people have different reasons for staying."

Owen's words carried a weight that heaped heavily onto my own thoughts. Even though I knew he was procrastinating, waxing philosophical while making his way through all my market shopping, I felt suddenly grateful for his company. He was right. I needed to figure out my motivations. I wasn't quite sure how I ended up in this condition. A bit disillusioned, a bit jaded, tired of all the research students, NGOs, and businesses that traipsed through here taking what they needed and leaving

villagers no better off. Sometimes even more resentful
or dependent. I was becoming weary of the internal
politics, the glad-handing, the competition for funding
and projects. The big companies, the small charities,
the well-intentioned but misled individuals. I thought
of the semantics of development, the hazy lines and the
ingratiating nepotism. In my time out here, I had moved
further from what I thought I was, and closer to what I
knew I was not.

I sat at the table, mulling over his words, over my
memories, staring past him, thoughtfully turning over
the ripe, pale fruit on my tongue. Outside, two Malagasy
children were climbing a tree, overreaching their tiny
brown bodies to snag a giant, bulbous fruit from the top
canopy. Their wiry bodies balanced on the branches like
acrobats on a high wire.

I had learned an immense cache of things about
development while being a volunteer in Madagascar,
and more than that, I had delved more deeply into the
fabric of the country itself. I had squatted in huts over
open fires, bathed in muddied rivers snaking through
sacred forests, roasted zebu meat under southern con-
stellations. I wrote scripts for educational radio, met
with schoolchildren and village elders, crouched under
tamarind trees drawing buildings with broken sticks
in the dense earth. I whiled away the downtime teaching English to Malagasy guides, while cataloguing my
abrupt fevers and erupting skin infections. I sank in the
soporific state of a place so heat-ridden that you didn't
do anything from eight in the morning until five in the
evening.

I tried to recall my last few months in Madagascar
with a kind of traveler's reverie, wilfully omitting all
moments of despair and heartache, and instead called

forth striking images of belief and humility. The murmuring talks with the Malagasy over rice tea, riding oxcarts through acres of Spiny Forest under an opal moon, watching traditional dances of spear and drum silhouetted by a fire. Within this dry, arid region of the south, I was graced for a time to see into the lives of the Antandroy people, or "The People of the Thorns;" a dark-skinned, proud people eking out a frugal living through cattle herding and agriculture, praying for the rain that rarely comes.

Being new and idealistic and fresh to all of this, I began entertaining the fact that I could do this forever. Wrapped in a headscarf, living a simple, Spartan existence, working under the ethos of development. But now I had to take stock, rethink, and try to make sense of everything I had experienced in a place so diametrically opposed to the life I knew. What was I actually doing here, and why did I want to stay? Was my work helping to make anything better, or did it merely aim to serve my own ends? When I looked at the state of Madagascar—environmentally, economically, and socially, and the amount of foreign aid that annually pours in, the idea that I could actually make a difference seemed remote. Outside my window, the sleepy town lay nestled between swathes of papaya plantations, and beyond, an escarpment of chaparral and palms, rising up to high mountainous peaks.

There are thousands of trappings that we lay down for ourselves, and perhaps if we noticed them a little more often, we would fall prey to them a little less. Maybe this was really a fool's paradise at the edge of the earth, lulling one into a false sense of piety that compels people into purpose. After all, in many ways Madagascar retains its savage beauty while coaxing Westerners to try to tame it. People arrive here and are shocked by what they see, and driven blindly by the idea of progress, succeed in convincing themselves that that they can reset the balance.

But what I saw over the last year was that money and philanthropy can equal all sorts of things, and imposing an imported model of development does not guarantee prosperity. No one told any smart director in his breezy office that sometimes people are not quantifiable—not the donors with their bank rolls, not the visitors from Washington with their rented four-wheel drives and their fly-by-night visits, not the expats who learn that their lives really belong somewhere else. Because out here, as in other places where development strives to survive, there is no course you can take that can prepare you for this. There is no module, nor model that can quantify these people of mixed and complicated histories. No theory or study that could ever strive to square this ever-widening circle.

This place, this southernmost tip exiled from mainland Africa, pushed beyond Asia, squatting below the Middle East, tiptoeing over Antarctica, has something important to say, though not in the way that we might say it. It welcomes workers, it patronizes visitors, it will give you the tastiest part of a zebu, the highest mound of rice, the softest, newest bread. It is a precious gemstone coveted in the raw. It is an evolutionary anomaly analyzed by scientists. It is the largest island nation on the planet and one of the poorest countries in the world. Despite this, it does not have civil war, a high crime rate, or massive epidemics. But it has a shocking degree of malnutrition, a tiny GNP, and an ample dose of corruption. Its inhabitants speak in dialects rooted in Arabic, Polynesian, and Bantu. People still fish in dugout canoes, practice subsistence agriculture, and keep their bank accounts grazing in the pasture. It is an indescribable masterpiece that is unfinished, unrecognized, and unappreciated.

As I sat there, contemplating my future, it was not the country itself, its politics or its potential, which caused me pause. I began to believe that why I was staying, or rather, why I could not leave, tethered to this place by some invisible thread, was because of the people. It was the people who drove my questions and, perhaps, in some way, I knew that they held the answers. I began thinking about all of those that I have met—some young, some naïve, buzzing around off the adrenaline of their own convictions. And others too, by years or by experience, full of wisdom and warnings from navigating the treacherous waters of development.

But ultimately, I stayed for the Malagasy themselves—who remain to this day like untold mysteries, sitting and waiting, amid an endless tangle of thorns.

Mei-Ling McNamara is a writer, travel guidebook author, advocacy journalist, and international development worker. Originally from the San Francisco Bay Area, she has lived the last ten years in Morocco, Madagascar, and the U.K. and has traveled to the South Pacific, Central America, South America, North Africa, sub-Saharan Africa, and Europe. She is writing a new travel guidebook to Senegal for Bradt Travel Guides, and is a contributing author on the current Bradt Guide to Madagascar. *This story was the Gold Medal winner in the Travel and Transformation Category in the Solas Awards for Best Travel Writing, 2007.*

JEAN TROUNSTINE

ℐℬ ℐℬ ℐℬ

The Memory We Call Home

Leaving Cincinnati was easy—the sting
was in the return.

I walk into the color gold. Ceiling chandeliers, paintings
of men, warm wood, and Persian rugs, an opulence
known to private clubs—Harvard, Stanford, Yale, to name
a few—all radiating the kind of light designed to highlight
hair, set off elegant gowns. I am in black, my dress-up color,
and I step carefully from the elevator onto the plush carpet
of Cincinnati's Queen City Club, a place my Jewish ancestors would not have been invited. A place even now where
women in gowns and men in tuxes hold glasses of wine as if
they'd stepped out of the artwork around them, descended
from a line of respectable souls immortalized in poetry.
They whisper to each other, eyes floating around the room
to walls or to well-appointed others who make entrances. In

182

the ballroom in front of me is a bar manned by black men who wear white gloves. Although these domestics don't bow like Milton, my grandmother's butler—head down, deferential, making me ache in my patent leather shoes as he served "Miss Jeannie" with a cool glass of punch—they hover by the bar in a corner of the room. Occasionally they noiselessly sweep around us, serving those who have come to hear me speak.

It is 2007, ten years after my father died, almost twenty since my mother slipped out of her coma. I have a few books by now, and like many children of the '60s, have left my parents' city and found my social conscience in work. Coming home is usually about business. I have never once driven by the house my parents built.

Connie, my father's second wife, belongs to the group that hired me, mostly because she likes the leader, a woman in her bridge game. I am secretly glad she is not in my mother's bridge game, the one where Lenore jokes that no one can see anymore to bid. Many are gone now, although my mother was one of the first, my mother who sought clubs like this one with every fiber of her being. She may have descended by marriage from Isaac Mayer Wise, the Germanic leader of Reform Judaism, but she preferred to say we came from Austria. While her parents divorced and she could not afford the Vassar of her mother, she married well. She bridged with women who went to Wellesley and Radcliffe; women who coined their own brand of feminism before Betty Freidan and Gloria Steinem; women who had secrets of the rich—alcoholism, affairs, disobedient children. She would have been amused at Connie's suit, just missing the mark, unfashionably below the knee.

As though she has never thought of it before, Connie nods when I say softly that almost no one in the room but me is Jewish. I want to tell her it is a strange feeling, a stab not so different from one I felt a few years ago in Vienna. There, illusions were dashed. Vienna seemed to hide its Jews, cover its brutal past in whitewashed subway walls and festivals. The concert halls, as decorative as this ballroom and filled with men and women in the grand style, were as serious as stone, more German than I had envisioned. Connie is Catholic, goes to church every Sunday, and reminds me how my father told her faithfully each week to give his regards to Jesus. She says this to me with a smile, but a smile on a face that is reminiscent of a Roualt clown—longing in her eyes for the years she's lost. No matter what I've lost, she has lost as much.

We mingle. Every member is at least seventy-five except for Connie who is almost sixty-four—the age my mother was...I say silently to myself. I am the teenager in this group. I chat. I am bemused. I pronounce names correctly. I earn credibility as the speaker. I laugh when someone introduces Connie as my mother. I don't laugh when a ball-gowned woman says, "You'll love this gathering; after dinner we dance! Oh no, wait!" she adds suddenly. "I forgot, that's my other group."

At the dinner, I am surprised that the wine is cheap. I pick at the food—some sort of chicken en brioche that flakes easily—and dabble in carefully guarded questions. I do not want to know what I know—that this gathering is more Republican than I can bear, that I have agreed to come here for money, for recognition; all that seems as tawdry as the merlot I am drinking. I wonder how I can speak to them about my passion—staging Shakespeare in prison—without feeling the fool.

I stare at the painting of Ulysses S. Grant beyond the podium, and remember a story. My distant relative,

Captain Philip Trounstine, had been ordered to expel all his fellow Jewish soldiers during the Civil War, something he found repugnant; he'd resigned in protest, refusing to internalize Grant's hatred. It is a noble story, something I want to claim as I sit here amidst the white gloves that pour water into my crystal glass. I could resign in protest too, get up from this table, crash into the front of the room and scream into the microphone that people in prison are no floorshow. But I am not so presumptuous to think that this small moment matters in a world where bombs of prejudice drop with the regularity of daybreak. I know too that tragedy lurks beneath the surface of these smiles. The woman to my right lost her husband last year, and a few years before he died, his parents hanged themselves—together. I know that the husband is the one who wandered into the room and found them. What can I say about prison that this woman doesn't already know? Oh Captain, my Captain, some youthful fury has fallen cold and dead. I'll stay.

It's time. I am at the podium. I feel my passion well up in spite of myself; I tell the story of my book *Shakespeare Behind Bars*. I sense the silence in the room, even some yearning in eyes to believe in change. The irony does not pass me by that I am talking about *The Merchant of Venice*, a play with undoubtedly anti-Semitic overtones, to a group whose ancestors never would have dined with mine. I read aloud Shylock's famous "Hath Not a Jew Hands" speech, portraying Rose, the character in my book who suffered from HIV and chose to play this outsider. I feel the wind of history.

The guests applaud. Some ask questions; a few credit Shakespeare with redemption. Within five minutes after we've ended, they have all kissed cheeks and donned wraps, whisking themselves away as if they'd lost their glass slippers. I drink my wine and think. How much I loved to watch my parents dance—the jitterbug, the fox trot, and most of all, the waltz.

Whenever settlers come to a new land, they find a place to bury their dead. In Cincinnati, the dead are scattered around the city, in landscaped acres of trees and streams. Christians lie with Christians, and Jews, with Jews. But separation in the Jewish community cuts deeper: the Orthodox, Conservative, and Reform each have different resting places for their beloved, and different customs for viewing their dead. Some Jews are from tribes that forbid their brethren from going inside the gates; they must visit from afar. Others weep openly or leave a stone on a gravesite—to outlast the elements. The body is always buried quickly and not viewed publicly after death. For some, a simple pine coffin suffices; for others, the body is buried in earth; so dust returns to dust.

Since 1850, Reform Jewish sons and daughters, parents and grandparents—even the ones we cannot stand—have lived underground on the hilly ten acres at the United Jewish Cemetery, and in spite of what we know, continued to exert some pull on the earth. Isaac Mayer Wise is there, and Murray Seasongood, former mayor of the city, has his tombstone as his tribute. Slabs of gray rise up from the ground for men and women who died in wars; some were senators; others judges, bankers, and businessmen. Mothers lie near babies who died in childbirth. Strausses and Bernsteins reside alongside Josephs and Kaufmanns.

My grandfather's sister Helen Trounstine is there. She founded the Juvenile Protection Agency, the Women's City Club, and fought for child welfare before she died at twenty-seven. She has weathered vandals who've come to the cemetery, turned over headstones and destroyed tombs. Helen was spared the desecration of a Joseph Steinhau, who like her relatives came to Cincinnati from Bavaria seeking refuge. His 1886 sandstone marker was separated from its sturdy foundation, sadly broken into three pieces, as if America weren't the land of the free.

It never occurred to me to visit a cemetery until we buried my mother. But now, almost every trip to the city, I go, kneeling at my parents' names. I speak without words to the grandfather I hated; sometimes I place flowers on a grave. I feel the pull of history at my feet.

Today, Connie is frantic as I drive up. She waves her arms in alarm, her pale face screwed up red. She can't find my father, she says, clutching at her camel hair coat and pacing the road that winds among the tombstones. Where is he, she wants to know, as if someone could take him once again, away from her. I drive by, knowing she's gone too far, letting her words of worry trail behind me. I pass the Friedmans and the Foxes, go beyond the Levinsons and the Kantors. I pass the small guard's house on my left and slow, sure of the spot. She has walked the road, found me, and before I can get out, I see her fear, a face trying to untwist itself. My father might have been moved, she says. Maybe it was her fault; she forgot to pay her dues.

I know irrationality when I see it, but I understand, want to tell her how the hundreds of souls who live here and in our hearts, could never be moved or forsaken, no matter how many tombstones are broken, how many times we drive by the spot. But instead, I step out of the car and stand by my mother. My father. My grandparents. The ones who died before I knew them. I touch the towering monument with my family name, leave two stones.

After lunch, I am to head to the airport. But here it gets tricky. Connie can't remember directions—the names of roads, the precise places to turn, the exact entrance to the highway. She decides to lead me, first so I can get gas, and then to the highway entrance, a generous offering to ease my way, a kinesthetic approach.

The ride down Reading Road begins. Within minutes we are in my old neighborhood, but it's bland, dirty. At a stoplight, I notice the buildings are shells of themselves as if bombed from the inside. The neighborhood's changed, they say, but that's not it. It's not just run down but uncared for, with streets bumpy and untarred, left for the poor. The light changes and the pink color of my old brown house flashes through trees behind the funeral home. We promised to take care of our city, the queen city. But wait, Marx's Drug Store has disappeared and the Chinese restaurant, and where is my dentist's building? I'm at the Belvedere Apartments, and here is where my father's mother moved after my grandfather died, still tall but somehow seedy, although I can't quite tell, it goes so fast this whirl of memory. I want to scream, stop the ride down the road that takes me past Wise Temple and the Orthodox synagogue, Feinberg, where I went for a Bar Mitzvah and wore of all things a pink yarmulke. Now I'm at my other grandmother's building, the yellow brick defaced, graffiti on the front, a chain link fence around the outside, broken windows. Gone her world—consommés, meringues—gone a life I had flying by me, and I can't catch my breath, I can't stop this car, this Wild Toad Ride through memory.

By the time I get to the highway, I'm in tears, a rage of tears that feels like I have to pull over. But I don't. I keep driving. I drive past the road that I'd take to the house above the river, the house my parents built where

Connie lived with my father, sold to strangers. Connie is waving me to the bridge. Oh Connie, I wave back, I understand how you thought my father was gone. The city is gone from me too, and I pass her car, waving, crossing over the bridge to Kentucky where we used to drive to the White Horse Inn for lobster on Sunday nights, over the bridge that took us to my father's favorite ribs joint, to Covington, where everyone knows there was a red light district, where Fred, my boyfriend, lived while he played the Wall in *The Fantastiks*. Connie's car is fading from my rear view window. I drive on and on, past the place our car broke down on the way to the airport where my sister stood on the curb with a suitcase, and a kind black man pulled over, gave us a lift, her to the airport, us to a phone. Past the new road that leads to the airport. Finally, I am at the car return. Cincinnati is behind me.

Jean Trounstine is a writer and professor at Middlesex Community College in Massachusetts. She worked at Framingham Women's Prison for ten years where she directed eight plays and wrote the highly-praised Shakespeare Behind Bars: The Power of Drama in a Women's Prison. *She has been featured on* The Today Show *and has written for publications such as* Boston Globe Magazine, Working Women Magazine, *and* Sojourner. *She is co-editor of* Why I'm Still Married: Women Write Their Hearts Out on Love, Loss, Sex, and Who Does the Dishes.

ఌ ఌ ఌ

Los Muertos

"The Mexican is familiar with death, jokes about it, caresses it, sleeps with it, celebrates it; it is one of his toys and his most steadfast love."—OCTAVIO PAZ

*T*his is what I remember: White sheets limp with sweat twisted around his naked body, a low mattress in a small white room, sun streaming through a window above the bed, the musky smell of sex, briny raw oysters sliding down my throat.

I might not have remembered at all had I not found his letter in an old desk drawer. I read, "We shared something special..." and my eyes leapt to the signature scrawled across the bottom of the page. I couldn't decipher it. I shook the letter as if that might cause it to speak. I checked the envelope. There was no return address.

I folded the letter back into the envelope and gazed out the window at my garden. The last rose of summer bravely held onto its petals as it wobbled in the light breeze. How could I not know who wrote such intimate words? Snapshot memories riffled behind my eyes. A woman patting tortillas. A copper-colored van. The silhouette of a small white hotel trimmed in blue. And in a flash, I knew.

"Why don't you come with us?" Helen had said, all those many years ago. "You'll love it." She and Claire were planning a trip to Mexico to meet their friends and former employers, Paul and Lorena, who had retired in Guadalajara. From Guadalajara, Paul would drive them to the little town of Pátzcuaro, high in the mountains of Michoacán for Día de los Muertos, the Day of the Dead. Claire explained that each year, on November 1 and 2, families throughout Mexico invited the spirits of the dead to visit them.

"It's a fiesta," she said. "I can't wait to see it. People decorate the graves. They bring food and spend the night."

I had traveled in Mexico, but only along the coast, to resort towns that felt American with a Latino accent and sometimes Mexican with an American accent. On this trip, Lorena exposed the interior. She led us into corners of Mexican culture, art, and cuisine that I didn't know existed.

At modern pottery studios, we admired hand-painted tiles and bought vases. In a Guadalajara market, we found soft woolen shawls. My tongue explored exotic new flavors: Velvety, dark chocolate mole sauce from Oaxaca that coated tender chicken, spicy salsa on fish from Jalisco served with icy crisp jicama, yellow squash blossoms wrapped in fresh tortillas from Uruapan. In the courtyard café of a small bed and breakfast, large birds with fanciful topknots strolled past our table as meat sizzled on a nearby barbecue. One night, Lorena took us to a popular tourist restaurant. She smiled at Paul and asked the mariachi band to play her favorite ballad, a love song, and the raucous music turned tender.

When we left Guadalajara in Paul's copper-colored van, the clanging energy of the city smoothed into a gentler pace. We drove through dusty villages and into lush tropical forests until at last we arrived in Pátzcuaro. I felt like I had moved from one dream into another.

In Pátzcuaro, narrow cobblestone streets wound past whitewashed buildings with red tile roofs. Lacey black railings enclosed second-floor windows rimmed in red. Wide plazas with splashing fountains, arched arcades, and ancient cathedrals affirmed the town's Spanish colonial heritage. It was cool at 7,200 feet. Tall pine trees curtained the town in one direction and spiced the air. When we looked the other way, we saw a lake so big that islands shimmered in the distance. One bump of an island supported an entire village.

Lorena, who spoke Spanish, had found rooms in a small inn. We ate *pescado blanco*, the delicate white fish unique to Lake Pátzcuaro, and watched the Purépechan Indian fishermen toss butterfly-shaped nets into the water while balancing in tiny wooden boats. The day of the festival, we walked to a plaza where women wrapped in blue *rebozos* and men in straw hats displayed crafts on soft blankets in the prickly grass. Lorena explained that in the 1500s, a Spanish bishop had convinced each of the Purépechan villages around Lake Pátzcuaro to specialize in one craft. Four hundred years later, I saw the result in finely woven cloth, fragile straw figures, and sturdy baskets. We fingered copper pots hammered by hand in Santa Clara del Cobre, and admired the elegant black-on-white pottery from Tzintzuntzan, a village named after the sound hummingbirds make.

But also, for Día de los Muertos, the people brought skeletons and skulls, devils and snakes. Claire picked up a cloth toy, I cradled a sculpture, and Helen bit into a sugar-candy skull. Men wearing masks, white shirts and pants, and long colored sashes performed the shaky Danza de los Viejitos, Dance of the Old Men. Giant bunches of orange and rust-colored marigolds hid the faces of women who walked through the plaza, their embroidered skirts as blue as the sky.

At night, we walked on narrow paths through a cemetery twinkling with candlelight. Families gathered around graves laden with fruit, bread, and bowls of the deceased's favorite food. We could hear murmurs and quiet singing as they waited for loved ones to rejoin them. Laughter, prayers perhaps. One family brought a band.

"Isn't that marvelous?" Lorena pointed to an arch of marigolds above a grave.

"I love the cross on the one next to it," Claire said.

"Do you think they eat the food?" Helen asked.

I grew uncomfortable. We weren't the only tourists, but even so, I felt like an intruder. I drifted a little from my chattering friends to get a better sense of the place, the people huddled near gravestones outlined with candlelight, the smell of tortillas and chilies, the sound of a woman gently shushing a child. A trace of sadness feathered through me like leaf shadows on a windy day, a shiver of a memory: a friend had died some months earlier. More than a friend. I had loved David. How do I explain this now? It was a time and a place when people moved in and out of relationships easily and we had chosen to live with other partners. But when we were in the same room, no one else existed. We'd look into each other's eyes and talk. For hours. And then, one day he died. He'd been sick and I hadn't paid attention and he was gone and I hadn't even said goodbye. Oh, I envied these families sitting in the candlelight waiting for their ghosts. I wanted my own midnight visitor.

I didn't say anything to Helen and Claire when I rejoined them. The feeling had caught me by surprise; I didn't know I was still grieving. I stuffed it back inside.

The next day, we all bustled into a van now loaded with serapes, copper pots, and devil sculptures. The grand adventure had ended; it was time to fly home. Or, maybe not. As we neared Guadalajara, Paul turned on the radio. We heard the news announcer say "*aero-puerto*" in an excited voice. Lorena translated. A strike had closed the airport. We couldn't fly home.

"Great!" I said.

"Oh no!" Claire anguished. "I have to go to work."

"You hate that job."

"I need the job. Maybe I can take a train. Or a bus."

Lorena called, but there were no seats available. She offered to let us stay with them, but it was a weak offer. Paul's son and his fiancé had arrived.

"We need to find a hotel," Claire said.

"No, wait," I said. An idea had popped into my head. "We're on vacation. Let's go to the beach."

"Now that's a dynamite plan," Helen said.

"I don't have enough money," Claire said. "And we aren't near a beach."

"I have American Express," I said. "We'll rent a car."

We left the next day. Claire drove. We barreled downhill, past ghostly blue agave plants that cast spiky shadows in the fields, past white egrets perched atop tall dead cornstalks, until we reached Barra de Navidad, the closest beach town on the map. We had reserved a cheap room in a small hotel on the outskirts of town.

A bare light bulb hung from the ceiling on a greasy cord. Flakes of sickly green paint curled off the walls to reveal a layer of putrid pink beneath. Rust and mold coated the sink. The floors were bare. The dream vacation had slid into a nightmare.

"I can't stay here," Helen said.

"We have to." Claire said. "I can't afford anything else."

"Well, you can stay, but I'm leaving," Helen huffed.

They sat across from each other, one on each bed, glaring. Claire gripped the car keys in her fist.

"We can always come back," I offered, "if we have to."

We drove into town and by sunset had checked into a tidy, blue-trimmed white hotel on the beach. We bought ripe melons at a fruit stand and ate them on our deck. Juice dribbled down our chins. Waves plashed softly. Helen made margaritas. We toasted the airline strike gods and American Express.

"Do you think the people in the cemeteries really believe that the dead people come back?" I asked, squeezing fresh lime juice into my drink.

"God, I hope not." Helen reached for the tequila.

"They might." Claire stretched her feet onto a spare chair. "They are very mystical people."

During the day, we bodysurfed in the warm waves, melted into the sand, and daydreamed. The beach was ours. There were no tourists, only a few fishermen. And one ghost.

He walked out of the sun when I was on my way to the market. People say that everyone has a twin. This

man was David's. The same golden hair. The same
moustache and dimples. The same teasing eyes. The
same size.

He had come to the town, as he did every autumn,
to fish. He had a room with white walls and a low mattress. Sun streamed through the window over his bed.
I stroked his chest and I held his face and I looked into
eyes that could have been David's. I poured all my grief
into acts of love.

And then I left.

I still don't remember his name. I tucked the letter
inside a musty journal and pushed the old desk drawer
closed. It was nearly sunset. I walked outside and put
summer's last rose in a Mexican vase. My husband was
calling me to dinner.

*Barbara Robertson's work as a journalist covering visual effects
and animation has provided the ticket for journeys to many countries over the years. When she's not peeking behind movie-making
curtains, she hangs out at home with her husband and her dogs.
She's won national and international awards for her articles,
and writes regularly for* The Hollywood Reporter, The Bark,
Animation Magazine, Film & Video, Computer Graphics
World, *and other publications.*

᪥ ᪥ ᪥

Which Side Are You On?

Neutrality can be the most difficult and
dangerous position in a civil war.

halatenango Province, El Salvador, May 1991. Driving
down to Las Vueltas at the end of the day, we met a
long column of *compas* walking slowly into the mountains.
Compa is short for *compañero,* friend, comrade, partner.
Compa is what the guerrillas in the FMLN called each other,
and one of the two ways we talked about them. The other
was *los muchachos,* the boys—*our* boys. We never referred
to them as soldiers, a term reserved for members of the
FAES, the government's army. Beneath the streaks of dirt,
the *compas'* faces communicated little. Their halting progress
was painful to watch. Several were carrying two rifles.

I put my foot on the brake while they passed us.
Only moments earlier I had been laughing with the
health promoters, Blanca and Panchita, and the North

American nurse, Lisa. We were giddy after nine hours of vaccinating in Tablón and El Portillo, two little communities in the hills above this town. Now, no one inside the car said a word. I heard the echo of our laughter and the emptiness where the roaring motor and jangling parts of the eight-year-old Toyota Land Cruiser had been. The *compas* did not speak either—not to us, nor each other. Just the slow steady padding of poorly shod feet on dirt and gravel. Watching the men and boys, some as young as nine or ten, it was hard to believe the rumors that the war, now in its twelfth year, would be over by Christmas.

The first rains had finally come, and it felt like we were watching the world turn from brown to green before our eyes. I caught the scent of perfume from a cluster of wild grasses before the odor of sweat and damp leather boots overpowered it. It was a time of growth and re-birth. In my own country it would have been a season of hope. But there was no sign in the *compas'* expressions that these changes would bring anything positive. When the last *compa* had trudged by, Lisa burst out, "*¡No es justo!* It's not right! They should be in school, or fighting at home with their brothers and sisters!"

I started the car and proceeded into Las Vueltas where I would part company with my three companions. Lisa and I worked together on the Diocesan Health Commission, CODIPSA, but she lived in Las Vueltas where Blanca and Panchita were on the village health team. I had picked up the three women early that morning.

I wondered if Padre Bernardo, the parish priest, was in town. He was the only person I felt safe asking what was going on with the *compas*. We had met in San José las Flores five years earlier when I was on a small delegation to El Salvador from Cambridge, Massachusetts. The delegation had been our response to a request for accompaniment, the Biblical concept of bearing witness, from the civilian residents of that village. They hoped the presence of internationals would protect them from the violence of their own government. I had seen Bernardo once in the three months since I'd come back to join CODIPSA, and the possibility of running into him made me forget, for a moment, how tired I was.

As soon as we entered the village, I knew something was wrong. No old men were sitting on the wooden benches in front of the small whitewashed church. No women hurried across the dirt path through the plaza balancing basins of cornmeal on their heads and pulling a child in each hand. In fact, there were no children in sight at all, except for the *compas* who were disappearing at a bend in the road behind us. The little plaza in front of the church was empty. I tried to figure out what had happened in the hours we had been gone.

Outside the clinic I stopped the car and waited while my passengers got out. Lisa mumbled something about being tired and walked off in the direction of the mud-brick house and her rented room.

I watched the health promoters, who were about eighteen—just a few years younger than Lisa—head toward the clinic. I saw no trace in their gait that suggested fatigue, nothing to indicate they had spent the entire day checking vaccination records, bribing timid kids with promises of candy, giving them polio drops and sticking needles into them to protect them from diphtheria, whooping cough, tetanus, and measles. I pulled the car off the narrow dirt road.

As I climbed down, my body complained. I was glad the long day was almost over. I followed Panchita and

Blanca to see if anyone in the clinic might want a ride to Chalatenango City, where I shared a little row house with four other diocesan workers.

That morning I had no trouble getting through the *retén*, the military roadblock, one of several that separated the city from the rest of the world. The soldiers on guard had been unusually friendly. They recognized the car and me, although I was surely not as memorable as the car, with its bright blue body and distinctive white trim and homemade roof carrier. I did not anticipate having a problem on the return trip. In fact, I allowed myself the happy thought that I would be resting in my hammock in little more than an hour.

I must have been mesmerized by the empty plaza because I didn't see the slender, almost frail-looking man, until I nearly bumped into him a few paces before the door to the clinic. He was wearing the black, long-sleeved shirt and black pants I recognized as the uniform of an FMLN *comandante*.

"*Con permiso.*" He excused himself in a voice so soft I had to lean closer to hear. "Would you be willing to take a wounded *compa* up the mountain to join his squadron?"

He told me the soldiers had attacked his company about a kilometer below the village. "We returned their gunfire and there was a battle," he said. "The soldiers were supported by mortars launched from Chalate, and a few of the mortars landed in Las Vueltas."

So that explains the lack of activity on the street, I thought.

"Several of my boys were wounded," he said.

And that explains why some of the kids moving up the mountain were carrying more than one rifle.

"I want to get all the *compas* into the hills, up to Zapotal, so the army doesn't attack the village."

He stood barely taller than my own five-feet-two, and there was a dark smudge across his forehead, as if he had mopped his brow with a dirty rag. Our eyes were on the same level, and I noticed that his were gray. In spite of the inflamed blood vessels and dark circles, something in his expression made me think of determined resignation, not exhaustion. Dried mud clung to his right sleeve and his once-black boots. The drumming of an invisible woodpecker took the place of my response.

Before I answered the *comandante*, I needed to think about the implications, about possible repercussions to other church workers who often used my car. I was not supposed to carry combatants. Period. I had been given this single directive, along with the vehicle, when I began working with the Diocesan Health Commission of Chalatenango Province three months earlier. It didn't matter whether they were *guerrillas* with the FMLN or soldiers in the Armed Forces of El Salvador, the FAES. The church was supposed to be neutral, and although my car was owned by Aesculapius International Medicine, the non-governmental organization sponsoring my work, it was registered to the Archdiocese in San Salvador.

Neutrality can be a sound ideological principle. Maybe it made sense here in El Salvador. After all, Catholic priests, nuns, lay workers, and parishioners had been targeted by the army. But I wasn't convinced of its practical merits in a civil war. I thought about civilians who had tried to stay out of the conflict only to be accused of helping "the enemy" and murdered by the other side. It had happened to the family of my friend, Magdalena. Her politically neutral cousin was shot and killed outside his village one night by the FMLN, and his body was left to rot where it fell. It was more than a week before his mother and brothers were able to collect the boy and give him a proper burial. Even though their sympathies were not with the army, they were terrified because it had become routine for relatives to be killed while they gathered a loved one's remains. Magdalena told me that later on they learned that a jealous rival had falsely denounced the boy to the FMLN.

I still had not answered the *comandante*. I sensed the merest displacement of mass as he shifted his weight from one foot to the other.

The woodpecker persevered with his *tap tap tap*, and the fragrance of sweet grass returned.

It was getting late and I wanted to be in Chalate before dark. I worried that the little diesel left in the tank might not get me there if I took a detour. And what about the consequences of ignoring the church's injunction? There were a million reasons why I should not do what the *comandante* asked. Although they had flashed through my mind in seconds, I felt apologetic, ashamed that I had hesitated too long.

"*Bueno. Sí,*" I said. "I'll take the *compa* to Zapotal." My voice came out small and I felt like a little girl.

"I'll tell them to get him ready," he said, and we both went into the clinic.

The main room of the cinder block building was empty except for the stench of rubbing alcohol and decomposing flesh and a thin coat of dirt on the concrete floor from mud that had been tracked in. No people, no furniture, no medical equipment or supplies.

In the only other room, a small one to the left of the front door, Blanca was sitting near a young man her age who was lying on his back on a makeshift cot. An attractive woman I had never seen before was standing next to him. She slipped the needle end of a syringe into a protective sheath so quickly that it looked as if she could do it in her sleep. There was something about her pale skin and blue eyes and the way she carried her body that commanded respect. She appeared to be more or less my age—late forties/early fifties—and her silver hair was pulled back into a ponytail. When she saw the *comandante,* she lifted her free hand and brushed away several unruly wisps that had fallen on her face.

She walked to the door with the *comandante,* leaving Blanca to clean and bandage the wounded *compa's* shoulder. I didn't hear what the *comandante* said to the doctor, but I recognized a faint German accent when she responded in otherwise perfect Spanish that the *compa* would be ready to travel in a few minutes.

In the meantime, Blanca helped the young man sit up while she wound a whole roll of surgical gauze across his chest, around his back, up under his left armpit, over the shoulder and again under the armpit, and across his chest a second time. She repeated the pattern until all the gauze sponges taped over his wounds were completely covered, but a dark stain started to seep through her handiwork before she managed to thread the *compa's* arms into the sleeves of his torn shirt.

The FMLN doctor supported him to stand. She either judged him steady enough to leave, or simply acquiesced due to the lack of options. With her arm around his waist and her body ready to bear his weight if necessary, doctor and patient walked to my car where she settled him into the passenger's seat. He had a dazed look in his eyes. I thought he might be in shock.

The *comandante* and another *compa* climbed into the back with Panchita and Blanca, who had decided to keep me company. My only concession to the church was to ask my new passengers to put their weapons on the floor. It crossed my mind that they would not see the logic in this request and might think I was overly cautious or out of touch with reality. To my relief, they complied.

I pushed more energy than usual into slamming the rear doors shut and then signaled Panchita to engage the safety latch from the inside before I took my seat behind the steering wheel. Otherwise, with my luck, the doors would swing open on the bumpy road and the *comandante* would probably fall out.

The *compa's* posture struck me as too straight and rigid. He must have been in a lot of pain, and perhaps he was fighting the urge to cry out. I smelled his blood.

We left the town behind. The car felt crowded although I had often carried twice as many people. The engine groaned and grumbled about the uphill climb, but my passengers said nothing. The rutted road wound past boulders through scrubby fields. With little more than an hour of daylight left, growing shadows speckled the ground. In front of us, white billowy clouds edged in amethyst floated on a peacock-blue canvas. Five minutes after leaving Las Vueltas the road leveled, and I felt everyone relax.

The *comandante* made an announcement for my benefit. "I'm an old friend of Eduardo Alas," he said. That was the Bishop's real name, even though he was always spoken of and addressed by his title, *Monseñor.* I caught the *comandante's* eye in my rear view mirror.

"*Sí,*" he said to my reflection, "we have spent a lot of time together. I know him well. Tell him that Juan Ramos sends his regards."

I aimed a forced smile at the mirror and said, "*¡Cómo no!* Sure, I'll tell him." Although I knew for certain that I was not going to say a thing to the Bishop, because if I did I would have to explain the circumstances to *Monseñor*—like how (in God's name!) I had run into Juan Ramos!

The drive back to Zapotal felt longer than it had on the way down. Perhaps I was traveling slower than before. Although we had not encountered mudslides earlier in the day, it was prudent to proceed with caution, but this time it seemed like there were twice as many twists and turns. As soon as I saw the *compas* ahead of us, I eased off the gas pedal. The *comandante* was quick to notice.

"Don't stop here," he instructed, "Drive past the next hill, and let us off on the other side."

I had an uncharitable thought about the *comandante* at that moment, since I was anxious to discharge my FMLN passengers, and the presence of *compas* on both sides of the road indicated to me that we had arrived at their destination.

"I don't want the soldiers to see us getting out of your car," he added, in a respectful tone of voice.

The *comandante's* words took my breath away. I became so distracted that I hardly noticed the *compas* getting out of the car when I stopped on the far side of the hill. During the drive back to Las Vueltas I was sweating a lot more than warranted at that hour.

The last reserves of energy drained from my body while I reviewed it in my head: No, I had not seen the government soldiers. Even after the *comandante's* revelation that they were near enough to see *us,* I still couldn't see *them.* I didn't know they were camped on a hill across the valley, facing the road. But since they were, they must have seen my car during the day. Even if they hadn't seen it going up to Tablón and El Portillo in the morning, they certainly must have noticed it descend from someplace above Zapotal heading toward Las

Vueltas when we came back from vaccinating. Then they saw it go up, again. This time only as far as Zapotal, where they also saw the FMLN. Then they saw it go down, again. I felt a new ache enter the hollow in the pit of my stomach.

It had been barely a week since I had gotten a stern scolding-cum-lecture from a good friend, a North American who had been working in El Salvador for several years before I arrived. He was visiting someone at the same hotel in San Salvador where I was meeting with a delegation of teachers from Cambridge. The teachers had not been able to deliver the material aid they had brought for the people in San José las Flores, which had become an official sister city to Cambridge a few months after that visit when I first met Padre Bernardo. Since I often worked in or near Las Flores, I agreed to take the books, clothes, and medicine.

When we carried the donations to my car, my friend, who had taught me survival skills for working in El Salvador, was standing in the hotel lobby. I was glad to see him, but he seemed reserved. He did not flash his familiar smile when he invited me to meet him the following day. I knew that I had done something wrong, but I wasn't sure what it was.

The next day he scolded me for the scene at the hotel. "Ten women filing through the hotel lobby carrying bags and boxes! Anyone could have been watching." He accused me of having a false sense of security.

He was right. I was not used to San Salvador. I had spent a total of four days in the city since February, when I started the job in Chalatenango. I felt anonymous in the capital, and because of that I probably did feel more secure than when I was in Chalate. It had felt good to let my guard down at the hotel. I had a passing acquaintance with almost everyone in the delegation, and four of the women were friends of mine. We talked and laughed together in their hotel rooms before putting their donations into my car. What sweet relief from the cloak and dagger life I led in the countryside.

After the meeting with my friend, however, I realized that my frivolity at the hotel the previous day could affect my entry back into Chalate, or my immigration status, or worse, it could affect the safety of the people with whom I worked.

Every international worker I knew in El Salvador was engaged in legitimate activities—popular education and teacher training, journalism, economic development projects, healthcare, legal aid. Unfortunately, if you were doing this work among the most needy you were under suspicion. Poor people in the countryside or in marginalized communities were, according to the government's definition, subversives. If the authorities targeted you, it was all over. You were *quemado,* burned, and news of your status spread like wildfire. Someone who got burned became a pariah. It was too dangerous to associate with a burned person because of the intense heat. Getting burned was therefore to be avoided at all costs because you could not continue your work or seek the comfort and support of friends without endangering them. You might as well go home. And since you never knew who might be an informer, you had to watch your back, a posture that I was finding quite difficult to maintain.

Now the *comandante's* last sentence about the soldiers seeing us repeated in my head. I was so absorbed in considering the consequences of my actions, or to be more precise, the consequences of my actions having been observed by the soldiers, that I almost missed Panchita's revelation about the *comandante*.

"Juan Ramos used to be a soldier in the Cavalry," she said. "You know, with the government."

She reacted to my expression of surprise by leaning forward across the back of the now-empty passenger's seat showing me that her usually smiling face could look quite serious, even under a veil of light brown freckles. She pursed her lips, widened her eyes, and nodded her head up and down. She said that Juan Ramos, the *comandante,* had been captured by the FMLN during their 1989 offensive.

"That was while we had this deal with the Red Cross that both sides would periodically turn prisoners over to them. But by the time the Red Cross came to take him back, he had decided not to leave. Instead he made a really dramatic speech about how he wouldn't fight against his brothers anymore."

"And he joined the FMLN," Blanca added, stealing Panchita's thunder by pre-empting her predictable last line.

Curiouser and curiouser, I thought, and for just a moment I forgot about my own predicament. Now I wished I *could* tell the Bishop, just to see his reaction.

Back in Las Vueltas, I shook hands with Panchita and Blanca—as is the custom in the countryside—although I felt like hugging them. I said goodbye and thanked them for staying with me while I ferried the *comandante* and the *compas* back to their squadron. I took a rag and a small bucket of water from the clinic and washed the wounded *compa's* blood off the front seat and the inside of the door. Already I missed the easy companionship of the health promoters.

I wiped a smear of blood off my arm, and wondered how long it would take for the *compa's* wounds to clot. I felt sad and angry that I had to consider so many angles before deciding to do the right thing. And still I hadn't thought of everything.

Fatigue ached through my body. I was as ready as I'd ever be for the home stretch. I had been sick with diarrhea and vomiting the night before. It was so violent and sustained that I feared I might be the first cholera case in the country. The epidemic began in Peru and had already reached Nicaragua. For weeks we had been preparing our villages for its imminent arrival. Every health promoter knew the symptoms and protocols, and had been given extra supplies of chlorine to purify drinking water, and salt, sugar, and baking soda to mix up batches of re-hydration drinks. By five in the morning I felt stable, but empty and weak. I decided it was either a passing case of food poisoning or the flu. There was no getting out of vaccinating, however, because there was no way to send word. If I hadn't arrived in Las Vueltas by seven, the health promoters would have worried that I had been detained or captured by the army.

I took my seat at the wheel. As the engine turned over and caught, I wondered what sort of communication the soldiers on the hill facing Zapotal might have with the soldiers at the *retén* outside the city. I felt like a lamb on her way to be slaughtered. The gas gauge indicated just enough diesel to get me to Chalate.

Before pulling onto the road, I glanced in the rear view mirror. It was a gesture of pure habit, since if a car were coming I would have heard it well before it came into view. The reflection revealed a man running across the plaza at full-speed in my direction. He was clutching a string bag in one hand, a battered straw hat in the other, and a daypack was bouncing wildly on his back. I felt a jolt of joy in my chest when I turned around and the figure became Padre Bernardo. He was waving the hat to get my attention.

When he reached the car, Bernardo said, between gulps of breath, "Susana, what luck! I have to be in San Salvador tonight."

I wished my pleasure to see him had been simple and uncompromised. I wished that I didn't feel compelled to provide the priest with a brief summary of the day's events before he risked riding in my car. I had to suppress my feelings of guilt and confusion in order to tell him about the vaccination campaign, the wounded *compa,* and the final vehicular ascent and descent of the day. I told him about the encampment of soldiers that was visible to the practiced eye of the FMLN *comandante,* and not to mine.

My litany was of secondary importance to Bernardo, who had been in Las Vueltas during the army's attack. Telling me that his primary need was to get to the capital, he did not hesitate to climb in beside me. The only way to San Salvador was through Chalatenango City. Bernardo would get his lift to the bus that would take him to the capital, and I had a companion on the ride back through the war zone and the roadblock.

After I reassured him that I hadn't been caught in cross fire, Bernardo said, "The army took us by surprise—even the *compas.* The battle lasted about an hour. It's a miracle no one was killed, and no villagers were hurt."

"Some of the *compas* were just children," I said.

"Yes," he said, and let out a sigh.

"Well, can't we do something? I mean, like getting them into civilian communities so they can attend school and have some kind of childhood?"

"They're orphans," he said. "The FMLN is all they know—and they do learn to read and write. That's more than can be said for the kids in some of your villages, isn't it?"

Bernardo knew that four of my CODIPSA communities were in a remote area of the mountains northwest of Las Vueltas, where the Sumpul River forms the border with Honduras. I was pretty sure the Salvadoran government had never provided educational or medical services to the people living there.

"Juan Ramos sent greetings to the Bishop," I said.

"Ah, so you know the history."

"I do, now," I said. "As if things weren't already complicated enough in this war—then they go and switch sides!"

There was some small talk about his parishioners and my latrines. After that we didn't say much. What more would we have said to each other? In Chalatenango in 1991 one had to trust that the person to whom one might tell something had the judgment and strength to be silent even under pressure. Maybe Bernardo trusted me, but he didn't know me very well, and although I was inclined to trust him, I had already revealed more than I wished had been required when he heard my initial confession.

A sidelong glance at the man with the reddish-brown beard sitting in my passenger's seat reminded me that he had walked four hours to Las Flores a few days after Christmas 1986, just because he heard there were three *gringos* in town and he was longing to speak his native language. Before we sat down to talk that day I noticed he had blue-green eyes with a particular twinkle that provided a clue about his origins even before I heard his brogue or learned that his given name was Brendan.

I was grateful for the memory. It helped me feel more confident when we got to the *retén,* where the same two young soldiers from the military base in Chalatenango were still on duty. Again they smiled at me, and didn't bother to search the car. Evidently, the soldiers up near Zapotal had not been able to alert the folks at the road-block about the car and me. Or else they had something else in mind.

When the soldiers asked to see the priest's ID, I was taken aback, but Bernardo managed to put them at ease with a joke I didn't understand. After that we were, as they say, home free. I dropped Bernardo at the bus stop and drove the last few blocks home where I climbed into my hammock without bothering to get undressed.

What happened around Las Vueltas that day weighed me down. I had violated the neutrality principle of the church and was now driving a marked car. I had no way to prepare for how this fact was going to play itself out, and it would be necessary to admit everything to the next person who asked to borrow it. It was as if the flames were already licking at my feet.

Two nights after returning from the vaccination cam-paign I had a vivid dream. In the dream I am collecting sheets and towels. While I am doing this, a young man is standing nearby, cautioning me that I should not do what I am planning to do. Then I am on a crowded bus with my laundry in my lap, and the same young man is sitting next to me, telling me to "watch myself." I look up from my seat, and I see that an armed soldier has gotten on the bus. He is working his way down the aisle, heading right for me.

My sense of inviolability drops away, and yes, my cockiness, which I had not acknowledged until that moment. I turn to the unknown young man in the seat beside me and, although I am aware it might be too late, I apologize for not paying attention to his warnings.

When I awoke, the message sunk in. During the three months I had been working in Chalatenango Province, I had made the transition. I was no longer bearing witness or accompanying other people in their struggle.

I had come to El Salvador because I wanted to do something useful that would benefit the civilians living in this war zone. I knew it would be dangerous, but I still believed in the "safety net" of working for the officially neutral Catholic Church—in spite of all the evidence to the contrary.

Like Magdalena's innocent cousin, my own beliefs and allegiances did not matter. Whether I wanted to or not, I had crossed the line. I had become a part of the struggle. Now I was subject to the same risks and dangers as everyone else.

෴ ෴ ෴

H. Susan Freireich went back to school to study public health after twenty-five years of teaching, community organizing, and political activism. She worked in the civilian communities caught in El Salvador's civil war and is writing a memoir about the experience. She is the recipient of the 1998 Frances Shaw Fellowship at The Ragdale Foundation, and the 2005 Mildred Sherrod Bissinger Memorial Endowed Fellowship at the Djerrasi Resident Artists Program. She has also received support and time for her work from Norcroft, Hedgebrook, Blue Mountain Center, and Casa Libre en la Solana. Her work has appeared in Poetic Voices Without Borders *and in* The Best Women's Travel Writing 2007.

ﾉﾓ ﾉﾓ ﾉﾓ

Tradition, Schmadition

A nosy tourist lands in Papua New Guinea.

G od bless their sensible footwear, matching t-shirts, and Ned Flanders-eclipsing good cheer. But missionaries (apparently flagged as my preferred seatmates by every international carrier) have always driven me to the silent, eye-rolling variety of self-righteous indignation. At least until I met one of their proselytes in the Western Highlands of Papua New Guinea.

The lobby minder at a lodge where—for several days last summer—I was the only guest, Michael was perpetually bored to tears and desperate to talk. And I was perfectly happy to exploit these conditions; a local, English-speaking contemporary was a rare find in the area, so I had a backlog of questions for him, all highly inappropriate, and most related to religion.

Though a magazine assignment had landed me in the Highlands less than a week earlier, I could already see what the obligatory packs of missionaries were doing to the local customs. While traditional dances and rituals were still on display for tourists, each performance came with the same basic intro: "A generation ago, the whole village knew how to do this. But since we've become Christian, only these five old guys do."

Nothing against Jesus—nor the schools, hospitals and social halls built in his name. Imposed beliefs and vaporized traditions are what I take issue with.

Granted, I'm part of the problem. If I learned nothing else in high school chemistry (and as the D- on my transcript would seem to suggest, I didn't), I *was* able to grasp this: The contents of an airtight container generally start to degrade the second you expose them to oxygen and light. And though perhaps never hermetically sealed, the Papua New Guinea Highlands were still basically untouched by outsiders until well into the twentieth century. So each tourist who shows up now—treading lightly or otherwise—is altering the local equation. (Unless, of course, the Huli tribe has instinctively favored Britney t-shirts since time immemorial.)

I would also concede that cultural degradation isn't always tragic—and some of what the missionaries want to stamp out very much deserves to go. Domestic violence and general female abasement come to mind. But centuries-old dances that pay homage to tribal ancestors? Gorgeous getups that happen to show a bit of skin? Come on. Where's the harm there?

Though I'd normally keep such views to myself among happy converts—and Michael seemed to fit the bill (something about his constant references to "the Light," perhaps)—he made me forget my manners. Between his gift of gab and intensely disarming smile, decorum stood no chance. And by the time I found myself walking to his village with him (out of sheer boredom, he had offered to give me a tour), I felt like I was chatting with an old crony.

So I asked the question that had been plaguing me most: "O.K. I understand that you're grateful for a lot of what Christianity has brought to the Highlands, but aren't you even a little resentful to see your own culture slipping away?"

"Our culture does need to be preserved," he answered. "Tourists really like it, and without it, they won't come."

Um…right then. Not exactly what I'd had in mind.

"Let me rephrase the question," I said. "Pretend, for a moment, that tourists don't exist. Just remove us from the equation. Now, aren't you at all sad that so many of your traditions are being destroyed?"

The answer that followed was even more jarring than the first:

"Frankly," he began, "I could do without them."

Then he turned the question around.

"Do you have any idea how much time it takes to go into the bush and track down all the seeds you need for the face paints, all the feathers you need for the costumes, etc., etc., etc.?"

No, actually, I didn't. So he went on to describe what a time- and labor-intensive pain-in-the-ass the whole culture thing can be.

"I'd rather be working at my *real* job, or emailing friends, or reading, or watching a movie," he added.

The guy had a point. So I shut up for a minute and tried to apply his logic to my own traditions. I started with bat mitzvahs—and had to wonder: Would mine ever have happened had I been required, say, to hunt down and pro- cess my own Torah parchment? Especially if the project entailed significant cutbacks to whatever I was doing for fun at the time? (A combination of Space Invaders and slow dancing with Dan Hirshfeld, as I recall.)

No matter how many analogies I thought through, I couldn't come up with a single legitimate rebuttal. The truth is, I was no more eager to forgo reading, movie-watching, and web-surfing than he was. And why were such pursuits my God-given rights, but not his? Who was I to tell him he should be foraging for face paint in the rainforest instead?

Mind you, he hadn't disavowed all "the old ways." In fact, his own bride price ceremony (basically, a wedding) was a mere two weeks off. Completely fascinated by the ritual—and frustrated that I'd be missing it by a matter of days—I grilled him for details.

I learned that at the appointed hour, both *wantoks* (the clans on which Papua New Guinea's society is based) would be gathering in front of his father's house, where his people would be offering her people the following: twenty to forty pigs, several thousand kina (the country's paper currency), and a pile of yams. If all went well, some spare pigs would be clubbed (though not by Michael; he's probably the only guy in the whole of the South Pacific who can't bring himself to do the deed), cooked, and eaten. Then, duly sated, the *wantoks* would part ways. No pageantry, no costumes, no sing-sings à la *National Geographic*—unless, of course, any tourists caught wind of the ceremony and wanted to attend, in which case the participants would happily oblige with a feathered accessory or two, and perhaps a little jig.

Again, my manners eluded me. I had to know: How did a university-educated woman (i.e., the bride) feel about being purchased for the contents of a pigpen, a money-market account, and a produce bin? And for that matter, how did a university-educated man (i.e., the groom) feel about buying her? His answer was that he and his intended would gladly have skipped the whole ordeal in favor of a simple, modern wedding, but that neither would inflict such heartache on the clans. (Cue Tevye and his *Fiddler on the Roof* castmates after some Pidgin lessons—though "*Tok Bilong ol Tumbuna!*" doesn't have quite the same ring as "Tradition!")

The next nosy question I couldn't help but ask: What would happen if one *wantok* rejected the other's offer?

"Brides from her province generally go for much less than those from mine," he said. "So our offer is going to seem really impressive, unless her family brings up their investment in her university education [read: her earning power, soon to be transferred to *his* family], and wants compensation for the lost returns."

Still, he seemed confident that with a bit of negotiation, all would go well. The only serious wild card was his girlfriend (not to be confused with his fiancée), who was threatening to disrupt the proceedings.

On a none-of-my-business roll—and fresh off the first season of HBO's "Big Love"—I asked, "Why not marry both?"

One of the few local customs Christianity hasn't managed to extinguish (to the outspoken consternation of the missionaries on my flight to the Highlands) is polygamy. Not to mention good, old-fashioned skirt-chasing. As one Highlander told me, he and his cohorts liked to "resign from Christianity once in a while to have fun with the ladies."

Sadly, Michael explained that his fiancée wasn't so interested in sharing. Hence the quandary in which he now found himself, and the longer we walked, the more its complexity emerged. I'll say only that a baby was involved, and the upcoming bride price ceremony was, at least in part, an effort to legitimize both mother and child—the

Christian thing to do, in his estimation. And when he asked my opinion, I had no idea how to respond.

Regardless of my thoughts (which weren't particularly illuminating anyway), what standing did I have at that point? Only hours earlier, I'd been prepared to relegate the guy to a life of seed gathering and loincloth feathering. Meanwhile, the missionaries who had essentially informed his decision to get hitched had provided education and health care along the way. And, last I checked, I hadn't built any clinics or schools in the neighborhood.

As if to underscore the point, my humble pie was served a la mode: By the time we reached the village, not a soul was around. Naturally, everyone had gone to church.

Touché, Flanders. And see you in the friendly skies.

A recovering beauty editor turned frequent travel writer, Abbie Kozolchyk divides her time between New York and wherever the assignment gods take her. She writes for National Geographic Traveler, Forbes Traveler, Allure, Martha Stewart's Body + Soul, Self, Redbook, *and others. For a random sampling of her work, visit her online at www.abbiekozolchyk.com.*

❧ ❧ ❧

A Blessing

The sacred river carries all that came before it.

"A *bebe*. See the *bebe*?" Abhay, my fourteen-year-old self-appointed "guide," gestured across the pea green water of the Ganges River toward a pile of detritus drifting near the boat. In the dim light of dusk, I could barely make out what appeared to be a large doll, its face in the water. It took a moment to connect what Abhay had just said and the doll-like form bobbing before my eyes. *It couldn't be. No, it couldn't possibly be.* But it was. A dead baby, bloated and pale, drifted in the water about ten feet from the dory's stern. I couldn't take my eyes off of it. Its body was a uniform gray-green, blending seamlessly with the dull color of the water but casting an eerie glow, as if announcing to the world that it indeed was something special. Within moments, another baby floated by, this one tiny, undoubtedly pre-term.

"A *bebe*," Abhay said again, smiling widely as his beautiful white teeth glowed in the fading light. "There are many."

I had seen dead cows, dogs, and rats, as well as human feces, condoms, and a rickshaw or two among the flotsam and jetsam that share the Ganges riverbed with the waters that drain the high mountain passes of the Himalayas. On the lookout for the rare Ganges River dolphin, a blind fresh water cetacean that negotiates its way through the river's murky waters by touch and sound, nothing had prepared me for a human baby.

Seeing my horrified look, Abhay first told me what I already knew. "Adults burn in fire," he said, pointing toward the west bank where cremation pyres dotted the river's edge. Smoke curled from one of them, an indication that a body was undergoing its transformation from flesh to ash. As the black cloud rose in the air, Abhay went on to explain what happens to babies when they die.

"They go whole," he said, motioning toward the water. "Rocks. No fire." I soon understood what he meant. Dead babies are taken out in a boat, tied to boulders, deposited mid-river and sunk. Burial in the Ganges in whatever form liberates dead souls from the interminable suffering of rebirth. Only then can there be eternal rest.

"Rocks come off sometimes," Abhay added as though I might not understand why the babies were floating in the water. "Bodies go up." I envisioned the tiny bundles detaching from their funereal anchors to join the dust and grit of their adult compatriots as they all wind slowly to the sea.

With the babies drifting off into the mounting gloom, I sat silently in the dory trying to get my mind around what I had just seen. Abhay and the boatman stared out across this, their home turf, fully at ease, as if witnessing decomposing babies floating down a river was as normal as the arrival of the postman. The air was tinged with the smell of smoke from the pyres, operated twenty-four hours a day by *doms*, those of lower caste, who, like their ancestors before them, spend their days carrying and placing shrouded bodies on stacks of wood. The sun, a white sphere hovering just above the river, was the only thing clearly marking the separation of earth and sky, the horizon a misty blend of ashen gray. As the luminous ball sank below the river, our boatman picked up the oars and with several long strokes of his muscular arms, propelled us across the water toward the ghats, the ceremonial stairs lining the west bank of the Ganges.

What am I doing here? I thought, as we slid quietly through the water. I don't need this. I had spent the last several years surrounded by death, or at least skirting it, as serious illness made its way into my life. Two years before, almost to the day, I had lain on an operating table as a nurse pumped Valium into my arm prior to a four-hour surgery to remove a malignant tumor from my lung. *This isn't happening*, I told myself as I faded into oblivion. One more surgery became two. Twice more I slipped under the anesthesia, thinking each time, this cannot be happening.

The surgeries were finally successful—I was cancer-free—but the sense of triumph was short-lived. Jane, my sister-in-law and good friend, was diagnosed with brain cancer and despite a valiant battle, was dying. My oldest friend Paula had recently told me she had breast cancer and was undergoing chemotherapy. Finally, my beloved dog Maggie, the one whose sweet and funny antics had helped me get through all this, died suddenly from an undetected illness. But even as Maggie slipped away in my arms, her death wasn't happening. Denial was my middle name.

I had lost my mother twenty years before, after a debilitating illness. My father was ninety-four years old, still healthy, but not destined to be around much longer. I yearned for an unchanging world, where the people and animals I loved would always be there.

As the two-year anniversary of my cancer surgery approached, I decided to go to India. The trip would be my reward to myself, an affirmation that I had in fact come out the other side and was getting back to normal. Yet here I found myself in Varanasi, a city that is anything but normal. A "must" on every tourist itinerary, Varanasi is one of the oldest and holiest cities in India. But it is also the place where people come or are brought to die if their families can afford to get them there. There are dying houses in Varanasi. If these are not affordable, it is perfectly fine to do your dying in public, along the ghats, in full view for all to see.

My first visit to the Ganges had been that morning. I rose before dawn, caught a taxi in the dark, then bumped to a halt a few minutes later as a tire went flat two blocks from the hotel. "No worry," the driver told me as I sat in the gloom, anxious to get to the river in time to witness the ceremonial bathing performed every morning by devout Hindus. He left me, then reappeared five minutes later on an ancient bicycle leading a bicycle rickshaw and driver in my direction. I climbed aboard, feeling foolish as the pencil-thin driver pushed hard on the peddles to get one more overfed Westerner down to the Ganges to view the morning spectacle. Off we went, the horns of early morning traffic honking noisily as we pulled out onto the pock-marked road, pariah dogs running underfoot and my nostrils smarting from the stench of Varanasi streets—dung, smoke, fumes, urine, and a sweet under-smell, unique to this city, pervading all.

The bathers had materialized that morning as they have for hundreds of years, women fully dressed in bright saris, merchants in tunics, sadhus—holy men who have renounced the world—in orange *dhotis*, most standing waist high in water so putrid it could have been an inlet to a sewage treatment plant. Arriving like royalty in the bicycle-powered rickshaw, I hurried through the alleys and

across the top of the ghats toward the river, stepping delicately over a half-decayed dog, tiptoeing through reeking
muck to the waiting boat. It was here that I first met young
Abhay, who appeared from nowhere and boarded for reasons not clear. "Who are you?" I asked him. He responded
with a cheerful shrug, as if nothing could be explained in
words. I was suspicious, but his wide smile and glittering
teeth were strangely comforting. As I leaped into the boat,
a bathing sadhu nearby picked up an aluminum kettle,
dipped it in the water, held it over his head and downed the
contents. This was my introduction to the Ganges.

That evening, as the boatman rowed through the muted
light of approaching night, I saw other boats bobbing in
clusters at the shore, their occupants watchful and expect-
ant. It was the week of Divali, the five-day festival of lights
celebrating the triumph of good over evil, a journey out of
shadow into luminosity. Divali commemorates an episode
of the *Ramayana*, the ancient Hindu saga, in which the
courageous Lord Rama returns home after his slaying of the
demon king Ravana, the embodiment of evil. Along Rama's
route, villagers light his path as he makes his way through
the dark.

As we neared the ghats, the sense of excitement was palpable. Curious tourists, locals, pilgrims, sadhus all milled
about on shore or spoke in low murmurs in the boats. It
was clear something was about to happen, but as usual
during my seven-week sojourn to India, exactly what was
lost on me.

We came to a stop in a backwater close to shore. Emerging
from the shadows, a dark-eyed, seven-year-old beauty skipped
across the nearby boats as if hopping on steppingstones. She
leaped onto ours and held before me a basket of tiny candles
set in equally tiny flower boats. "Blessings," she said, "for
loved ones."

"Dead loved ones or loved ones still here?" I asked.

"Both," she replied.

I bought five and set them on the gunwale of the boat. Just as I did, eight shirtless young men appeared on a huge platform above the shore, the lights went up on the ghats, and music from loudspeakers began to blare. The men held up burning fire sticks and positioned their sturdy bodies in a line. Swirling the fire in giant arcs, they swayed to the rhythms of Hindu chants while bells, cymbals, and drums clattered and boomed into the night. A hush came over the boats, and the milling people on shore seemed to freeze in place. I felt myself fade into the shadows, as the lights, the sweating men, the music, the fire, the chants, drowned out my perception of almost everything else. I awakened from my trance only when Abhay, his eyes alight with flames, whispered in my ear. "A puja," he said. "A blessing. For the dead." Again, he gestured with his hand away from the boat, a nonchalant wave toward the shore.

I squinted through the greenish light and searched the shore where Abhay's flapping hand seemed to point. Below the large platform, and directly above the river, were what looked like large white tubes. I got out my binoculars. Shrouded forms came into view, about five or six feet long, narrow, raised at one end and descending at the other. Rows of bodies, laid out on stretchers and covered in stiff white cloth, two deep and about eight across, rested on the shore.

A puja for the dead, Abhay had said. The ashes of these bodies would soon join the thick rich soup we floated upon. As I peered into the watery graveyard, I felt an intense urge to flee this messy place. But at the same time, I knew I was exactly where I needed to be. Denial was out of the question. Death and decay occupied the same space and received equal billing as the glorious and celebratory life that whirled all around me—the young and healthy bodies of the dancing men, the brilliant saris of the women who joined them, the dark eyes of the flower girl, the beautiful teeth of Abhay, and the music and chants that thwarted any turn of deaf ears.

When the puja was over, we rowed in silence through the now black water toward the boat docks. Puffs of smoke rose from the funeral pyres to the north. As they did, a single, staccato note punctuated the great silence that had descended on the ghats, a distinct popping like the bursting of a giant balloon. I looked over at Abhay. "Head," he said as he pointed to his. "Explode in fire. Soul coming out." His teeth glistened in the dark as his smile broadened wider than ever. In Hindi, I learned later, the name Abhay means fearless. Abhay, my intrepid guide, was lighting my way.

As we approached the shore, I remembered the candles on the gunwale that I had put aside earlier. One by one I held them in my hands as Abhay leaned over with a match. I set them gently in the water, calling the names of loved ones as I let them go. "Jane. Paula. Maggie. Mom. Dad." Over the heads of blind dolphins, following the babies to the sea, the tiny flames drifted down the river, becoming smaller and smaller until their pinpricks of light merged with the night and disappeared.

Carol J. Arnold is a California environmental and travel writer and photographer interested in exploring the relationship of culture to landscape. Her work has appeared in Coast & Ocean *magazine, the* San Francisco Chronicle, Fourth River, Windham Hill, *and* Hallmark Editions, *among others. Her favorite thing in life is to get lost in a landscape or mindscape—and to keep a little of the lost with her wherever she may be.*

※ ※ ※

Keep Breathing

The train ride from Istanbul to Bucharest
included one primitive toilet, one border stop,
and the best breakfast on earth.

*I*stanbul's Sirkeci station was spooky and nearly deserted at 9 P.M. It was clear which train was mine: the only one around, the one that looked ready for the scrap heap. Several people had suggested I fly to Bucharest instead: for the first time, I wondered whether I should have listened to them.

The compartment that held my assigned seat number was filled with chain-smoking Turkish men. One of them agreed that my ticket did in fact specify seat number 76. Nonetheless, this was his seat and he wasn't budging.

It took half an hour of consultation with sleepy ticket office men, German university students, and a grouchy old guy in a sweater vest before the mess was straightened out and my new ticket issued, for a sleeping compartment in a section of the train that was actually going all the way to Romania.

The grouchy guy turned out to be the conductor, and he conducted me to my new seat. My last day in Istanbul had been long and emotional, so I hoped I'd have the compartment to myself.

But it was full, with a stocky, dark-haired, older woman who had two teenage boys with her, and about seventy-seven pieces of luggage—most of them piled on my seat.

She didn't look very happy to see me either. The conductor said a few words, and she frowned and barked at the boys, who set about stowing her luggage in the overhead bins. When her bags were put away, they grabbed my big pack and hoisted it up. One of them was reaching for my overnighter, when I said, "Whoa, I need that one!"

He handed it over with a shy smile, and I thanked him for his help. The boys lingered for a few minutes, then went to their own compartment.

The woman sat down in her place. I sat in mine. If we were going to share this tiny space for the next twenty hours, we'd need to make the best of it. I pulled out a wet wipe to clean my grubby face and hands and offered her one from the packet. She accepted it, then held out a bag of sunflower seeds. I took a handful, and we smiled at each other.

The train pulled out of the station exactly at 10 P.M., under a steady rain.

She started making her bed the minute we were underway. She cleared her seat, pulled down the back, sat on it a few times to make sure it latched into place, then snapped out the bundle of linen we'd each been given and made a neat bed for herself.

I followed suit, glad to have a guide.

When our beds were made, I went to explore. I'd noticed that there was no dining car on this train. I should have been more serious about my provisioning. I had plenty of snacks, but only one liter of water.

Once I'd checked out the facilities at either end of the coach, I was glad I hadn't brought much water. The bathrooms were dank, smelly, and completely without toilet paper—or paper of any kind. The toilets were of the infamous "squat" variety. This wasn't the first time I'd ever seen one, but it was the first time I had no other options. I turned and fled.

Back in my compartment, the woman offered her bag of sunflower seeds. I held out my bag of raisins and the train rattled on through the rain.

Eventually, we introduced ourselves by exchanging passports. Her name was "Akcharla," she was Bulgarian, and I was surprised to see that she was only three years older than me. She spoke no English, German, or French—just Bulgarian and a bit of Russian.

Given the language barrier, I can't explain how we talked through half the night. I wished I'd had pictures to share. I'd have shown her a postcard of Austin, and some photos of my family, cats, or house. And I'd have loved confirmation of my guess that she was telling me about her daughters, and a new baby in the family.

Eventually, I had to go face the bathroom.

I told myself that if it weren't possible for a wide range of humans to use these things, the bathroom would be awash in shit, piss, and blood. And it wasn't: it was merely stinky.

"Be methodical," I muttered. With my personal toilet paper supply in my bag, I took a deep breath, entered, and locked the bathroom door behind me. The train lurched and swayed as I stood contemplating the problem. I noted the handgrips screwed into the walls about eighteen inches up, the footrests, and the hole itself.

I managed it, and returned to the compartment feeling proud for having used the toilet without major incident.

I prepared to sleep. Just as I kicked off my clogs and settled into a doze, Akcharla began to bustle around, then waved her passport at me. We must be nearing the Bulgarian border. Since the conductor hadn't taken our passports away, I'd figured we weren't going to be lucky enough to sleep through the night. I pulled my papers out.

The train slowed, then stopped. I sat back and waited for the border guards to come through. Akcharla looked quizzically at me, and made a "Let's go!" gesture.

The exit stairs seemed even steeper without a platform to step onto. We jumped down to the wet ground, followed the tracks to an opening cut in the chain link fence, crossed another set of tracks, then lumbered up onto the station platform. I went first, then turned to haul Akcharla up.

She said, "*Merci*."

Soon about fifty of us huddled under the eaves of the ancient station, trying to keep out of the rain. I saw only one other man I recognized as American. He was wandering around in a t-shirt, and looked very cold. Half of the passengers looked as if this was entirely routine for them. The rest of us stood around in various states of confusion and alarm, until a sleepy functionary wandered up and opened the passport office.

Once inside, everyone pulled out passports of different colors and waited in line. The official studied each one, then inspected the face of its bearer and asked a question or two.

All he asked me was, "Mary Ellen?"

Only my mother called me by my full name, and only when she was angry. I gulped and nodded. He looked at me for a minute more, then stamped my passport.

Back on the train, I wondered what had happened to Akcharla. When she finally showed up, she was laden with bags. She showed me cartons of Marlboros, three bottles of Johnnie Walker Red, and assorted boxes of chocolates. I don't know how she found a duty-free shop in that desolate train station when I couldn't even find a soda.

"You are amazing." I told her.

I imagined that her reply meant, "Yes, I am."

Now that I'd gotten my transit visa, I was ready to sleep. But when I lay down, she shook her head at me and said, "Passport Kontroll!"

I thought we'd just finished with passport control, but she knew the drill. Within ten minutes uniformed border guards moved through the compartments, confirming that each passport was in order and had a stamp.

The men looked at mine, and nodded. They looked at Akcharla's, and ordered her to open her luggage for inspection. She had a lot of interesting goods among the usual stuff: carded socks, packaged toys, bags of candy, and t-shirts. They pawed through it all, then re-closed her bags and moved on to the next compartment.

We stowed her bags on the overhead racks, but she kept one case on her lap: the guard had busted the zipper. I was indignant over the careless search that had broken it, but she just shrugged and tried to set it right. Finally, she sighed, gave up, and slid it carefully under her seat.

The rain pounded down harder as we sat and waited. Finally the train shuddered to life, clattering into

Bulgaria. I leaned back against my little pillow and took my shoes off. "Can I sleep now?" I asked her.

She looked puzzled till I made snoring noises, then she laughed, and said, "*Da*—sleep."

The narrow bed was actually comfortable, once I stretched out. The rain was pleasant, as long as I didn't have to stand in it. The rattling could be re-framed as rocking. I told myself, "This is the exotica you wanted. Relax into it."

I must have slept, though I also lay comfortably awake for periods, rocked in the arms of the dark old train.

By 8:30 A.M., Akcharla and I were both awake enough to sit up, pull the curtains open, and say good morning. I was hungry. She left the compartment and I poked around to see what I had for breakfast. I settled on pretzels and a few sips of water.

When Akcharla returned, she laughed at my offer to share pretzels. She opened a bag, pulled down the little table between us, and set out a feast: a loaf of bread, several boiled eggs, three types of cheese, a big cucumber and tomato, and black olives.

When she'd laid it all out, she said, "Eat!" I didn't know the Bulgarian word, but it couldn't possibly have meant anything else.

"Oh, I couldn't possibly," didn't fly with her. She repeated, "Eat!"

It was the best food I'd ever had.

"You are a goddess!" I told her in English.

"Yes, I am," she replied in Bulgarian.

She'd saved the best for last. When we'd finished and cleared away the debris, she brought out a bottle of Pepsi, an individual packet of Nescafe, and two plastic cups. The operation was complex, but Akcharla was a patient, determined woman.

She'd pour some Pepsi into the cup, then add Nescafe granules. The mixture would bubble and threaten to overflow, but she never let it. She'd wait for the foam to subside before she added more Pepsi or coffee. Finally, she had both cups mixed to her liking, and handed one to me. We toasted the sunny morning with warm, coffee-laden Pepsi.

She taught me the most important word in the tourist's vocabulary. In Bulgarian, "Thank you" sounds like "*Blah-go-dir-ay*."

The train crossed a plain, then started to climb hills that turned into mountains. Akcharla found a scrap of paper and drew me a map of Bulgaria and its mountain ranges. I asked her where she lived, and she drew a small cross to indicate her town.

As we went into one of a long series of tunnels, she tensed up.

"Claustrophobia?" I asked her. She didn't understand, so I mimed breathless anxiety. She nodded.

"Breathe," I told her, "keep breathing. Don't lose your nerve."

The words, I realized, were a quote from a Radiohead song. In the next tunnel, I sang it to her and she laughed her wonderful laugh.

Laughing at me seemed to keep her mind off her fear, so I repeated it whenever I saw her hand clutch at her collar in the darkness of a tunnel. I wondered whether the memory of a nutty American would help her laugh through tunnels of the future.

She got off the train at an isolated stop. The boys reappeared to help her with her seventy-seven bags, and we said goodbye. I watched through the window as a burly man and several dark-haired young women met her and took the luggage. One of the women had a new baby on her hip, but still managed to carry the bag with the broken zip.

She turned once and waved at me, before the group engulfed her.

With abandoned oil paints drying in their tubes in the closet and unpainted canvases in the hall, Mary Day Long fills the space with all the traveling she can manage, all the photos she can take, and all the experiences she can wrestle into words.

❒ ❒ ❒

Tsunami

In Thailand, a traveler comes face-to-face with death—
and the meaninglessness of "identity."

*L*eaving a trail of footprints in the sand, I walked bare-
foot along the water's edge to a thinly thatched bamboo
bungalow that I would call home for the next month, or so
I thought. It was early December 2004, and I was laden
with an overly stuffed North Face backpack worn thin from
carrying my belongings almost everywhere I traveled. Its
woven material had absorbed, just as I had, a unique fusion
of essences from Asia, North America, the Caribbean, the
South Pacific, and now Thailand. Constantly shifting the
straps on my back to find a comfortable equilibrium, I let
the texture of the sand exfoliate the soles of my feet and the
heat from the late afternoon sun radiate through my body.

With a slower than usual pace, I realized how undeni-
ably exhausted I was from the crowded overnight bus ride
south from Bangkok. The sleepless night was followed by

a longtail boat ride to Railay beach in a tropical downpour, and finally this twenty minute walk across the peninsula and around the point to Ton Sai beach, my final destination. Although physically fatigued, I was eager to experience the exotica of what was for me yet another unfamiliar part of the world.

I arrived at some bungalows set against a backdrop of limestone rock formations jetting fiercely into the sky. They stood in an idyllic corner of Ton Sai beach, overlooking the expanse of ocean that formed the Andaman Sea. I paid the owner for the first week's stay. She had one of those smiles that undoubtedly blessed whomever she shared it with. I dropped my pack into bungalow Number Eight, and quickly returned to the water's edge to watch the rain clouds dissipate and the sun dip lower and lower in the sky, tangerine hues reflecting on the ripples of water and vertical faces of rock. Enchanted by that moment, I spent almost every night for the next month in a hammock on the beach, watching the sun sink down and waiting for the stars to illuminate the night. This time was sacred to me, hailing the end of another day and the beginning of the next day, unknown and mysterious.

I had spent the previous three months in Chiang Mai, a populous city in the northern part of the country. There I was able to immerse myself in Thai culture and way of life, as best I could. But even though I felt at home in my metropolitan apartment on Nimanhamen Road, navigated the dusty congested streets on a five-speed motorbike, ate local spicy cuisine at the street markets on tables shared with ants, and spoke conversational Thai, I would always stand out as a *farang* (foreigner).

Now and again, I allowed myself the smallest familiarities of home. One afternoon, I sat indulging in a *café yen* (iced coffee) at a trendy Internet coffee house. While connecting with loved ones half way around the world, I sat beside young monks with cleanly shaven scalps and clad in their distinctive orange garb, playing video games during their free time away from the *wats* (temples). I had never witnessed such an extreme cultural juxtaposition. Here I was, a *farang,* enjoying a familiar iced coffee while more-over adopting what I thought it meant to be Thai, amidst a generation of Thai youth who were adopting what they thought it meant to be American.

Leaving the north and traveling to Krabi province in the south, I wondered if westernization was in fact encroaching on all corners of Thailand and whether or not it had the same effect on the people, dialect, cuisine, and livelihoods I had seen in the north. Was the increase in tourism growing their economy while destroying their traditions? Did the average tourist know their direct and indirect effects? Were modernization and tradition really clashing, or was it more of an amalgamation than I let myself believe?

On Ton Sai beach, I settled in comfortably in my thatched dwelling amid the majestic limestone cliffs, white sand beaches, and translucent aquamarine abyss. I explored the region's natural beauty both above and under water, easily falling into the rhythm of the ocean as it dictated a way of life for many of the locals. In the morning I heard the fishermen kibitz with their partners as they prepared to set out for the day. And in the evening, as the sun dropped toward the sea, I watched from my hammock their return with the day's catch. I learned that casting the nets from wooden longtail boats, both canoe style and non-motorized, was a traditional way of life that remained very much intact, even amid the insurgence of modernization, and was passed on through the generations. Each day, as I lay suspended by woven cloth above the sand, I felt a more intimate connection with the fishermen as we exchanged familiar smiles.

As the month of December waned, decorations for an "American" Christmas celebration were listlessly being strung around, adopting American culture and simultaneously appeasing one kind of Western tourist, at least, who seem to need the comforts and familiarity of home everywhere they go. Colored lights, plastic wreaths, and images of Santa Claus cluttered the naturally aesthetic coastline. The raw beauty to which I arrived, and the traditional culture I had been experiencing, were glaringly altered.

On Christmas day, carols were sung on the beach late into the night. I celebrated with friends at their bungalows on the other side of the peninsula—independent units elevated from the beach and shadowed by the limestone rocks. We sipped piña coladas and rum punches at the water's edge under the hot night sky. Although the rhythms of familiar tunes filled the air, I was somewhat nostalgic about previous "traditional" white Christmases in my hometown in New England. That lasted for only a moment before I simply let that spirit from home transcend to this continent and felt truly blessed to be sharing it with the people who inhabited it.

I awoke the following morning to a gentle tremor. Not knowing whether it was a dream or not, I didn't think anything of it as my friend and I strolled the dirt pathway down to the veranda where breakfast was served. The jagged limestone cliffs pierced the cloudless sky breaking the horizon. Rock climbers scaled the formations suspended by ropes and harnesses. Fishermen had already left for the day navigating their wooden boats across the familiar aqua expanse. Tourists settled into their favorite spots on the beach marking their territory with bright towels, folding chairs, and straw mats.

In no hurry for a beginning or end, my friend and I were later than most to start the day. We sat on the veranda enjoying the moment, sipping fresh pineapple juice, reminiscing about the previous night, and making plans for the day and upcoming night's full moon celebrations. The heat was palpable and the ocean was placid. There was not a breath of wind as the daily ferryboat to Koh Phi Phi left the shore and sliced through the calm water, taking passengers to explore what was boasted as one of the world's most beautiful beaches.

Suddenly, the ocean receded from high to low tide in a matter of moments. Although I've lived by the ocean all my life and know its rhythms well, I ignorantly commented that this irregular tidal flow must be because of the full moon that night. But before we could say another word, a wall of water appeared from nowhere, looking like an endless white cloud stretching the length of the horizon. It then took shape, becoming the most perfect wave I have ever seen. This mysteriously beautiful wave peeled from left to right creating a hollow barrel and expelling a white spray as it crashed on the contoured bottom of the ocean.

Before we knew what was happening, we heard a Thai woman yelling, "Tsunami! Tsunami!" in a tone suggestive of her worst nightmare. In seconds, the water violently enveloped the beach, taking everything in its way with a force only Mother Nature could claim. It stopped for nothing.

Without a moment to connect my thoughts with my body, I began to run from the unforgiving flood that was suddenly upon us, swirling and bubbling. Looking back I saw that nothing in its path was spared—it destroyed trees and plants, homes and buildings alike. I didn't think I could run far enough or fast enough. I didn't think the water would ever stop. No matter how deeply I breathed,

I felt like I couldn't get enough oxygen to my lungs. There was a moment when the present became incomprehensible and the textures of my surroundings changed and became surreal—smell, sounds, colors, shapes, and sizes blurred together as I ran to higher and higher ground.

I made it somehow to the highest peak of the peninsula, where others who had escaped the tsunami had all grouped together. There was a chaotic muddle of questions and conversations pierced by frantic screams and loud cries. People's faces held both the gravest fear and absolute disbelief. I knew that everything below us that had been in the path of this one wave and the vast ocean it carried with it, without any exceptions, was destroyed. We found comfort in each others' beating hearts and human presence; on some level we shed the skins of our inconsequential identities as Thai or American, young or old, Buddhist or Christian, rich or poor. We all connected as humans alike, having just moments before obliviously witnessed the largest natural disaster in recent years. I calmly held the hand of my closest friend, and we comforted each other, moment by moment.

We spent that night on top of the peninsula under the stars in fear of a second wave, as that was the science that was commonly known about tsunamis. Any unfamiliar sound that broke the night's silence alarmed us. People cried and became more anxious as plans for surviving the impending second wave were made. My eyes burned from trying to stay open, and by morning were glazed over having spent every moment of the night staring out toward the black horizon, just waiting—waiting for Mother Nature to display her force again. My emotions were numbed to a state I had never experienced before.

I can barely remember the events that took place after we knew for certain that a second wave was not coming and that our lives were indeed going to be spared. I do remember that it wasn't until I was at the airport when I realized the gravity of the event. I was accosted by a barrage of news clips on the television. The death toll was horrifically rising by the moment as the catastrophic destruction was revealed in Sri Lanka, India, and Thailand. Frantic people were rushing around asking if anybody had seen their particular loved one, their faces full of hope for someone to say "yes." The flags and representatives from foreign embassies were herding everyone to check in by their national identities. How meaningless "identity" seemed to me in the face of this event that stole so many lives.

The mixture of chaos, anxiety, and despair culminated in a cacophony that overwhelmed the conformation of Bangkok's Don Muang International Airport. I boarded the plane with the same North Face backpack with which I'd arrived. This time it was empty, with the exception of my U.S. passport, which I had left hidden deep within its seams. It had absorbed yet another essence: the combination of salt and sand from being caught by the tsunami. It was my only belonging that I found washed up on the beach amidst an array of debris. It lay, in a horrific wreckage of splintered bamboo that had once been my bungalow, where the ocean again had returned to its rhythm of gently kissing the sand.

Upon my arrival home I was surrounded by a palpable energy of love from my family and friends. Still, for a while I felt a lingering numbness and disconnect from the home and everything that had always been familiar to me. After what I'd been through, it was as if my soul literally needed to warm and my body to reawaken to the blessings of life. I had come face-to-face with death, and I had seen how quickly a person's identity, even the place we call home, can be rendered meaningless, obsolete, in one obliterating act of nature. I learned that we all, as living individuals, have the ability to transcend our cultural, racial, and religious barriers and just be humans breathing the same air, loving in the same presence, and leaving impermanent footprints wherever we may be and wherever we may travel.

No longer than a week passed before I booked my flight, and two weeks later I returned to Thailand.

Kira Coonley returned to Thailand just weeks after the tsunami to work on reconstruction efforts with Heifer International. Her background in anthropology and her spirit for travel have taken her around the globe. A passionate surfer, kayaker, and sailor, her respect for the ocean has only grown deeper after coming face-to-face with the tsunami. Most recently she sailed with her sister from Gibraltar to the Canary Islands and across the Atlantic Ocean to Antigua, BWI. Currently she is working with a women's travel company, Serendipity Traveler, in Rockport, Massachusetts.

≈ ≈ ≈

Solo on a Spare

Where's the line between safety and danger?

As I pull into the gravel parking lot of Wind River Sales, I barely notice that the place is almost deserted. My body is moving automatically, and my mind is focused on one word. *Tire*. It is only after I have killed the engine (and my Johnny Cash CD), and I begin to roll down my window, that my surroundings slam me hard: rows of random for-sale autos, desolate highway, a billboard announcing Thermopolis, Wyoming, and a half dozen men hanging around a shabby sign reading "Office." And now add me, a thirty-two-year-old woman wearing jeans and a white t-shirt, traveling solo on a spare tire.

My stomach tightens and I check the time: 4:30. *Shit*. No time for nerves. There are no other options. I am nowhere near home or my destination, this is the *first day* of my road trip, I have been turned away by the only two other mechanics in town, and I am fully aware that if Saturday is a hard day to get help, Sunday will be even worse.

The local who sent me here said, without smiling, "I guess you can try Ed's place on the edge of town." To me it feels like this place is *falling off* the edge.

I glance up at the billboard. It shows a family frolicking in a hot spring pool. I wonder where the hot springs could be located. As far as I can tell, Thermopolis consists of scorched ridges, rock outcroppings, and sagebrush.

My arrival is a distraction. The men, dressed in jeans, boots, and an array of pale work shirts, break from their slumped gathering, glance at one another, and fix their eyes on the spare tire adorning my rear passenger tire well. Nobody moves. My fingers linger on my door handle, and I catch sight of my wedding ring glimmering in the late afternoon sun. I swallow hard and tuck my hair behind my ear.

Suddenly, a skinny man in a one-piece navy blue jumpsuit appears in the doorway of the office, and he strides toward me. As he gets closer, I see that his nametag reads "ED." *Yes, Ed. Wonderful.*

But before I can speak, Ed does. "Honey, I can't help you."

I suck in my breath and stick my head out the window. "What do you mean?"

"Honey, I don't have tires that size." Ed's hair is black and slicked close to his scalp, and his skin looks like a piece of paper that has been crumpled up and then stretched taut. I have always wanted to be called "honey," but not like this.

"Maybe my tire can be patched," I offer, trying to sound cheerful. "I ran over something the diameter of a tent stake about thirty miles back. Will you take a look?"

Ed tries not to smile. He shrugs. "All right, I'll look."

In order to dig my bum tire out of the trunk, I have to unload all of my gear for the second time today: tent, sleeping bag, food box, backpack, hiking boots, swimsuit, and towel. I try to make light conversation while everyone looks on, about my hometown of Fort Collins, Colorado, and my husband and the hot springs that apparently exist in Thermopolis. But really I feel like I am being forced to turn the pages of a story I don't want to tell. My mouth feels dry from the effort.

In the chaos, I notice that one of my backpack straps is loose (oh no, don't let my underwear fall out), and I drop my keys on the ground and run over to fasten it. Out of the corner of my eye, I see Ed pick the keys up and slip them in his shirt pocket. My stomach tightens. Unsure what to do (what can I do?), I pretend not to notice. My story is laid out before me. I am surrounded by six strange men and a vacant lot, and it is clear that Ed has just moved his pawn and whispered, "Checkmate."

Ten days solo through Wyoming and Montana: that was the plan. Just me, my Subaru, and endless open road. The mere idea of the trip delighted my senses. A month before my departure I could close my eyes and hear the sound of rubber skimming asphalt, and the voice of Bob Dylan trembling through my speakers. I could see the sky punctuated by stars as I sat outside my tent at night sipping Fat Tire. I could taste a greasy hamburger in a dingy diner. I could feel sunshine on my bare shoulders. I could smell horses pawing the earth.

This trip would be all about freedom and romance and wonder. The desire to travel solo had always been there, burning deep inside me, and over the years I had found ways to half-heartedly meet the need: a three-month stint in Germany teaching English, a one-bedroom apartment in a notoriously bad neighborhood in downtown Minneapolis, an immersion experience in Oaxaca, Mexico.

But then I moved to Colorado, and I fell hard for the West and its symbols: evocative country music, the short stories of Annie Proulx, riding horses and the irresistible cowboys from the novel *Lonesome Dove*. I found a place to be fully alive—finally, a home. And the desire to explore and discover and dream only grew stronger.

Then I got married, which was a scary step for me, considering my tendency to roam. But Chris is a man who supports my independence and my adventures, and he smiles, nods, and says, "Go for it," when I tell him about my dreams.

"I'll be right back." Ed lifts his index finger and disappears toward his office, and I wonder (hope) that he is going to check into options for my tire. Patching, it seems, is impossible, and my tires have sixteen-inch rims, which is apparently not standard.

I want to call Chris; I need advice. But my cell phone has no service. I've been out of range most of the day. I silently curse Sprint and their stupid promises. I didn't even want a cell phone, but Chris told me it would save my life some day.

I stand in my small sea of belongings and decide that my best strategy is to re-load. As I am doing this, a too-skinny man in a peach shirt with the arms cut off struts over and leans on my trunk. His shirt reads "National Cowboy Poet Gathering." He kicks at the gravel with his boots, but he doesn't speak (or lend a hand).

To cut the silence, I ask the obvious, "Are you a cowboy poet?"

He turns his head and spits. "Nope, I just went to the gathering."

"Oh." I heave my backpack into the trunk and wipe the sweat off my forehead. My packing is sloppy, and I shove things toward the back to ensure that the trunk will close. I look toward the west. The sun is hanging low in the sky, but the air doesn't feel any cooler.

The guy smiles. "Me? I'm in the movie business."

I almost laugh out loud, but then I realize he is serious, and I look away to conceal my shock. Inside I cringe. *What kind of movie business operates in Thermopolis, Wyoming?* I don't ask questions, and I hope he won't elaborate.

Just then, Ed waves at me from the office door and beckons me over. It is a welcome distraction (at this point it's all relative). I slam my trunk. The movie producer grins and rests his elbows on my car, and I can feel his eyes staring through my shirt as I walk away.

When I told people I was planning this road trip, they mostly responded with blank stares and baffled looks. Women asked things like, *Who will you talk to? Are you really going to sleep in a tent? Won't you be lonely?* Men, on the other hand, focused on the practical. *Get your oil changed. Never tell people you are alone. Keep a knife inside your tent at night.* My response was always the same: *I'll be fine. I'm good on my own.*

I wanted to go for the sake of going, to travel 700 miles without feeling obligated to anyone in the passenger seat, to talk to local people and explore the rich history of the region and to operate wholly without an agenda.

I spent a lot of time arranging the details of this trip. As a person who prefers spontaneity, this was not easy. But I am a woman, and my life experience has taught me that my gender alone (beauty is irrelevant) presents a unique vulnerability. I'd be traveling through Wyoming and Montana, a "known *man's* land," and I was not looking to get laid, or lost, so I knew a plan, even a loose one, would be better than none.

Even Chris was impressed when I sat him down to discuss my preparations.

"I'm going to drive our sedan instead of the flashy red WRX," I said. "I'll be low profile, like an undercover agent."

"Good idea," he said.

"And I've got a map of my route, and lists of potential campgrounds. The oil is changed. I've got food, my cell phone, bear spray, and a knife. I'll keep all my weapons in my tent at night. Oh, and I'll wear a bra."

At this, he smiled and rolled his eyes, but he seemed satisfied that I was appropriately prepared for my little expedition.

So it was a bit of a shock when on day one of the trip, on a two-lane highway in desolate Wyoming, I suddenly heard a clanking sound on the passenger side of my car. My first instinct was to turn up the radio and ignore it. Unfortunately, the sound didn't magically stop, so I made myself veer off onto the shoulder. The sun was hot and high, and pick-up trucks were flying by like racecars. In the middle of the road, a crow was pecking at a dead rabbit.

As I stood on the passenger side of my car, listening to the air hissing out of my tire, wondering if I *really* knew how to change a flat on my own, all I could think was, "I want help, but I don't want help."

"Great news!" Ed is beaming. My heart leaps. Maybe he has found me a tire, and I can get on with my trip.

"There's a place in Cody that has a tire your size."

I open my mouth to say, "Great!" but then my excitement fades. Cody is eighty miles away.

"You're gonna need a place to stay the next couple of nights," says Ed. "And I was thinking. Honey, why don't you stay at my place?"

I step back. "What?"

I had already accepted the fact that I wouldn't make my destination, Meeteetse, tonight, but I'd certainly find a campground near Thermopolis. At this point, I was even considering the Holiday Inn.

"I've got a mansion on the river," says Ed. "It'll be just you and me, and you can set up your tent in the backyard or stay in the house. You'll be just as safe as if you were staying at your dad's place."

My jaw drops, and I am stunned that he is serious.

I know I need to remain calm. I look Ed straight in the eye. "I doubt my dad would agree with you."

Ed smirks. "Oh honey, I'm a good guy. Ask my friend, here." He points to a guy about my age who looks like he wrestles bulls 24/7.

"My friend's a cop from Casper. He'll vouch for me," says Ed.

The man strides over. "Ed's okay," he says, his mouth a rope-thin line. "You'll be safe." He crosses his arms. "If you want, I can show you my badge."

I squint. "No, thanks." I can hardly believe this is happening. *Do women really fall for this stuff?* I look over at the movie producer and wonder if I've ended up on the set of some bad B movie. But the movie producer is just leaning on my trunk, and his face is scrunched up, as if he is worried.

I take another step back. The image of the dead rabbit creeps into my mind.

I look at Ed. "Well, I'd better head toward Cody. Can I have my keys back?"

Ed fumbles around in his pockets, as if his fingers are made of spaghetti. He chuckles, as if he didn't even know he had them. But he does toss them to me, and I'm nothing less than ecstatic.

As I approach my car, the movie producer waves me over. He looks me straight in the eye. "Hey, there's a campground just north of town," he says. "It's run by a good Christian family. You'll be safe there."

He glances at Ed, and then back at me. Then he repeats his last sentence. "You'll be safe there."

A shiver runs down my spine, and I feel the full weight of the situation. My feet are cement, and my shoulders are iron weights. I take a deep breath, and I feel tears welling in the corners of my eyes.

"Thanks," I say, grasping for my door handle.

As I slide into the driver's seat, the guy walks around to my side. After locking the doors, I crack my window.

"Hey, why isn't your husband with you?" he says.

"Solo road trip," I respond.

He smiles. "You did good."

Carrie Visintainer lives in Fort Collins, Colorado. Her essays have appeared in various local publications. Carrie spends plenty of time searching for solitude in the mountains, where she gets down to life. A believer in whimsy, Carrie often "writes" from the seat of her blue cruiser bicycle.

❧ ❧ ❧

A Fare to Remember

Can food replace foreplay?

I wake up much later than I had planned on my last day in Italy. It is my first time ever outside of North America, and I am on the homestretch of my first real taste of travel in almost ten years. I commit to opening my eyes and see that Will, who will be my traveling companion from Florence to Milan, has already placed the last of his belongings neatly in his pack. I'm groggy from the previous night's debauchery, from which I retired just in time to avoid the capture and stealing of a life-sized Santa and the chase that ensued. I'm achy from sleeping on the wafer thin, twin-sized mattress of my hostel cot and, as is typical after a night of drinking, I'm famished. I take a quick, cold shower, and then Will, a seasoned backpacker, coaches me through the process of leaving behind the clothing, books, and shoes necessary to make room for things European that I have accumulated…and so I won't be quite so wobbly.

I have been freeloading my way around Western Europe for five weeks, staying in homes of people who I had met via hospitality exchange web sites in order to reserve most of my budget for splurges: namely, food. I come from a sophisticated breed of gluttony, and most of my strongest childhood memories are defined by the meals that augmented them. There were times during my youth where my parents were barely scraping by, yet they brought me along to fine restaurants and encouraged me to order whatever my "big eyes" found appealing on the menu. They were grateful I never really did like lobster.

Appreciation of good food is so deeply woven into my fabric that I knew I could never do something as big as my first trip to Europe without *really* doing it. Perhaps it's why I waited till thirty to wet my feet. I'm just not the kind to stand on the shore and not jump in. And how can you truly experience a milieu without *tasting* it?

My routine, up to that point, had been to hit the local supermarket upon arrival in a city and stock up on local foods. I packed bagged lunches for most days, and pre-pared at least one elaborate dinner for each of my hosts. I was very selective about what I treated myself to. In Brussels, my monies went to mussels and Chimay; in Paris, to Chablis, Escargot and Brie; in Amsterdam... well, we'll keep that in Amsterdam. In Rome, Mozzarella di Buffalo was my focal point. Perugian chocolate and Montefalco wine sucked up their share of my dwindling funds.

When it came to food, Italy was a whole other animal. In other countries, while their native cuisines dominated the restaurant scene, there were other options. You could locate a Chinese take-out in France, or a falafel joint in Holland. In Italy, there is *only* Italian food. I offered to cook a meal for Andrea, a filmmaker whose couch I would be crashing on in Rome. After my long day of exploring the inexhaustible outdoor museum of a city, I found that even the markets carried only indigenous foods. Although I was elated at the ingredients I had at my disposal and quite confident in my grasp of Italian cuisine, I cringed at the thought of any comparisons Andrea might make. But I stuck with what I knew, cooked my heart out and any anxiety I had was quelled by his mix of silence and contented groans.

"How do you know how to cook like that?" he asked after he'd practically licked the plate.

"I'm a born and bred New Yorker," I replied. "I've been eating good Italian food since I was in the womb."

As I made my way through Italy, each meal became a work of art. Breakfast was my only meal that never varied, as you can't really top starting your day by biting into a croissant and having warm Nutella ooze onto your tongue. Upon arrival at my hostel in Florence, I stocked "my" drawer of the fridge and "my" shelf in the communal kitchen with crisp arugula, gorgeous tomatoes, fresh mozzarella, basil-infused olive oil, local bread, big jugs of Tuscan wine, and a jar of roasted peppers. As I unloaded my grocery bag, I noticed that the other guests, mostly Canadian and American students, had loaded up on generic brand packaged foods. I was appalled. Who are these people? Don't they know they're in Italy?

On my trip thus far, I had only stayed in people's homes, and had become accustomed to hanging with the locals. Europeans have a deep respect for food, so I was always in my element, if not humbled by people who would be revolted by the thought of eating just for sustenance—or not eating for the sake of vanity—or missing a meal to a business call. I immediately knew what I had to do: latch myself onto the people who worked at the hostel.

As it turned out, Nino and Simon were more than willing to show me *their* Florence...its underbelly. Simon was a self-proclaimed chef, and he let me tag along on his excursion to the massive market next to the Duomo, packed two stories high with food stalls proffering fresh produce, handmade pastas, and cured meats. If I were a guy, I would've had a hard-on. That morning, cognac and hashish got added to my pastry and espresso breakfast.

After eating Simon's O.K.-at-best meal off the cigarette-butt- and dog-hair-covered kitchen table in his apartment, I realized I should probably pry myself away from these environs before I missed Florence altogether. I mean, I love grit, but not as a trade in for The Boboli Gardens and The Uffizi Gallery.

So I sucked it up and did the tourist thing with my dorm mates at the David Inn. And it wasn't so bad. In fact, it was kind of nice to take in a monumental piece of artwork and have someone to discuss it with. They were all a little too budget conscious to spring for any of the cheap, abundant wine, so I bought some more and shared it. I didn't offer up any of my bread, as I have an almost dog-like territoriality about food. So I just enjoyed the flickers of envy in their eyes as I ate my Caprese salads in the hostel kitchen, licking my lips for extra effect.

By the fourth of my six days in Florence, I was ready for my big meal out. I could have dined out solo, just as I had been doing...but a big Italian meal alone just wouldn't be right. The *perfect* Italian dining experience needs a little love. It requires hands in other people's plates. It entails talking with mouths full, elbow rubbing, eye contact with someone tasting what you're tasting.

It took me an entire afternoon of half lecturing, half whining to convince my new cohorts that a proper Steak Florentine really *was* necessary. I had wrangled up six reluctant backpackers, promising them no more than a twenty-euro meal. We were just getting ready to leave when Will showed up.

He was about my age, dressed simply, but well. With a quick "what's up" he sat down in a corner of the room and began to unpack his necessities. Knowing the sluggishness of Italian trains, I suspected he must be a man in need of a meal. Eager to spread the food love, I asked him if he wanted to join us for dinner.

"Hell yeah. Just let me wash up."

From that moment on, it was as if Will and I had become chaperones on a class trip. Neither of us had been to Florence before, but we walked ahead of the group with conviction and perused menus with critical eyes. We finally agreed on a tourist-trappy spot that offered a three-course meal with wine for eighteen euros.

Will and I guided the ordering process and watched proudly as our protégées *oohed* and *ahhed*, sopping up sauces with bread. However, we were both aware that this meal, as far as Italy was concerned, was child's play. As we walked slowly back over the Ponte Vecchio with, but separate from, the rest of the group, Will whispered to me, "We can do better. Tomorrow night we'll find a *really* good place and go to town." Our friendship was a done deal, sealed with marinara sauce.

After spending the day apart—Will had been traveling for quite some time and had to attend to life management stuff and I had some watercolors I needed to play with—we met up for a sunset at the Michelangelo Piazzella. Our life stories unraveled with the sky's light, words and laughter spilling forth with ease. Our perspectives on almost everything were uncannily similar. Then, the conversation started to go "there," and it came time to disclose my boyfriend of nearly two years, Gregg, who was to meet me in Barcelona, my next and last city. As the cosmos would have it, Will was also headed to Barcelona. We were both leaving out of Milan; he by train and me by air, and we had the entire next day to get there.

We went to freshen up at the hostel and ask Nino for directions to his cousin's restaurant. We were met in our room with shouts of recognition from Richie, a blustering blond Aussie, and Danny, a brooding Mexican-American filmmaker. Will had met them in a hostel in Rome several days before and, based on the slaps on the backs and guilty snickers, I assumed they had done some drinking together.

And then we were four.

We stuffed our faces and probably made the restaurant doubt their all-you-can-drink wine policy, then we hit the nearest piazza and fed each other gelato. Then came the bar with one euro shots, where Will and I decided on an 8:30 departure to Pisa. I'd masqueraded as "one of the guys" for long enough to know to get out when night had peaked. So I ducked out just before aforementioned Santa incident and now here I was, disoriented and lethargic, yet knowing the early start would be worth the extra time spent in Will's company.

My repack cuts into our time, and we have to jet to the station. Will makes fun of the bounce the backpack adds to my walk and I fix his tucked-in pant leg. He is beginning to look a lot like trouble for my already deteriorating relationship. We hustle into the Stazione Santa Maria Novella with just enough time left over after we buy our tickets to grab some food for the train.

We spot it at the same time. We lock eyes and look away, guilt washing over us both. This is the kind of epicurean crime that neither Will nor I would normally commit, yet we are drawn forward. We hang our heads to avoid being seen and traverse the marble between the ticket machine and those dubious golden arches.

As we stand in line, we whisper a pact to never disclose to anyone that we so much as set foot in this wretched place. We order OJ, coffee, and Sausage Egg McMuffin, then race to the platform to find the track empty. There is a message on the departure board next to our train time that simply reads: *REPRESSO*. Overconfident in our translation skills, we assume this means delayed, and we plop down next to our packs. By this time, our hunger outweighs our shame and we rapaciously unwrap our sandwiches and bite down. Will's face almost reflects my own disgust. I chew slowly; swallow reluctantly.

"What kind of meat is this?"

Will simply shrugs, that "whatever" type of shrug that only guys are capable of, and then quickly devours the rest of his sandwich. I, on the other hand, can only manage to get through two more bites of what is, perhaps, the vilest thing I have ever tasted.

An hour passes and the next train to Pisa is also "represso," and we discover that this means "cancelled." We poke our fingers around on a map for a few minutes and come up with Bologna. The train leaves in four minutes. We bolt to the platform, tickets to the wrong destination in hand. Will whips out a little broken Italian and a little more of his unadulterated charm and talks us onto the train for no extra charge.

The ride is quick and we make use of it well, arrive in Bologna another three years into our friendship. The weather is fantastic and the quaint little city welcomes us with open arms and a giant flea market. I do a little dance inside until I remember that unless you've got a ring on your finger, it's not that easy to rope an American guy into browsing the racks. But give him a blue ribbon, because it turns out my boy likes to shop. Will is in the market for a snakeskin belt and a pair of red sneakers; me, for anything under thirty euros that looks like it belongs in my world. We find none of the above and head to the city center.

We come upon the open square, framed by outdoor cafés. The cityscape is punctuated by two buildings that are humbly reminiscent of the ones recently robbed from the cityscape in my hometown. We wander past the terracotta archways and aesthetically wonderful buildings that line the streets, both entranced by the play of sunlight on the rich colors. We pick a spot, I share my art supplies, and Will and I experience something that rarely exists between close friends, let alone practical strangers: a shared, comfortable silence, which lasts until it is broken by the grumbling of our stomachs.

Now here's a pickle. Two foodish, indecisive people coming down from bad McDonalds, with only two meals left in Italia, trying to pick one of the gazillion cute little cafés we've passed. We hastily settle at a table on an outdoor terrace. A waiter greets us as we open the menu—way out of our budget. We apologize and get up, walk around the square several times and settle on another, more affordable, place. We order drinks and study the menu, and then the food arrives at a neighboring table. "Bullshit tourist food," we agree. We apologize to yet another server, pay for our drinks and exit the café.

By this time we are so hungry that our standards slide from snobbish to sensible, and we find an indoor, cafeteria-style joint that looks promising. We both order the spaghetti bolognaise and the house red wine on tap. It's not until we're halfway through our meal that we glance up at each other and shrug. The flavor of the sauce is way off, the bread is stale and the wine is crap. We are not as disappointed in the food as we are in ourselves.

We fill our train ride to Milan with animated discussions of our favorite films, our funniest travel stories, and endorsements of books that the other absolutely must read. We create playlists on our iPods and exchange headsets, write down all of our crucial contact information. We promise to hang out in Barcelona, and I assure Will that he and my beau will hit it off. The train compartment fills with a different breed of shared silence, one that is bloated with sadness, that toys with the idea of alternate realities, with "what ifs."

We have less than an hour to kill in Milan before Will's train departs. We're both aching for good food and we decide that, with our track record, it's best not to take any chances. We enter a nearby supermarket and purchase fresh rolls, an avocado, a ripe tomato, a hunk of smoked scamorza cheese, and a bottle of cheap wine. While looking for a spot outdoors to tackle our makeshift meal, we get a whiff of sauce from a small pizza stand and buy a slice to share.

With forty minutes left, we find a bench outside the station, inhale the pizza, pop open the wine and slug it directly from the bottle. We realize we have forgotten one crucial item…a plastic knife. Will, ever the boy scout, produces a Swiss army knife from his bag, and by the time we finish making our sandwiches, our hands are slathered in green mush. As we hunker down over our pizza box table and bite down, the wind kicks up about five notches, blowing apart the windshield of a Vespa parked nearby. We laugh as we dodge glass, pieces of tomato and breadcrumbs flying from our mouths, causing us to laugh even harder. It is here that we finally have that food moment…the kind you'd normally have in a four star eatery. That intense eye contact that says, "There are no words to acknowledge how good this is."

Although we are to meet again in two days, we both struggle to hold back tears when it's time for Will to board his train. Our love affair, in which we have substituted foreplay with appetizers and sex with entrees, has reached its conclusion. As I turn and walk away, the tears start to flow, and I glance back to see that Will's eyes have also grown wet and puffy.

Gregg and I do meet up with Will in Barcelona. The boys get along famously and Gregg, oblivious to any of the quick, mournful glances exchanged between Will and me, offers to treat us all to a proper meal. As we slurp oysters, sip Rioja and scarf down tapas, I wonder how the finest meal I've had in six weeks could possibly pale in comparison to a sloppy sandwich on a park bench.

Jen Sotham is a freelance writer and New York native, who currently teaches English in Busan, South Korea. Her words have appeared in New York Resident, *The Citizen Travel Guides, iToors travel podcasts, and she was a core food writer for* LIC Ins&Outs. *When she's not writing, teaching or playing guitar, she can usually be found with a mouthful of kimchi.*

TERRI TRESPICIO

ɷ ɷ ɷ

Out the Other Side

A pilgrim braves Hezekiah's Tunnel in Jerusalem.

*F*rom the moment I left it at the check-in counter at
Newark International Airport, I knew my bag wasn't
going to get to Tel Aviv. I kept looking back over my shoulder, blinking dumbly, as you do at something you may never
see again. So it was a confirmation of my worst assumptions
about chaos and human flaw when my oversized duffel
didn't tumble out with the rest of our group's luggage onto
the carousel when we arrived. At that point, having flown
countless hours and eaten only foil-wrapped salty foods for
the past day and a half, I was short on resilience. I started to
well up and then all-out sobbed at the inhumanity of it all.

Losing your luggage can be traumatic, especially on a
trip to a foreign country. Because you don't lose just your
luggage. You lose the one string tying you to anything
and everything that you know for sure exists: a yellow
hairbrush, a tube of moisturizer, sandals that have taken

on the shape of your feet. You don't lose your bag. It loses you. The system, the gods, fail you. And when your bag, that symbol of all you possess in the world, fails to appear, the string breaks, hurling you into the unknown.

For the first day or so, as I waited for my brain and body to catch up to the local time, I tried in vain to push the luggage-worry out of my head. I felt regret, though I hadn't done anything wrong. "It'll show up," everyone said. As if my wayward duffel had just taken the long way, made a stop in Paris, and that I shouldn't take it personally. Then the guilt emerged; after all, given the rare opportunity to travel so far, many would gladly go with just the clothes on their back, and not work themselves into a lather because they didn't have an alternate pair of shoes. I tried to assume a Buddhist posture of non-attachment. And then went back to pining for my hair gel. It was an extreme and tiring exercise in faith.

This, of course, was fitting, as I was on a ten-day study tour through the Holy Land, led by my uncle, Father Robert Barone, a professor at the University of Scranton. I was one of fifteen or so travelers (assorted priests, nuns, and lay folk) whom he'd handpicked for the journey, many of whom had made this trip before. I was twenty-four years old, and this was my first trip with my uncle, my first time to Israel. Being the newbie of the group, I kept hoping this was some kind of initiation, a Catholic hazing, and that as soon as I gave up my material longings, someone would come trotting out of the kitchen, with my duffel in tow. "You passed the test!" No chance. Not yet, anyway.

My roommate Arlene felt particularly sorry for me. Sweet Arlene, whose husband owned a sub shop outside Scranton, and who had arrived at the airport armed with a sack of ham and turkey sandwiches. She wore red glasses à la Sally Jessy and a soft blonde bob, and spoke in a way that made you believe she'd never done a careless thing in her life. "I'm so sorry about your bag," she whispered tragically, digging through her immense Samsonite. "I don't know what I'd do if that happened to me." She handed me a billowy flowered nightgown with ruffled sleeves straight out of Betty White's trailer on the *Golden Girls* (when I'm stressed, I go straight to my '80s-TV happy place). "I know it'll show up, sweetie. They always do."

We were staying at the White Sisters, a convent and rooming house run by French nuns who catered to pilgrims. Located just outside the Old City, it was, as you'd imagine, a clean, sparse setting: polished linoleum floors, tiny, hard beds, blank walls, a crucifix in every room. The White Sisters were warm and hospitable hosts, starched and scrubbed, with such a soft step they seemed to float through the halls. Here's how the days went: rise before dawn, mass in the garden at 6 A.M., and breakfast at 7 A.M.—a delicious meal of ripe tomatoes, warm, fresh-baked bread, cheese, jam, and cold cuts. Meet my Uncle Bob for a morning lecture tour in the Old City, return for lunch, siesta, and then out again in the afternoon.

One of our first and most memorable excursions was to Hezekiah's Tunnel, for which, without my blasted luggage, I was somewhat unprepared. We set out in the morning for the City of David, where the ancient passageway awaited. Dug by hand around 700 B.C., the mile-long tunnel runs beneath an ancient hill in Jerusalem called the Ophel Hill, transporting water from the Gihon spring to the Pool of Siloam in the southwest corner of the city. Two teams simply started digging toward each other and met up somewhere in the middle, led by the sound of each other's shouts. When Jerusalem was attacked by Assyria in 701 B.C., this tunnel (named for King Hezekiah) saved the city from destruction and capture by its enemies. With a constant supply of fresh water, the inhabitants could resist surrender, and not, as the Assyrians had hoped, get trapped "like birds in a cage."

I feared that we might very well get trapped like birds—in a cave. Did I mention that once inside, you're wading through water of ever-varying depths? That water levels may be at your knees one minute, mid-thigh the next? And no sign outside indicating that you must be "this high" to enter? My uncle, a large man at six feet, 275 pounds, with a bad knee, had gone through alone years before, with water up to his chin—something I wish he had waited until afterwards to tell me.

We walked a half mile to get to the tunnel through a depressing landscape, a littered and largely abandoned valley of scrap-metal shacks, and as we got closer, I instinctively started looking around for, I don't know, a ticket booth, some big fanfare, a bored-looking employee collecting stubs. But there was no governing presence to be seen. That is, unless you count the two questionable fellows slinking around the entrance selling t-shirts that read "I Survive [sic] Hezekiah's Tunnel." They flashed glinty, dangerous smiles and said they'd wait for us on the other end—"in case" we made it through.

We weren't the only people there for a little off-road adventure. A small cluster of Asian tourists—complete with backpacks, cameras, and hats—was collecting at the mouth of the dark cave, moving downward into the roar of water. You'd have to be crazy to go in there, I thought. And in we went.

This kind of unpredictable outdoor activity was the very reason I had packed the way I had, and without my suitcase, my efforts were all for naught. I fantasized about how much more ready I'd be with my own flashlight, amphibious footwear, and vaguely appropriate clothing. If the mounting anxiety about being in a closed, dark, water-filled tunnel wasn't enough, I looked and felt ridiculous. Lorraine from two doors down at the convent, a fellow traveler, had taken it upon herself to dress me, since we happened to wear the same size ("Well how do you like that!"). I had politely declined, but she'd insisted, and I was taking on the day's challenge in a pink-striped babydoll dress that she said was "just darling" on me. I looked as if I was about to launch into a rendition of "On the Good Ship Lollipop," not brave an ancient ruin. My shoes, a pair of imported blue rubber Chinese flip-flops, were a half size too small, on loan from Sister Margaret.

To get into the tunnel, we walked down a set of steps, but we couldn't see them beneath the cold, rushing spring. We had to hold the single handrail and feel our way down through the current. Absent the hot sun, the temperature dropped by ten or fifteen degrees, and the cool, damp air, while a relief, raised every hair on my arms. I stuck close to the front of the line with Ed, my uncle's former student and right-hand man, and one of the few people with a flashlight. And I tell you I have never seen darkness like that. Not during a new moon, not in a closet, not anywhere. Even Ed's flashlight beam seemed to get swallowed up by the inky black atmosphere. Because we were beneath the holy City of David, Bob said, we were essentially in holy water. I told myself no one could die in holy water. I didn't know if that was true. It didn't matter.

Walking proved tricky because I wasn't walking at all but rather wading through knee-high water on an uneven and rocky path, the hem of my silly sundress flapping with each step. Sister Margaret's flip-flops were clearly not up to the task, designed more for strolls on the boardwalk than offshore excursions. With each slip over the stones, the hard rubber jammed into the webbing between my toes and threw my balance, but luckily there wasn't anywhere to fall. I could flatten my palms against the walls without fully extending my arms. In some places, the ceiling hovered just inches above my head. For the claustrophobe, it was the kind of scenario you might spend a lifetime trying to avoid.

While I struggle with my own long history of generalized anxiety, I'm not a textbook claustrophobe. I stride into elevators or tight spaces with relative ease. But I do consider myself somewhat adventure-averse—and I'm a lousy person to have around at an amusement park. There's something taunting and horrid about their manufactured thrills, and even as a kid, I felt no desire whatsoever to strap myself into a plunging basket or a perilous, zipping tube. But while this tunnel walk was more vigorous sightseeing than amusement ride, they had one thing in common: once you started, there was no getting off until it was over. There were no exit signs, and no way out; turning around was not an option. Which made this little jaunt through Hezekiah's tunnel fairly metaphorical. Here, as in life, there was just no going back out the way you came in.

Given that this was a pilgrimage to the Holy Land, I expected sightseeing, academic lectures, interesting discourse on the roots of the Catholic faith. I even expected prayer—some internal dialogue, self-reflection. I did not, however, anticipate having an existential crisis that hovered somewhere between travel gear and fear of the dark. I wasn't sure if I was testing my mettle or indulging some *Goonies*-esque fantasy in which I brave feats of danger for buried treasure (and the '80s hits keep on coming). And I must confess: back at the tour bus, when I realized what I was in for, I'd downed half of a Lorazepam—just enough to stave off any disengaged moments of panic that might befall me underground. Faith could only take me so far.

And yet in many ways this tunnel was a testament to faith—certainly of the men who dug it in hopes of resisting their enemies. On this trip, I would go on to visit many churches, temples, and mosques, beautiful, awe-inspiring houses of prayer. But nothing came close to the kind of religious experience I felt moving through that narrow passage under the Ophel Hill. Ed snapped off his flashlight, plunging us into pitch black, like the inside of a velvet pocket. "Look at that," Ed said. "I mean, is this incredible or what?"

The rushing water was long behind us now, and the tunnel grew quiet, save for the drag and splash of our legs moving through it. No one spoke. For a few long moments we moved in silence, and the initial fear and disorientation fell away. I was strangely comforted by the notion that, even without a light to see by or any tangible idea of how far we'd come, we all knew where we were going, and that we weren't alone. What shoes I had on hardly seemed to matter.

Because of the twists and turns, there wasn't a sign of light until the very end, which took us about forty-five minutes to reach. I was used to walking a mile to the train station in far less time, but this wasn't a mindless commuter jag; it was a sacred delivery from one end of darkness to the other. And when the first break of light appeared, we cheered and yipped as if we'd been traveling for days. It occurred to me that this was the kind of experience every twelve-step program, ropes course, and trust fall aims to replicate, but I can't imagine any coming close. To be struck, then and there, with the realization that you would make it through, after all.

As we emerged, one by one, blinking in the daylight, we became giddy in the heat, and grateful beyond words. The spring water was a clear, jade green in the sunlight as it poured from the tunnel into the Pool of Siloam, where, as told in the Gospel of John, Jesus rubbed mud on the eyes of a blind man, and gave him sight.

Later, over vegetables that had been boiled to within an inch of their lives, we regaled each other with tales of our own fright and fearlessness. The front desk attendant interrupted the meal with an announcement. "Terri?" he said tentatively. I raised my hand. "The airline called. Your luggage will be here in one hour." And I was seized with such joy I leapt up and hugged him, which scared him half to death. A whoop of applause and laughter went up from the group, and for a moment we reveled in the peace that comes when things return to their natural order.

Back in my room, I opened my bag: there were my worldly possessions, just as I'd left them. And yet, I felt oddly disappointed. Not sure why—after all, what did I expect would be in there? The Holy Grail? Some sacred talisman? A treasure? Nope. Just some socks, extra shirts, my amphibious sandals, dry as a bone. A bottle of styling gel (which in truth I was glad to have). My luggage, in some ways, had become a moot point. And that night I slept soundly, in a t-shirt that smelled like home.

Terri Trespicio is an award-winning poet who earned her MFA in Creative Writing from Emerson College, where she also taught writing and editing. She currently teaches in the publishing certificate program at Boston University, and works full time as a senior editor at Body+Soul *magazine, where she also hosts a weekly radio show for Martha Stewart Living Radio on Sirius. After many years of traveling with her uncle, Rev. Robert Barone of the University of Scranton, she now happily tags along with her adventurous mother, Jeanne, a leisure travel consultant, in her journeys abroad.*

🪶 🪶 🪶

The Widow Dines Alone

A traveler revisits the Paris she knew with her husband.

*T*hree years and some months after Richard's death, I am in the rooftop restaurant of a pleasant small hotel on the Upper East Side of Manhattan. The view is a spectacular panorama of the East River, the Queensboro Bridge, the Roosevelt Island tramway, and the Manhattan skyline. The lights are dim in the room, emphasizing the lit skyline outside. I like the sleek urban black and chrome décor, the red accents. I am tired, relaxed, and happy to be here. I order a martini while I look at the menu. I'll have the chicken with artichoke hearts and mushrooms in wine sauce and a glass of pinot grigio. I'll look around and observe the other diners.

It's a weeknight in January, not crowded. A well-dressed African-American woman and her teenaged son sit at one table. They bow their heads briefly before they pick up their forks. A blond family in jeans, admiring the view, probably tourists. A group of businessmen and women gathered over drinks in the lounge area by the windows. A single man in a t-shirt and jeans, talking on his cell phone, eating a salad. Another single man, dressed in jacket and slacks, glass of wine and a finger food appetizer. The t-shirt and jeans guy goes out on the roof to smoke. Jacket and slacks guy makes a call, then leaves. I order coffee, reflect on my day, consider my plans for tomorrow. I am dining alone.

I remember the first time I was aware of a woman eating at a restaurant by herself. I was twenty-two, traveling in Great Britain with a woman friend. We were in a pleasant hotel restaurant in Scotland. A woman sat alone at a table, eating a meal. I was impressed. I had never eaten dinner at a restaurant by myself, wouldn't have even considered doing so. A woman eating alone in a restaurant, dining, not having a grilled cheese sandwich at a lunch counter, vaguely seemed to belong in the same category of accidental indignity as the woman my mother had warned me against, the woman who left the house with rollers in her hair and got into an automobile accident. But this woman seemed comfortable. I particularly remember the half-bottle of red wine she was enjoying. I never forgot her, though years passed before I ever had the occasion to eat alone in a restaurant.

Thirty years later, six months after my beloved husband's death, I was on a pilgrimage to Paris, visiting people and places that were important to Richard. I didn't want him to simply disappear after twenty years of visiting at least once a year.

I walked into one of our favorite restaurants in the neighborhood we considered our home away from home. It's an Asian restaurant, typical Parisian style: small, intimate, white lace curtains, no more than a dozen tables, mixed clientele of locals and students from the nearby American University. The proprietor, Kam Tin, has become a friend over the years, inviting us to his son's birthday party, offering assorted gifts to take home. On my birthday the previous June, he had opened a bottle of old cognac and joined us for a drink.

Kam Tin greeted me with a kiss on both cheeks, and looked over my shoulder for Richard. I took a deep breath.

"Kam Tin, I am very sorry to tell you that my husband has died."

"Oh, Madame," his voice was sympathetic, concerned. "When? How?"

Then he led me to a table in the back, the one next to the fish tank, the one where his family sits. Kam Tin sat down after pouring two aperitifs, one for me, one for himself.

"You are my guest tonight. We must talk."

Kam Tin was up and down that night, greeting his regular customers, but he always returned to my table. After he had opened a bottle of his best wine for me, his wineglass was at the place opposite mine. I stayed a long time, feeling cared for and comfortable. I will never forget Kam Tin's kindness. And from that evening on, I have never felt uncomfortable or lonely while dining alone.

Twenty years ago, before Richard, I was a young divorcee. Once-divorced and once-widowed, I am acutely aware of the difference in the two states. One is a single woman whether widowed or divorced, but I find that while both states require a level of self-sufficiency, the state of widowhood allows for more, rather than less, peace of mind. The divorced woman, I believe, has the matter of failure to overcome. No matter what the circumstances of the divorce, a marriage has failed. Being alone in a restaurant or especially a bar is a visible witness to that failure. There's an almost biological imperative to prove oneself capable of catching and holding another man. One is not in the restaurant to enjoy a meal, one is in the restaurant to make oneself available to men. One is hunting, or issuing an invitation to be hunted. There's tension always. I imagine myself back in the rooftop restaurant as a divorcee. The scene is the same, but I am restless, edgy. The two single men? Are they looking at me? Are they wearing wedding rings?

Kam Tin helped a great deal. He wasn't the only one, either. There was Alain, who simply kissed me, said, "You have a great deal of courage, Madame," and brought me my morning coffee. There was Michel, who asked about my friends in the south of France, and suggested excursions to gardens he knew I would like. "Don't be afraid," he said. And, "I can see your husband's smile in my mind right now." One of the things I have come to like about dining alone is conversation with waiters and restaurant proprietors. Divorced, you're self-conscious and hoping for conversation with another, hopefully eligible male, patron. You don't want to waste your time with the waiter or the owner of the establishment. Widowed, if the conversation is reasonable and genuine, you're glad of it, whatever the source. Your goal is to enjoy a good meal in a congenial atmosphere.

Paris helped a great deal. Now, after a good and satisfying day of working at home, I'll ask myself: "What would I do now if I were in Paris?" Go out for a salad and a beer. So I do it. Or on my way home from a Sunday afternoon concert, I'll stop for a nice dinner at a restaurant with a view of the city skyline across the bay. Maybe even have a martini or a glass of champagne.

Do I bring a book? I say, loud and clear: NO. I bring a book to a café or coffee shop, where I go for the purpose of reading or working. A book at dinner is a mask to hide behind. It's braver, stronger, to simply sit and eat. No book. Besides, I've come to enjoy the opportunity to observe. When I was divorced, I was self-conscious, aware of being observed. Widowed, I can look around, even write down my observations.

Do men approach you? Yes, sometimes. I can take them or leave them, as I please. On a second trip alone to Paris, about a year later, I was once again having dinner at Kam Tin's. It was busy in the restaurant for most of the evening. Kam Tin spoke to me off and on, but didn't sit down. I was tired out after walking all day, enjoying my dinner, daydreaming. The man who had been sitting at the next table approached me, a British guy with a dark ponytail and a diamond earring, also eating alone.

"Would you join me for a drink in the neighborhood?" he asked. "I overheard your conversation with Kam Tin. My mother is also recently widowed. I hate to think of her eating alone."

"No, thank you," I said very politely, "I am comfortable here."

Kam Tin came over shortly afterwards with two glasses and the bottle of Chinese liqueur. "Why didn't you go for a drink with him?" he asked me.

To Kam Tin, I said sincerely: "I'd rather have a drink with you." To myself, I thought with some amusement: "What you should never say to a woman: You remind me of my mother."

Another thing that's easier about being widowed rather than divorced: You haven't lost your sense of humor.

Susan Butterworth teaches English at Salem State College and is an ardent traveler, reader, and writer of travel essays and literary biography. She firmly believes that nonfiction is an artful, creative genre as worthy of respect as fiction or poetry. So, for that matter, is teaching. Attentive reading and living are the practice; writing and teaching are the performance.

፨ ፨ ፨

A Life Together, Worlds Apart

Transnational lovers make the best of it.

The morning I leave, I wake at five, my belly churning with both dread and anticipation. I let the shower soak my skin, the heat loosening my limbs in preparation for my long trip. At 5:50, I glance outside and see the taxi sitting in the seeping light, the driver motionless behind the wheel.

It's not until I get to the airport that the churning in my gut lurches with unexpected intensity, and suddenly I have to stifle tears. It's more real now than it's been in the long months I've planned this departure, the weeks of back-and-forth in my head. I'm actually going now, tracing some uncertain arc over an ocean and two continents, voyaging across what feels like a whole new world, to a different life, trailing a lost one behind.

Twenty-two hours later, the last leg of my trip to Osaka almost finished, I pass through immigration, collect my bags, clear customs, then round the corner into the main terminal.

And there he is.

He starts towards me with a hesitant smile, his face moving in a sea of other Japanese people, some holding signs written in sloping English, others standing still and straight. His black hair and dark eyes blend with the others', but the familiarity of his face and gait stand out unmistakably to me. And then I'm huddled against his chest, this man I love, this one I've crossed a planet to see.

It's been six weeks since we've touched, the longest by far we've ever been apart, and the first time I've leaned into him since he moved back to his native Japan after a year with me in Boston. When I look at his face again, his tentative smile has broken into a relieved grin. It's a relief we share, not just—or even mostly—in seeing each other again, but in the assurance that we've not become too much like strangers, that our embrace feels comfortable. Somehow we're still bonded, even after this time apart, and even if the people we each call kin and the lands we call our own will always, inexorably, be foreign to the other.

It's this mixture of belonging to each other and being from worlds apart, this quandary of love and loss, that has made me hesitant to take this trip—and yet has also made my tie to him more visceral than any I've ever forged. Despite all the fears, our connection has endured, each embrace holding both the promise of loss and the pledge to soothe each other through it. Ours is a longing steeped in desire and alienation, merging and separation, so that my yearning for him comes like an echo from some inchoate state, where self and other coexist in a peace made fiercer by the inevitable severing to come.

In the months before he returned to this country where he wants to grow old, I anguished over whether just to cut contact or stay in a relationship that feels safer than anything I've known, but whose logistics loom like a sharp cliff from which one of us may have to push the other. And eventually, to my mother's horror, I, a thirty-eight-year-old woman, a nice Jewish girl from the suburbs who should be fretting over her biological clock, not winging her way to the land of a former Axis-power, choose the latter. I decide to go to Osaka to explore the possibility of living there and building a life with a man who calls a world apart his home.

I had met Toru fifteen months earlier, on the second day I ever set foot on the Asian continent. It was in a graduate program for executives that included a short module held in a corporate training center in Kobe. He was a student and I one of two professors, although a professor years younger than almost all the businessmen in my class. The night before I traveled to Japan this first time, to teach in this program, I lay awake for hours in my apartment in Boston, listening to the sounds of ambulances going by, cars rushing past. As on most nights, my mind turned in its tussle. I am an eternal pessimist, a Jewish American who grew up watching live footage from the Holocaust, the horror of those black-and-white films indelibly carving itself, in some emotional or existential way, into the skin of my worldview.

And so on this night, my mind did what it always tends to do: dwell on every possible disaster, from the local to the global. With every sound of tires on the road or ambulance's wail, I thought of all the potential misery waiting at their destinations. A crash victim dying on the way to the hospital. A crying lover, swerving down the street after some late-night desolation, the betrayal that always comes. Next door, I imagine the TV on, scenes of genocide in Darfur burning the pixels on its screen.

Just before I slip beyond consciousness, I dwell once more on this first voyage to Japan I'm about to take, remembering stories of my grandmother's youngest brother, the nineteen-year-old soldier who died off the coast of its southernmost island in 1945. Across my brain skid pictures from the tangled history of that war, of our two countries, of our allies, sins, and sufferings. Eyeglasses from the victims at Auschwitz pile on a floor; a bomb billows over Hiroshima; Japanese soldiers bayonet Chinese prisoners in Nanking; Okinawan citizens jump from cliffs as American forces arrive. Eventually these images fade too, and the lights go down on this mental scrim of misery that teeters just beyond the brink of my privileged, twenty-first century American existence. Then I slide fully into sleep, a deeper but gentler darkness.

When two nights later I meet Toru for the first time, I notice him immediately, not for his sharp-cheeked beauty or black-pooled eyes or honey skin, but because his hair is so spiky. It's not until I've spent a few days watching him move, tilt his head slowly in thought, search through his computerized dictionary for translations to English words, and smile gently, that I realize I'm drawn to him. He has a quietness about him, a calmness, a lack of apparent freneticism that seems soothing, even though we've barely spoken one-to-one. I confide this small crush to a co-teacher, and we gossip and giggle, then go to our own rooms and fall asleep.

I don't remember exactly what I dreamt that night, but I know it was about Toru, and there was comfort and warmth and shelter in his presence. I woke feeling not so much excited as calm and safe. And my first thought was, "I'm in love. And for once I'm not convinced it will end disastrously."

Eventually, we spend more time together, sneak off separately one weekend to Kyoto but meet up and spend it together. We keep our relationship a secret, and during the week, when we have classes and live at the Japanese corporate training center, we are alone together very little. But on weekends we get away, lying entwined for hours. One night, he stirs in his sleep, and I wake and tense, get ready for him to cry out, wonder what sort of nightmare he's having. Instead, he laughs, chuckling at some phantom dream joke. And I'm astonished. This is a man who laughs in his sleep, I think, amazed. In the inky black of night, he doesn't dream of Nagasaki or Birkenau; he giggles.

And so he comes back to Boston with me for a year and finishes his graduate program there, and then, when his mother is killed in an accident and his father is left alone, he goes back to Japan. And despite all my certainty to the contrary, he convinces me that there may actually be a way to work out our international relationship, and I should at least come to Osaka, where he grew up, for a visit. We spend a month together there, eating tofu and tempura, adjusting to our first extended experience of him being at home and me standing out as "the other." I watch the ease with which he moves through crushing crowds, shoots off rapid, sharp-edged syllables; he sees me search street signs for the curve of a letter I can recognize, bow stiffly to strangers, and gaze wide-eyed at trucks that buzz the streets like toys, fire engines one-fifth the size of those at home.

One evening, his aunt and uncle hold a dinner for me, a special honor to welcome me to their city, their home, perhaps even to their nephew's heart. This is a rare privilege in Japan, this country with houses so small and boundaries so cherished that rarely is anyone other than family welcomed. After dinner, which his aunt serves while barely taking a bite herself—she jumps up constantly to bring another course, pour more tea or sake, adjust the stove's heat—she walks us to the door. And then, before we step into our shoes lined neatly in a row, she drops to her knees and bends so low her forehead grazes the floor.

I bend with her, because I think she's dropped a contact lens, or perhaps cut her toe on some piece of jagged glass. "Stand up!" Toru whispers hurriedly, yet it takes me a few seconds to fully understand that she is bowing, not searching for something missing or staunching a wound. And so I wait uncomfortably for her to rise, certain that when she does, she'll stand with shame etched across her features—shame that as a woman she's expected to bend so low, to curve her aging body in self-effacement until she's eyeing nothing but her blank and spotless floor.

Yet instead, she straightens in a fluid sweep, her limbs agile, her movements graced with tranquility, and on her face, a gentle yet fierce pride: pride that she has welcomed me to her house, that she has given this honor to me and her nephew—her dead sister's only son—and herself. Proud that this is her culture and her home and she has welcomed me so beautifully to it. And I realize, as I will again so many times in this land a hemisphere away from my home, that my feelings and judgments map imperfectly here, that I can no longer use them so fluently to circumscribe experiences with meaning. I feel lost, yet also strangely released, freed for the first time in my life from the expectation to navigate the world and its dimensions with acuity, to anticipate it slights and wounds and guard against them.

That night when I sleep, I dream I find Toru on a cold, wooded stretch that's unfamiliar, the forest's unknown shadow slicing a dark edge along my path. But instead of turning back, I turn towards him fully, and he extends his arm to me, a whole new world in the dip of his smooth palm. And because he holds it in his steady hand, that world seems warm to me, its orbed heat welcoming me in.

When I return to Boston, Toru comes two weeks later for a holiday, and then I'm back in Japan again a season later, this time for four months, and then again a quarter of a year later for another extended stay. I learn that in Japan, they have a term, *tanshin-funin*, that roughly translates into "single-married-person-who-moves-for-work," referring to husbands and wives who live apart for much or even all the year, one (usually the husband) in a distant location for his job.

And eventually, this is the life we decide to try, molded into a version that fits our resolve to be together with my desire to be at least part-time in Boston. I have lived all of my life in this Northeastern U.S. city—have never known any other home—and I cannot imagine feeling grounded in any other place. But I also cannot imagine feeling grounded with any other man. And so I will, I tell friends and family, try being a new kind of bi: bi-continental. Six-to-eight months a year in Osaka, four-to-six in Boston.

"Give it a try, at your age?" my mother asks, alarmed. "You'll be almost forty after you experiment like this for just one year," she points out. "And how will you have children if you spend six months a year alone in Boston? You'll be a single parent half the year and a foreigner the rest," she warns me—and she's right. "And if it doesn't work," she continues, "if it falls apart—and in my world, spouses do not plan to live half their lives apart; it's a sure recipe for disaster—what will you have then?"

The answers, I must confess, are "not much" and "I don't know." My mother's warning is now three years old, and as of today we've lived together, and apart, for almost sixteen seasons. We've both grown to love this lifestyle, this ability to have a home together while maintaining time and space just for ourselves. But if our satisfaction with the arrangement wears off? If our seven-year itch starts to feel like the chafe of some frayed rope? What then? It's true that I'll have, in that case, to adjust not just to the loss of a great love, but to leaving a country that has already started to seduce me. If we break up, I'll probably be too old to have children with someone else by the time I've nursed my broken heart back into a state strong enough to give new passion a try. And if we stay together, we may have to forgo offspring altogether, my not being, I fear, the single-parent-even-for-a-day type. I have no map for a relationship like ours, no compass that can show me where the road will lead a decade down the line, no one to tell me, from personal experience, what the odds are in a partnership whose contours skew like ours.

But I know one thing for sure: if we don't try to build this life together—and episodically estranged—I'll regret it forever. And perhaps this is the only assurance we can ever have in life or love: the assurance of what we'll miss, not what we'll have or what will happen. Ultimately, I reason, we never know how things will work. We never know if the new worlds we inherit every day, as the future morphs into the present, are worlds in which we'll be happy or sad, safe or in danger, lost or found. We never know if a risk will be worth taking, but we do know which risks we'll regret not trying, and which we can pass up. And for me, the answer to the former spans two continents.

So as I finish these lines, I'll turn off my computer, call my husband in Japan—who will be just waking up as I prepare my dinner—and print my boarding pass: round-trip to our home in Osaka, and then back again, four months later, to my other home in Boston.

Tracy Slater is a freelance writer and the founder of the Four Stories Boston and Four Stories Japan literary series. She lives part-time in Boston, where she teaches writing on the main campus of Boston University, as well as literature and gender studies at various prisons in Massachusetts through the Boston University Prison Education Program. She also lives part-time in Osaka, Japan, where she writes for the Asahi Weekly *newspaper, among other English-language publications. Tracy holds a Ph.D. in English and American Literature from Brandeis University.*

෨ ෨ ෨

Alive in Lisbon

The lights have come on, the night is falling,
life changes its face.
One way or another I have to keep on living.
My soul burns like a hand, physically.
I'm on the road of all men and they bump against me.
—Fernando Pessoa

My hotel is as I pictured it, simple with all the comforts: nice bed, private bath (with bidet and tub), phone, desk, and best: terrace and wide-angle view of the red-tiled roofs of the vast city of Lisbon. The light of late afternoon is soft-focus and otherworldly. At night circus/calliope rhythms reach my windows from a courtyard below, where a large group of teenagers practice a line dance, march, grapevine, side step, swing your partner, singing along in Portuguese.

Leaving in the morning on foot from the inn's hilltop

perch near Miradouro do Monte means following a wind-
ing path downhill through Graça and Alfama's narrow
neighborhood streets. Looking into doorways, walking the
cobbled alleys, I lose track of how to retrace my steps, and
can only go forward, on a self-paced stroll with no destination.

Glimpses of Tagus River provide orientation and I head
toward the water to gain my bearings. The beaded sandals work well on the stones, stable ground. Knee-length
skirt a comfort, glad to have sweater on turns into sudden
gusts. I walk along the wide riverfront boulevard toward
Municipal Plaza, and now I appreciate the comfort of
being where tourists are expected. The pedestrian shopping street, Rua Agosto, leads to Rossio Plaza and a stop
for *café con natas* at a sidewalk café for people watching.

I sit among street musicians, beggars, tourists, artists.
Here I am, author of a book on end-of-life ethics and the
right to die, whose publisher invited me to present my
story at four venues in Portugal, and agreed to pay my
flight and three nights hotel. I have no check in hand yet,
and I worry a little about everything.

I observe the Human Statue at work nearby his collection jar, standing on a high box, white garb draped at
length so he appears extra tall, in white face, white hands,
cloth wrapped like gauze, facial expression of a sad clown.
A crowd gathers, awaiting his act. But the act is simply
this: to stand perfectly still, be like Pessoa, no one, empty, a
blank canvas on whom the observer can toss a personality,
empty so perhaps a soul can appear.

At the corner: a mysterious figure seated on a doorstep—Is he wearing a mask? What does it signify? What
does he mean for us to make of it, to think?

A closer look reveals that it is his face, his actual face!
Visible purple and red tumors, bursting vessels that are

twice as big as his face, grow there obscuring his humanity.

Attempting to understand what I'm seeing, I catch his
eye, barely detectible amidst the unworked red clay of his
face.

He has eyes! He's human!

Not soulless like the white-draped statue, but fully present, and stricken by this disease, his fate, which renders
him a beggar. Who could love such a being?

I do, I love him, the eye connects his humanity to mine.
I drop a coin then join a stream of others passing by him
without seeing.

Later I describe him to my doctor hosts and learn it's
true there's nothing medicine can do for his particular
affliction. The society of neonatologists wants to know why
this is so: why do some newborns arrive with *anomalias*—
defects, predispositions, imbalances—that will render their
lives miserable or short, or both? Death is everyone's fate,
but the whims and will of expected natural order include
this percentage of chaos and extremes at the edges of com-
monness.

Doctors do not respond with the "why" of philosophy
or religion, they face off anomalies with science, analyze
statistics for where and why there arise clusters of experience, use microscopes to examine close-up the details of
the misshaped kidney, trace back in sonograms to which
prenatal period initiates the "wrong turn," present find-
ings in PowerPoint in darkened hotel conference rooms (as
outside the sun blazes, wind pushes air, waves pound the
rocky Viana do Castelo coast).

The audience takes notes. Where can the doctor inter-
vene to prevent this, or if not, to treat it, to right the
wrong? Research is assessed, conclusions offered: these are
the possibilities, this is what we might be able to control.

The rest—what is out of control—is not the subject of these meetings.

I'm introduced into the conversation to tell my story. My 1995 biography *Silvie's Life* was translated in 2006 as *Estar Grávida É Estar de Esperanças;* "Being pregnant is called expecting," the first sentence, is the new Portuguese title. I read from a chapter set in the Neonatal Intensive Care Unit (NICU), a place I call "God out of control," and the book says, "This is not supposed to happen."

My daughter's case was extreme. After ten days of tests, trauma, and assessment, doctors concluded she'd suffered severe brain damage and that death was "her best hope." Our task became how to accomplish this within the boundaries of law, morality, and our unbounded love for our newborn.

"I needed an explanation. No one could explain it," I read.

Does the distinguished lady doctor wearing the cross necklace cringe when I call God out of control? *Silvie's Life* wonders what kind of faith can allow for belief in a God who designs *anomalias,* or, if not designs them, permits them to exist? Belief that suggests this is part of our lesson here: imperfection.

Only God is perfect?—and perhaps even God is still learning.

The churches of Portugal are fortresses, walls three feet thick, interiors a kind of hubris, prideful reaching toward some perceived conferred power—priests' throne-like seats, bishops' tombs, velvet robes, worship-me rituals—I feel both awe and cynicism inside these monuments to power.

The University of Coimbra's grand plaza overlooks the city and river, and to step inside the ancient library requires an appointment. My group enters the temperature-controlled, sacred space with its ladders to high shelves, books in cages, grand conformity of spines and colors, grand depository of knowledge on medicine, law, physics, mathematics, the arts. Climbing through the buildings, the steps are unevenly sunken and slippery from thousands of footprints, weight of centuries; I can feel my fleeting presence and my permanent mark as well.

At Café A Brasileira in Lisbon, Portugal's most famous poet, Fernando Pessoa, appears as a bronze man in a hat and suit seated at a bronzed outdoor café table, with an empty seat where everyone who passes feels compelled to sit and pose for photos. I regard this parade: the traveler observes, the writer records these observations, the ordinary person wants her picture taken with Pessoa, and I hand my camera to a café neighbor, gesturing the shutter click as we don't speak the same language.

Then I enter the café and head toward the back to watch comings and goings. All is chatter, animated, relaxed, nothing going on that doesn't happen here on any given afternoon. I see four men in the front doorway, one pushes the other, who returns a punch to the shoulder, which causes the first one to stumble, then retaliate. Portuguese is tossed in the air, some insult or threat, and the four go at it, a regular brouhaha, and the patrons shout, stand up from their seats (myself among them), as the tinkle of breaking glass is heard—the mirror at the entrance? glass in the doors? port glasses at tables? A roar goes up, the waiters shout, one hurls a bottle at them, the bartender is on the phone to *Policia* as is the fat lady on her cell.

Outside, there's a row of sidewalk cafés full of people who leap up shouting as the men "take it outside," and proceed with the fight down the block.

Inside, the café settles into an excited bustle—Ah, how

the energy of the afternoon can change, the moment of
danger reinvigorates the ordinary; emotional tenor shifts.

We've just dodged "what could have happened" (one
pulls a gun, or the tumble falls in my direction; I am, after
all, trapped in the back of the café, the fight at its entrance;
we were all forced to witness and wait to see where danger
might strike, be prepared to defend our space and lives).
Everyone is shaking their heads, reliving excitement,
speculating, dismissing them as ruffians, laughing about
it now, fear gone and replaced with some new elation that
coffee and wine can't offer. Only the adrenalin of fear gives
this spark.

At my hotel I overhear the clerk, José Manuel, describing
his "problem child." Later, we get to talking and I show
him my book, "This is why I'm here."

(He speaks some English, I employ my little
Portuguese.)

Soon he is pulling pictures from his wallet, one of his son
now at age five, and the dreaded NICU shot with the newborn attached to all the tubes and wearing the too-familiar
cap and blanket with the same pink and turquoise stripes
used in the States.

I gulp. "Yes, my baby looked like this. But listen, her
situation was extreme. She didn't live."

His baby, his boy, lives, and his problems will be ongoing (I don't diagnose but it sounds like autism, or obsessive-
compulsive disorder; José Manuel says *hyperactive*). He
and his wife disagree about how to respond, and I worry
for their marriage; I've been through all this, death and
divorce, and feel like I'm on the other side.

I point to Teresa Botelho's name in the preface, "Maybe
she can help you; she works with these children and families."

He has no faith in psychologists, he says, doesn't read books, but accepts my gift of the book, maybe for his wife.

On Monday morning I'm scheduled to tour the public hospital where Maria do Ceu Machado, who wrote the other preface, Alexandra Dias, my translator, and Teresa Botelho, all work. Dr. Machado heads the department of pediatrics and neonatology, Dr. Botelho leads the psychology team, Dr. Dias is a respected pediatrician.

Two young psychologists-in-training accompany us as we visit the children's library and playroom, staff offices, wards, and intensive care. We pass through waiting rooms for day service appointments, noisy with hordes of the needy, all races.

It is a squelching hot day and the hospital is not an air-conditioned place; the air is stifling with the smell of bodies, illness, fear. On the wards the smell of bleach and disinfectants; in the cafeteria, hospital food.

My hosts, used to the smells, the air, the sight of the needy hordes, walk past as if guiding me through a cathedral or museum, casually (kindly, respectfully) pointing out children with pneumonia, those with long-term care needs, one with possible lymphoma or is it edema that will respond to medication given one more day?

All is well, *tudo bem,* I'm in stride, O.K., until I'm invited in, inside, in closer, to see the newborns in their cubicles.

Alone in a blanketed cubby, there's Matilda, teeny, bruised, connected by wires, holding on by a thread, alive. Breathing!

I bend close to peer inside, a spectator, and feel ashamed for looking, for being on tour. Gulps of emotion are swallowed then rise like air as I cross the room to meet the young Portuguese mother lovingly hovering over her perfectly beautiful baby boy. He is so so small, desperately yet calmly attempting to live with his intricate hands and complex brain waves, internal organs striving to do their work of coming into life and sustaining life before he is fully formed and ready. He's been here three months so far. This mother has been here too, in this darkened room with the busy nurses, doctors, and monitors, in love with this new being, faithfully conjuring hopeful thoughts.

This is when I start to cry, seeing that young mother. Looking into the more dire condition of the fist-sized African preemie, grasping a hand in camaraderie with the stoic, broad mother, I mumble, "*Compreendo,* I understand," want to offer prayers, can offer only empathy.

As we exit, wells of old feelings engulf me as I fall, weeping, down the well.

My guides seem surprised and I am too.

"It's been eighteen years, I didn't expect to feel this way."

"You haven't been in a NICU since?"

"No."

Why would I?

I ran as far from the place as I could get, avoided thoughts of this becoming my life's work. Yet I wrote the book, and attention was being paid to the story, again, after all these years, and it is my work here now.

One neonatologist down the hall realizes it's me, the author, here in their midst, and hurries over, drops everything to catch up with me, to tell me, *this is an important book*—she read it last week on a plane—how meaningful it is for doctors to hear from the patient's side of the bed.

Someone has brought me tissues and I stand in the hallway crying and dabbing at eye makeup, as I try to absorb this praise. Aware I could sob all day, bottomless buckets even after all this time, I recuperate enough to move through the cafeteria line with these fine people, swallow a few mouthfuls of bad food, attempt to keep track of conversation about the newest baby in crisis.

My other appointment on my last day in Lisbon is at the offices of Gradiva Publishers with the formal Sr. Begonha, who has most efficiently arranged for my check.

Generous Sr. Begonha inquires how I'll spend the rest of the day.

"Wander the neighborhood, drink coffee, process everything that's happened."

He locates a city map and highlights his recommended path to tranquility, then walks me to the corner and his favorite café, points downhill to Jardim da Estrela (beautiful, shaded benches to rest on, gazebo, wide walking paths), and beyond to his secret garden—Jardim Botanico, an oasis of palm trees, labyrinth hedges, giant-root ancient *arbols*.

There, in the silence at the center of Lisbon city, I will find a shaded bench and release all my tears, shed mascara, snot, façades of composure.

I'm crying for many reasons, I realize, not least my pleasure and shock that my deceased baby girl herself has led me here, to this dark green garden. Silvie, her fictional name, means *sylvan,* green dark forest.

Aha.

Her mother smiles at the image of herself weeping wetly in the garden in the city, blows her nose, wipes sweat, persists in walking through the heat onward toward the rest of her life.

Back at the hotel I pay my bill with the Gradiva check, shy around José Manuel.

Business settled, he says, "I read your book today."

"You finished it?"

"Yes. In three sessions. I had to stop when guests arrived of course, and when I had to cry."

His experience was exactly the same in the beginning, he tells me, it brought all the memories back.

"But of course my son is alive, and for that I can be grateful."

Guests come in and need his attention.

He nods to me, embraces my hand, and I bow good night.

Boa noite.

I ride the elevator to the rooftop bar and buy two bottles of water to drink in my room while I ponder the nighttime view.

Outside, the calliope dance loudly proceeds.

Marianne Rogoff's true story "Raven" was selected for Best Travel Writing 2006. *Her 1995 biography* Silvie's Life *has been optioned for movies, adopted for ethics courses, and translated in 2006 by Gradiva, Lisbon. She has published numerous short stories, essays, and book reviews, and teaches writing and literature at California College of the Arts in Oakland and San Francisco.*

🐚 🐚 🐚

But I Only Wanted One Photo

Behind every picture lie a thousand words—
well, two-and-a-half thousand in this instance.

"Now we're *really* in trouble!" said my driver, a tall, lean ni-Vanuatu, native to the island of Tanna in the South Pacific island nation of Vanuatu.

I thought he was joking. I really didn't believe the torch batteries had died and we were stuck on the side of a crumbling cliff in the middle of the Tannese rainforest on the side of an active—*very* active—volcano, in the wee hours of a wind-swept, coal-black night, with neither spare torch, battery, nor match between the four of us.

"Sorry missus. No joke." It had been a bad night for batteries. In fact it had been a bad day, period.

Like most things, it had begun simply enough. A printer in Singapore had lost one of my favorite photos and the client wanted a replacement shot as similar as possible. The photo was of a young Tannese girl in the famous Toka ceremony's Women's Drum Dance, during the "night of free love." I had more or less risked life, limb, and what remains of my long since shredded virtue to get the photo, by weaving through over a thousand adrenal-hyped, near-naked, stomping Tannese males surrounding the women. After suffering more than just bruises in all the wrong places, I was almightily peeved when the printer sent the bland apology and request for just one replacement photo. That couldn't be much trouble, could it?

A few days later, a friend and fellow photographer called to tell me that a major circumcision ceremony would be held on Tanna in a few days. It wasn't a Toka ceremony—they only take place every six or seven years—but I'd get some good portraits and maybe one photo of a young Tannese girl in full make-up, dancing.

As with all traditional circumcision ceremonies the world over, in Vanuatu this is the most important ritual in a young man's life. Leaving the things of childhood behind, they take with them into the jungle nothing more than a half coconut shell provided by their mother. The shell is for food, for their uncles will provide them with all their other needs. Living in the jungle for up to three months, the boys learn the secret ways of men and, at some point, have their foreskins removed. If a boy dies during circumcision, from bleeding or infection, the mother is wordlessly handed back his bowl—broken.

Fortunately such deaths are rare these days, and when the boy emerges from the jungle following his initiation into manhood, a full day's celebrations follow. Mothers give gifts of food, kava, baskets, mats, pigs, and other goods to the uncles in an elaborate and colorful ritual. Each bundle of gifts is laid out in the grounds of the *nakamal*. As the boy—now a man—emerges in traditional face paint and not so traditional but extremely colorful decorations, the gifts are taken and pigs killed with an almighty wallop to their heads. Platters of *lap lap*—taro and yam mixed with coconut milk and baked in banana leaves—are broken open and served to all, starting with the very serious young men, some of whom are no more than four years old. Each man-child proudly wears a *nambas*—penis sheath—to proclaim his manhood. No more will he run naked with the children.

Interestingly, circumcision ceremonies do not take place when a boy reaches a certain age. They are purely a function of wealth and only occur when the mothers can afford the necessary gifts to the uncles. Following a cyclone or severe volcanic ash rains that ruin gardens, it can be years before a lad's circumcision can be sponsored.

So my fellow photographer and I flew down to Tanna in a mad rush. We spent the day being broiled by the sun on the ash plains around Yasur volcano (guess who forgot the sun cream). I lost a tripod into the bowels of the earth following a particularly violent eruption (I should know better, that's the second time that's happened) and later wrote off a couple of lenses when we were showered in a particularly nasty sulfurous ash rain. Finally, at about 3 A.M. we conceded we had become totally lost on the craggy slopes of the volcano while vainly searching for our "taxi" driver, who had long since given up and gone home. On the upside, I managed to get a couple of nice dawn photos over the volcano, one of which was sold to *National Geographic*.

However, by the time we arrived in the village for the boys' "coming out" ceremony, my companion had come down with malaria—probably as a result of the previous night's volcanic forays. I ended up spending the day scraping caked ash from cameras and fetching countless half coconut shells of water from a nearby creek for my fevered fellow photographer.

So much for the photo.

About a month later, the same photographer called to tell me he'd just heard about a huge Yam ceremony on Tanna. I agreed to go on the condition he take a *very* large bottle of chloroquinine tablets.

I'd just checked in my bags at the ticket counter, when my photographer pal, standing in the line behind me, opened his hastily collected mail, took one look at a bill and decided he couldn't go. He grabbed his bags and rushed out of the airport.

Now, that should have been sufficient warning, but I was still half asleep—it was 2 A.M. and we were catching the redeye flight—my bags were checked, the line behind me was getting longer. By 8 A.M. I was standing in the middle of the *nakamal* grounds talking to an old chief.

"Yam ceremony, oh yes! Sometime this month," he said with a toothless smile. "Yes, definitely this month! Today? Oh no, nothing today."

Never travel with French photographers who get malaria and nasty bills in the mail.

However, being a Friday and being Tanna, there was a reasonable chance of finding some sort of *kastom* ceremony or dance somewhere. All I had to do was wander around the only post office in the only town, Lenakel, and ask enough people. With a bit of luck...

Sure enough, about three hours later I learned that a circumcision ceremony was taking place *long way tumas*. How far? One-and-a-half hours by four-wheel drive.

Now, functioning four-wheel drives are hard to come

by on Tanna, but with a bit of patience...though there was another condition.

The driver had to have no fear of heights.

Everyone on Tanna who owns a vehicle seems to make a point of passing Lenakel at least once a day. Eventually a four-wheel-drive truck was dragooned into taking me to the village, conditional on his returning to Lenakel before dark. No way was he going to negotiate *that* road at night!

All went well. Much to my surprise we did not fall off the side of the cliff on the way to the village. It didn't rain despite the glowering thunderclouds, and even the mosquitoes were almost reasonable (you guessed it, I forgot the mosquito-repellent). But I didn't get shots of the semi-controlled riot loosely referred to as "dancing" that would begin at sunset and continue until the wee hours of the following morning. No amount of money would convince my driver to hang around until after dark. Coming back down the hill, I can't say I blamed him. I couldn't risk staying there without guaranteed return transport as I might be stuck for days. But I was determined to get the photos. Someone, somewhere would take me back.

By sheer chance I stumbled across the same utility driver who had taken my photographer buddy and me under wing last time we were in Tanna—the same guy who left us stranded on the volcano. His truck had aged considerably in a few months, and it was not a four-wheel drive, but he felt bad about the volcano incident and assured me that he knew a shortcut to the village, and that we would make it.

We didn't.

About half way along the same road I'd taken that afternoon, my driver stopped and picked up three Tannese women in custom dress and full-face paint, looking more than ready for the night out. They would, he told me cheerfully, act as necessary ballast to the rear axle of the utility. Fine, I thought, no problem, nothing like being prepared.

I have to admit the journey was not nearly so bad at night. It was far too dark to see the crumbling cliffs dropping off into oblivion on my side of the truck. I admit there were a few nervous moments when I felt the rear axle sliding over the edge, but I'm sure it was just my imagination, even though the three women in the back went shrieking over to the far side of the rear tray and tried to leap out into the bush.

When we crossed over the same boulder-strewn creek bed as I'd traversed twice that day, I began to have my suspicions about this shortcut. But then we turned off into a black hole in the jungle and my faith in my driver returned...for about five minutes. We hit another boulder-strewn river, this time with water. I know it was water because it came up around my thighs through the holes in the floorboards. (To be truthful, they were not holes so much as the gaps between the narrow planks where I rested my feet.) Then, as we roared across and up the sixty-degree slope on the far side of the river, the utility, justifiably I feel, refused to climb the goat track up yet another impossibly steep hill. It stalled. It would not start again. My driver made absolutely certain of this by flattening the battery with countless attempts to restart the engine.

No problem, we'll use a torch and follow the goat track to the village. So what if the flashlight died about the same time as we realized that we were on the wrong track because it suddenly dropped 10,000 feet into nowhere? Why worry? I was with four Tannese who knew the jungle backwards.

That was when my driver said: "Now we're *really* in trouble."

We squatted on the track. Somewhere, in one direction, there was this cliff dropping into oblivion, but with a thick, overcast sky it was impossible to see where. In fact I think it is safe to say that I have never seen such total blackness in my entire life.

Have you ever been in limestone caves where the guide turns off the flashlight and says we'll all suffer sensory deprivation and go mad unless she turns the light back on? Well it was darker than that and I had no problem with the mad bit, I was already there.

I mean my *darkroom* isn't that black!

Still, of one thing I could be absolutely certain: four sets of eyes were staring intently at me.

No one was willing to get up, walk around, and try to establish which way was down—the track, I mean, not via free fall. Then it began to rain. Not much, at first, but enough to establish that the "track" was probably a creek bed that would no doubt turn into the top bit of a waterfall. You know, the bit that crumbles away at the edge during really heavy downpours? That might sound unlikely, but on Tanna, near Yasur volcano where the topsoil is just thick, uncompressed ash, mudslides from tropical downpours have buried entire villages. The most recent was only last year.

With eyes boring holes into me, I felt duty bound to come up with a solution. I remembered seeing a small fire down the side of the cliff about two hundred yards back in the direction we had come. If I could just figure out which direction was back, we could probably feel our way along the creek bed and find the fire.

In a sudden inspiration, brought on by me trying to protect my now sodden camera bag, I grabbed one of my trusty Nikon flashes. It fires off at about 1/10,000th of a second, but that's enough to give some sense of direction.

This allowed us to stumble down the side of the gully-cum-goat track-cum-potential-waterfall, find the fire, and light a torch of damp coconut leaves.

Now that all sounds amazingly simple when you read it on paper but believe me, it wasn't. Still, about four thousand AA batteries and an hour later, we found the soggy fire which, not surprisingly, turned out to have been caused by a particularly enthusiastic blob of lava.

I am not making this up. We were on the "wrong" side of Yasur volcano. While you can walk around sections of the crater in reasonable safety, periodically blobs of lava the size of a Buick spit out over the rim and land a considerable distance away. These lava bombs rarely kill anyone because most people avoid the dangerous downwind side.

Which is another reason why we were all keen to move around to the safe side of the vent, and the village, which was nearer to the rim. My driver, fortunately, was adept at making a torch of coconut husk fiber, and lo! What should we see but another goat track heading up in a different direction. The Shortcut!

Around 3 A.M. we arrived at the village. Despite the drizzle down on the side of the volcano resulting in me being caked in soggy volcanic ash with the consistency of cement, it hadn't rained in the village. For two hours I battled through clouds of dust and a mass of boldly dancing bodies for my shots. Problem was, because it was mid-winter none of the dancers were made up in traditional costume. Between that and the dust, not one photo was of any value.

As to the eventual fate of my driver, his truck, and the female ballast, I confess I have no idea. I paid him the agreed upon sum and hitched a ride back with the only other truck to climb to the village (by a different route) that night.

There was a message from my publisher waiting for me on return, wondering when I was sending the replacement shot. I blinked a few times then the phone rang. It was my photographer mate. I went to hang up when he accused me of lacking a sense of humor, but then heard him say the Yam ceremony is definitely on this Friday.

It should be simple. I mean, I only need one photo.

Sonny Whitelaw, an Australian, worked for twenty years as a freelance photojournalist and travel writer for several international magazines before deciding that writing novels involved traipsing through less mud. She is the author of seven novels including four Stargate SG-1 *and* Stargate Atlantis *titles. Visit her at www. sonnywhitelaw.com.*

⁊⁊ ⁊⁊ ⁊⁊

Crossing the River

With a leap of faith, she fulfilled her dream—
and her mother's.

*T*he trip wasn't supposed to be this way. Life wasn't
supposed to be this way. How much can get thrown your
way, and you still manage to keep your kayak upright?

Ah, the kayak. Now that's another story. I got it into
my brain (and body) about a year ago that I'd learn how to
kayak. It was the sight from my train window while rolling
through the Rockies that got to me—white water tripping
madly over rock. I can remember the precise moment. The
mountains were breathtaking enough, especially to the girl
from Eastern Ontario who thought she knew mountains.
But the hilly peaks of my childhood hometown with its
staunch United Empire Loyalist churches atop every one
of those peaks, and far-reaching steeples atop every one of
those churches, were really just that—hills. The Rockies,
now these were *mountains.*

But even so, even in the midst of such towering rock, it wasn't until I saw that raging river spitting white water that I was moved to action—or to consider action. To contemplate moving my own mountains, so to speak.

Which river did this to me, I don't know. But that nameless river was enough to make a forty-seven-year-old woman suddenly contemplate doing something completely outside the normal realm of her experience, something say, rash. Like putting her large frame into the tiny cockpit of a white-water kayak, sealing herself in with the spray skirt, and throwing herself down a river.

Note the choice of the word. I *contemplated* such an action.

But still, the idea took hold. Found a permanent place within my brain, but just as much within my body. I physically felt the urge to go down such a river, as if the idea to kayak was somehow directly linked to my bones and flesh and muscle, part of the river-rush of blood streaming through the chambers of my heart, the oxygen streaming through the capillaries of my lungs. It was most odd.

Now it wasn't a large river that I saw from the train window somewhere in the Rockies. A large river never prompted this kind of reaction in me. I know large rivers. Lived my early years on the shores of the St. Lawrence, a river large enough to hold a thousand islands.

Large rivers stir within me something akin to hearth and home: bread rising in the oven, chestnuts roasting on an open fire. But then, I grew up in a household where something wonderful was called "the next best thing to sliced bread"—store bought, of course. And chestnuts, well, I never saw a chestnut (let alone one roasting on an open fire) until I was an adult and moved into a house where every second year the gigantic tree growing next to the porch with the corrugated roof produced a banner crop of chestnuts. They sounded like bombs dropping.

So needless to say home-baked bread and chestnuts aren't the stuff of metaphors to make me think of home. The tangy smell of dead fish and seaweed that rise from big rivers, well, that's another thing. But viewed from the train window while rolling across the Rockies, this other river stirred new and unusual feelings—feelings of adventure and unlikely daring. Small in comparison to the St. Lawrence, the river raged and foamed and twisted through the steep rock, tumbled through the rapids, churned white, and in the moments when it was quiet, flowed with the color of the great blue heron.

Six months later, I stood at the edge of the YMCA swimming pool staring down at a bright orange kayak bobbing at my feet.

A classic Canadian winter swirled outside the pool windows and here I was, in a bathing suit and tucking in my tummy muscles. Vanity, yes, but also practicality. The kayak was much smaller than I had imagined. How would I fit into it? And once in, get out?

But there were more pressing matters. Malcolm, the kayak instructor, tossed me a black, kinky number to wear. He called it a sprayskirt. It was a skirt like none in my closet. Tight. Slinky. I tried to squeeze the neoprene material over my hips. Malcolm waited in full kayak attire, looking almost Scottish, bare knees showing beneath the hem. Time passed. I finally admitted defeat and asked for a larger size. By now, the others were sitting on the deck and shimmying gracefully into their kayaks. They all fit, but what could I expect? They were men with genetically narrower body types.

I imitated the chubby kid in front of me, laid the paddle across the back of the cockpit, lowered my weight to the deck, leaned on my paddle and somehow slid my butt from the deck into the kayak. The boat rocked, but didn't spill. I felt smug, even daring. Then Malcolm skirted me in. Pulled the hem so that it fit snugly over the kayak cockpit.

Not only was I in, I was sealed in. Malcolm pointed at the bright yellow loop at the far end of the cockpit and attached to the sprayskirt. "Pull that if you need to get out," he said. His instructions reminded me of the ripcord of a parachute. The RIP cord. We've all heard stories of the parachute not opening.

I played bumper cars for most of that first lesson, crashing into the other kayaks, apologizing to the men, smashing into them again, hitting the pool deck, scaring the lifeguard. Malcolm kayaked over with two strong strokes and turned my paddle around the other way. "The power blade faces the water," he said. "And use your right hand control grip, it'll help you handle the offset of the paddle."

Yeah, right.

"Hug the kayak," he instructed next. "Put your arms around it, bend at the waist as if you're kissing the deck, and roll upside down. Slap the bottom of the boat three times, and then pull on the loop and somersault out."

Yeah, right again.

But I did it, rolled over. Slapped the hull like a beaver slapping its tail against the surface. Tugged that loop. Somersaulted underwater like an otter. Left the pool that night feeling the Zen of it all. *Hug the kayak. Be the kayak.* Hey, I could do this.

It was the following week that the parachute didn't open. I rolled over and lost my bearings. Forgot to hug the kayak. Kept reaching for that loop in all the wrong places. Just kept reaching...

Panic set in, raged through me like that white-water river through the Rockies. I used my hands to dogpaddle the boat upright. Gasped a bite of air, tipped back underwater. Tried again. Another bite of air, then rolled back upside down.

Blindly reached for that damn rip cord.

So how much *can* get thrown your way, and you still keep your kayak upright?

My story started with a journey and that's where it will end. Not on the train, but another trip a few months after Malcolm flipped my boat upright. I finished the pool course, but pushed from my brain and body all thought of traveling down a river in a kayak.

In the spring, my mother was lonely so I drove out west to visit her. The evening I arrived she didn't get out of bed. I went into the kitchen to make tea, and that's when I heard the thud, found her crumpled on the floor. "Stroke," the paramedics told me as they tried to find a hospital that would take her.

What came next is a blur: intensive care, intravenous, brain scans, convulsions racking my mother's body, discussions with doctors about life and death. But against all odds, against all predictions, my mother wouldn't die. Refused to do what was expected of her. "There's the funniest-looking little man standing in a river over there," she said one day from her hospital bed, peering into the distance over my shoulder. "Keeps waving for me to join him, but I'm not crossing that river."

Probably Malcolm. "Is he wearing a skirt?" I asked, but mother had already drifted back into unconsciousness.

Later that week, I asked my mother what she wanted to do. My father had died the year before, and the family house sold.

Mother's eyes once again looked over my shoulder into the distance. "I want to go *home*," she said. "I want to see the St. Lawrence River again."

Two months later, still in the hospital, her recovery akin to a rollercoaster ride, she called me on the telephone, her voice small and despairing. I had already returned to Ontario. "The doctors say I can't travel, it's too dangerous. I could die on the way, heart failure or a stroke, and Air Canada won't risk it either."

They had her in restraints, across her waist and her wrists. She had bruised her face quite badly, falling while getting out of bed against orders. But I knew what she was doing—trying to gain the muscle strength to walk again. The strength she'd need to convince them to let her come home. They saw it as the belligerence that comes from losing touch with reality, hallucinating men-sightings in rivers and such.

Mother had some money left from the estate, but not much. Father worked his whole life in a factory. They had scrimped and saved in order to make ends meet for us— their family of five children. Even in their "golden years," dining out meant McDonald's, and going shopping meant buying thrift shop. Mother had a closet full of second-hand clothes.

But if she were going to die anyway in the very near future, like the doctors predicted, for what did she need to save her money?

And if she were going to die anyway in the very near future, like the doctors predicted, why not die trying to make the trip home? She had stubbornly not died yet. Maybe she *would* live to see her river again.

"A personal jet and nursing care on the plane will cost $30,000." I tested the waters, waiting for her reaction. I had done the research, knew the figures, but it was a huge amount of money for her. Much more than my father had made in a year's wages anytime throughout his life.

"You'll book the jet? You'll do that for me?" she said.

There was something new in her voice. Hope, but also daring. The thrill of adventure. She would fly home in her own jet. She knew the risks as much as I did, but chose to take them.

Yes, I would do that for her. I would do that for *me*.

I hung up and made the arrangements. She would fly two days later, an ambulance taking her to the airport, pilot and plane waiting, her own nursing staff, an ambulance meeting her when she landed.

Then I made another call—to a white-water kayak outfitter.

Booked a trip down a river.

Marianne Paul currently lives in Kitchener, Ontario, although she grew up along the mighty St. Lawrence River. For gentle adventure, Marianne kayaks, and for wild adventure, she writes. Marianne is the author of the novel, Tending Memory, *published in 2007. Her favorite travels include a train trip solo across Canada, a road trip to New Orleans with the girls, and a "quest" to Kentucky with her husband on the night of a full moon to see the moon-bow at Cumberland Falls. Visit Marianne's web site at www.mariannepaul.com.*

Acknowledgments

Many, many thanks to all of the folks who worked to put this collection together, especially my friends and mentors Larry Habegger and James O'Reilly, Travelers' Tales' founding editors. Many thanks as well to Sean O'Reilly for superb editorial help and contributions. Endless gratitude to Susan Brady, Travelers' Tales' long-time production manager, who leaves some very big shoes to fill. Many thanks to Christy Quinto who has so seamlessly taken over the job from Susan. Many thanks also to Amy Krynak, who volunteered her time and talent to work with me as an intern and contributed to the resulting book you hold in your hands.

"La Zisa, La Cuba, and La Cubula" by Natalie Galli published with permission from the author. Copyright © 2007 by Natalie Galli.

"Dipping Fork, Flying Girl, Heart Attack" by Christine Sarkis published with permission from the author. Copyright © 2008 by Christine Sarkis.

"My *Ex-Novio's* Mother" by Laura Resau published with permission from the author. Copyright © 2008 by Laura Resau.

"Cave with a View" by Kate Wheeler first appeared in the summer 2007 issue of *Tricycle: The Buddhist Review*, www.tricycle.com. Published with permission from the author. Copyright © 2007 by Kate Wheeler.

"Eros in Venice" by Jennifer Carol Cook published with permission from the author. Copyright © 2008 by Jennifer Carol Cook.

"On the Dark Side" by Kari Bodnarchuk published with permission from the author. Copyright © 2008 by Kari Bodnarchuk.

About the Editor

Lucy McCauley's travel essays have appeared in such publications as *The Atlantic Monthly, The Los Angeles Times, Fast Company Magazine, Harvard Review, Science & Spirit*, and Salon.com.

She is series editor of the annual *Best Women's Travel Writing*, and editor of three other Travelers' Tales anthologies—*Spain, Women in the Wild*, and *A Woman's Path*. In addition, she has written case studies in Latin America for Harvard's Kennedy School of Government, and now works as a developmental editor for publishers such as Harvard Business School Press.